Other ʼ
Kit

www.dommee.co.uk
facebook: Dom Mee

Other Titles by Mark Time:
Going Commando
Going All The Way
Going Around The Bend

www.marktimedia.com
facebook: Mark Time Author
instagram: marktimetravel

Dom Mee and Mark Time first met in 1989 as young commandos on a warship bound for the Caribbean to reassure the islands' inhabitants that the UK still cared. The pair ended up following similar routes into the murky world of intelligence, but in different units they soon lost touch. A chance encounter with a mutual friend running a Middle Eastern sniper school reunited them, and as both had exchanged the sword for the pen, it seemed serendipity was at work.

Dom Mee is a renowned maritime adventurer who rowed the North Pacific and the Atlantic oceans, kayaked solo in the Arctic's Northwest Passage and attempted to be the first person to kite sail across an ocean. For his expeditions he was made a Fellow of the Royal Geographical Society. After founding Protection Vessels International he was voted world shipping's 30th most influential person by Lloyds of London. Now semi-retired on his island paradise, Dom commentates on security issues for the BBC, CNN and Sky News.

Mark Time is also a former Royal Marines Commando. Post service, he furthered his adventures by travelling to over 100 countries and is often found dabbling with danger on the road less travelled. From an initial self-published title, Mark has evolved into an internationally acclaimed author. Now in demand as a ghostwriter and co-author, Mark is currently collaborating with a number of international clients while also writing for the UK national press and various satirical websites under yet another pseudonym.

WARLORD
OF THE
SEAS

Integritatem implicat fraternitatis

DOM MEE

MARK TIME

"There are men in Mogadishu who want to fish in Somali waters but it is too dangerous. Will you protect them? They say you are the Warlord of the Seas."

Abdirahman Sheikh Ibrahim, Minister of Fisheries, Marine Resources and Environment in Somalia, to PVI President, Dom Mee in 2011

Published by Smashed Plate
Davington Mill, Bysing Wood Road
Favershan, Kent ME13 7UD

www.smashedplate.co.uk

ISBN: 978-0-9935470-4-1

Cover design by www.golden-rivet.com

To Leon Green

Acknowledgments

It would be impossible to thank all those who joined me on the voyage south to the dark waters around the Horn of Africa as there were so many of you who believed in our honourable quest. To the onboard teams and the patrol boat crews, it was a privilege to work by your side. Brothers, thank you.

None paid a higher price through these times than Al Sims, Adrian Troy, Taff Falvey and Chris Collinson detained in Eritrea. To their families who kept the home fires alight, I thank you for your fortitude and for your understanding towards me as the man responsible for their ordeal and to the Foreign & Commonwealth Office for their support, in particular Sandra Tyler-Haywood, along with the Qatari Royal Family and Foreign Minister to Eritrea. To the Eritrean people, we never meant you harm.

For those who relayed their experiences, I hope this book does you justice. Our stories may differ as they are unique through our eyes.

To David Fulgate for pushing me to write.

For my wife Anna looking after newborn twins and a two-year-old while I bunkered down in the office. Without you there would be no book.

To Mum, Dad and Sian, thank you for my moral compass and never holding me back.

To those no longer with us, stand easy men we'll meet at the final RV.

For the pirates we dispatched. Unlucky.

And finally, I raise a glass to those who still ride the wild ocean far over the horizon.

~Dom

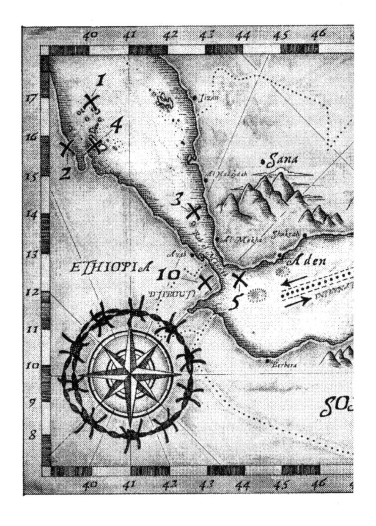

YEMEN

Ghubbat al Qamar

Nishtun

Al Mukalla

6
GULF OF ADEN

TRANSIT CORRIDOR RECOMMENDED

Abd-al-Kuri

7

Suqutra

8
Salalah

Qandala

Boosaaso

SOMALIA

9

LEGEND

1. Ramiya Inlet
2. Massawa
3. Hanish Islands
4. Prison on Dhalak Island
5. Hijack of Asian Glory
6. Hijack St James Park
7. Sucutra, Island
8. Salalah, Oman
9. Pirate Anchorage
10. Djibouti

Prologue
Pirate Alley
14'13N 53'00E

Beer bottles
Unleaded Petrol
Funnel
Motor oil
Cotton skirt
Kerosene

A simple list of innocent items. Together, they would burn them alive. What else could I do? They're armed, we aren't, and I can't just walk into my local store and buy a gun. This isn't America.

I check the stored crates of empty beer bottles to ensure all are intact. I place the fire axes on the dented metal worktop that reflects the flickering fluorescent strip above giving the workshop a surgical feel—apt considering we are sharpening implements to open bodies.

I watch intently as my brother works the oily steel into submission on the grinding stone. He prefers a machete and long knife combination in combat. An upward thrust deep into a hollow belly, followed by a machete hack to the head; few survive such a frenzied onslaught. He looks peaceful, almost transcendental, sharpening a weapon—a primordial task undertaken for thousands of years by our ancestors. We still have a lot to learn from them.

It's now my turn. The hairs on my arms are matted black with dirt and sweat, and rivulets tickle my soaking back. There's no thermometer; it would be an unnecessary distraction from the task at hand, and it's only going to get hotter. I wipe my brow. It's time to prepare death.

Fire axes are great for crashing through doors. They're also fantastic for severing limbs. I love my short-handled axe; it's perfect in a confined space where I'll only get one chance to split his head like a watermelon. My goggles, already lathered in sweat, slide on my face as I grind the axe until razor sharp. There's nothing worse than having to swing an axe twice to cut through bone—it's a waste of energy. My mind slips to a severed head. I cringe. Beheading is not my style; it's a fashion statement and takes up vital time when facing an electric-paced enemy. I slide my thumb across the edge. *That'll do.* I repeat with three more axes.

I pick up a steel rod from the pile on the floor and grind an end. This simple material takes on a sinister medieval appearance once a point is formed—a lance to impale anyone stupid enough to invade my personal space. I push it into the adjacent leatherette stool to test it. It pierces immediately like a spear through a rib cage, just as it should. The chair's owner may not be happy, but it's preferable to the outcome should things go wrong.

My lungs are now filling with metallic fumes; the air vents recirculate little in the way of fresh air, and the claustrophobia of the small compartment doesn't help the stickiness of my tainted palate.

A loud clank on the metal bulkhead in the shadows makes me jump a little, but I finish the final lance without slicing off my hand, an ironic injury in the circumstances. It's time to get these bad boys to the surface; I've had enough of darkness and stifling heat. It's time to go outside. I ascend the echoing metal steps carrying a beer crate and undo the final hatch. From the obsidian bowels of Hades, I step into the bright blue rainbow of nature's grandest sight—the ocean.

***

There is little finer than a sea breeze drying a sweated brow. An endless horizon surrounds me, my last stand on terra firma a forgotten vanishing point. The vibrating hulk of metal below me the only indication I live in a modern world. Without it, I could be a sailor of yore.

I ascend higher up the superstructure and place the crate down on the rough painted flat that makes an ideal vantage point to repel any intruder. My other brother, currently preparing barbed wire, is an advocate of fire as a weapon, and these bigger beer bottles are an ideal medium—thin enough to smash easily and hold enough fuel to cause damage no one could walk away from. I'd already found a place shaded from the wind to prepare my fiery friends, and the serenity of the ocean I move through offers a surreal juxtaposition to these devilish devices I now hold. Inserting the funnel neck into the first bottle, I pour it half full of unleaded petrol—my favourite fuel for such an occasion. It's plentiful and destroys skin quickly enough to cook the flesh underneath. I fill the rest, careful not to overfill or spill a drop.

I add motor oil to each. I could use laundry detergent instead, but I like to wear clean clothes. Oil helps flames stick to the target. I'm an honourable man so hate to see prolonged suffering; it's fairer to both parties if they die quickly.

The cotton dress has already been ripped to shreds for the wicks. Dresses are the easiest clothing to tear—less hem work, double stitching or seams. Each pile of wicks is accompanied by a small plastic tub of kerosene, a perfectly light hydrocarbon with a low flashpoint to quickly light a wick, yet burns at too low a heat to burn skin at sufficient speed. I take a crate of bottles, the wicks, and tubs to each firing point where already sits a pile of scrap metal so dirty that just looking at it gives my eyes tetanus.

Below me, I see the fruits of the last 48 hours' labour. The ship is old and thankful to be scrapped later in the year. On the plus side, she carries plenty of spares and holds an extensive workshop. Without the requested defence stores, we'd worked tirelessly to MacGyver her from a jaded old tanker to a medieval super fortress of the seas:

Fire axes and knives – sharpened. *Check*.

Portholes – welded up with thick steel. *Check*.

Stairwells – blocked with barbed wire and oil drums. *Check*.

Access points – sealed with steel bars. *Check*.

Decks greased. *Check*.

Railings – Oil drums grinded in half and placed on the rails to prevent ladders being hooked on. *Check*.

Hull perimeter – Steel rods fashioned into lances surrounding the ship ready to skewer any would-be attacker. *Check*. *Check*. *Check*.

It may be unthinkable for unarmed men to challenge drug-addled pirates wielding AK47s and rocket launchers trying to board, but our improvised defences level this most brutal playing field. Flares have been doctored, the parachutes replaced by jagged metal just to add scything shrapnel to molten magnesium. To make them more accurate, they are inserted into improvised steel launching tubes placed at potential boarding points along the ship's rails. A direct hit on a skiff laden with fuel would take the pirates out of play in a burning inferno of petrol-covered screams.

The obstacles and entanglements are placed strategically to channel any boarding pirates into an area of our choosing—a killing zone. The pirate would follow the easiest path we've created to the accommodation block, only to hit a dead end directly below where I now stand, a vertical target for the 200kgs of sharp scrap metal piled beside me. We'd drop these shards of doom onto him, followed by two Molotov cocktails to burn him to death while he lay bleeding. Repeat if necessary.

If they want a war, they can have it. PVI is ready for business.

CHAPTER 1
St Tropez, France
43'16N 06'37E

"STARBOARD!!"

My eyes shot across to the panicked yells from the bowman of the maxi yacht hurtling closer. If hit, she'd slice through us like an 80-foot scimitar. Justin looked concerned. He acted as my danger barometer and his reading was close to popping the tube. Misha stood at the wheel. Highly adept as a helmsman, he hadn't yet mastered how to handle the errant charter boat.

"GET OUT OF THE WAY!" The maxi yacht bowman screamed, now too panicked to use proper terminology. He was fifty metres away and closing fast. Even through heavily polarised sunglasses I could see the glare on his face.

I dived across to the opposite side of the yacht for safety and readied myself to assist when the inevitable collision happened. Self-preservation to help others—it was kicked into me when a commando.

Misha finally hauled the wheel over as if wrenching it from its pedestal. Inches of sea spray separated us as the maxi yacht's own emergency tack turned them to relative safety. Their red protest flag waved frantically to our front as we span round in a self imposed penalty to avoid disqualification. Now facing the wrong way, our mistake had literally taken the wind from our sails.

Our boat now sat dead in the water. It could have been worse; it could have been me. Our sails flogged as if trying to avoid catching the wind from the shouting on board. Parked fifty metres from the start line we watched the sun reflect a contagious gold upon Kevlar sails as the rest of the fleet pulled away to start the race in earnest. We would continue on in the spirit of the regatta but would certainly come last in class.

A near death collision wasn't an unusual occurrence. A yacht racing start line is a notoriously dangerous place, a mental asylum of millionaires' yachts all jockeying for position. Here there were a hundred ego-fuelled vessels aggressively funnelling through a 300-metre wide start line, so avoiding another boat was always the biggest issue. Getting to the front was just a bonus.

This mayhem was the perfect environment for our supplementary passengers—a gang of Russian oligarchs and media moguls—all with networks wide enough to include President Putin and my friend Misha who'd invited them on board to drum up interest in a Russian America's Cup campaign. Our job was to make sure they enjoyed the experience—it's unwise to upset a Russian oligarch. It meant our boat was bigger than our usual racing yacht *Murka* owned by Misha and his wife Olga. The previous three years crewing for them had been extremely pleasurable and their Swan 45 remained my favourite boat to sail in. I'd grown incredibly attached to her and promised if I ever owned a boat she'd be named in *Murka's* honour. This 20-metre Swan Delphi we now plodded in was definitely not a racer but sadly the only vessel available. It was skippered by Alfonso the silver-haired sea dog, his face leathered by the tannery of sea winds and the only one on board with real knowledge of the boat yet couldn't impart it as he spoke so little English.

Despite these issues we settled into the race and soon catching the smaller yachts nearing the first downwind mark. Justin and I set up the foredeck ready to drop the Genoa sail and hoist the spinnaker to round the busy mark ahead, now full of the smaller yachts that we'd normally be leading should we have not started so abysmally.

"I don't like this at all," said Justin. "We'll need to do an early gybe and get into clean air."

While not my regular bowman, Justin and I had done our fair share of sailing together in the Royal Navy's offshore sailing team so were fairly synchronised. I couldn't say the same about Alfonso. His speciality seemed to be recruiting the most beautiful of stewardesses in the form of Claudia who jumped like a scalded cat around the foredeck trying to help while I positioned myself to hoist with the Russian bear I called Big G who wasn't quite so attractive.

"This is going to be a shit fight," I said looking ahead.

Justin agreed. We could already hear angry shouts from the smaller yachts entangled in the maelstrom jostling round the mark. We were coming in way too fast, preventing us from yielding to the five yachts closing in from starboard. I threw Claudia from the foredeck. This was dangerous—a manic bar brawl of yachts without the manoeuvrability to dodge punches.

"Justin, watch your back!"

Again Misha wrenched the wheel, but this old crone couldn't turn like my beloved *Murka*. We hit the first yacht with an ear splitting crunch throwing everyone to the deck. We then luffed up a French yacht, causing it to lose wind and alter course, a crewmember communicated through over emotional hand gestures and unintelligible screaming before stomping to his rear to unfurl his red protest flag.

"I am protesting you," he yelled in an accent so French it spat croissants.

Undeterred, we barged further into the hornets' nest of red flags and French yachts. We hit two more vessels, receiving a 'merde' from one and a 'putain' from another. We were running the gauntlet of insults yet Justin and I, both of military descent found the smiles to brush away the pandemonium.

We battered further towards the mark in a very Russian style, but as we rounded the mark two small yachts sailed right under our bows. As we'd already hoisted the spinnaker we were already charging down the waves, a twenty-ton bull of teak and fibreglass trampling down these two yachts like runners at Pamplona. Their confused cockpit crew, slow to react could only duck as we broached. With Misha thrown from the wheel, the yacht turned uncontrollably and the Delphi's gybe swung the boom violently across the deck like a quarter-ton executioner's axe. The crew, now wise to the danger, lay on the deck covering the VIPs as if protecting them from assassination.

Misha regained control of the wheel. I waded in to try and tame the wild spinnaker ropes that had turned into angry cobras lashing out at anyone who dared near them. At last, sanity befell the boat and calmness, of sorts, returned.

We finished last. It was a wonder we'd finished at all. I peeked into the cockpit where sat the oligarchs. Never ones to lose, I wondered whether they'd enjoyed the race. Owners of race yachts were normally cut throat businessmen, some taking the phrase too literally. These incredibly successful guys didn't take prisoners on the water and, like in business, only a win would suffice. The oligarchs had loved it. If they could smile at near decapitation they were perfect for the high-class insanity of the yacht racing world.

We drifted into St Tropez, the sun contrasting the pastel colours of the Provençal buildings surrounding the old harbour. Like in the race, boats hackled for a berth like seagulls nesting at sunset. We tied up, conducted our post race admin and readied the yacht for the next day.

"Beer?" It was as much a demand as a question from Justin.

"After today, several," I replied.

***

She had the body of a Bond girl and the smile of an assassin.

"Claudia certainly adds glamour to the foredeck," I said to Justin.

"She sure does. But her and Alfonso are an item."

"Fair play." I tried not to convey envy. "There's life in the old dog yet."

In normal circumstances she would have turned every head. Not here. This was *Les Voiles De St Tropez* regatta week where sexual anticipation charged the air, the quayside transformed into an international catwalk of *agents provocateur* keen to hypnotise billionaire super yacht voyeurs.

We took another swig of Nastro Azzuro or Nasty Astro as I called it. I shouldn't have been so ungrateful, it was free and it quenched my parched throat. Being on the water all day made me feel as though I'd eaten a never-ending bag of salted pretzels. As per usual, the atmosphere bubbled with laughter at the day's events on the water. I enjoyed being lampooned by other competitors—familiar faces and friends with whom I competed on the regatta circuit, their light-hearted ribbing made a disastrous day all the more bearable. I felt far more comfortable here in the carefree surroundings of a crowded sponsored beer tent than outside on St Tropez's exclusive promenade where I'd encountered many a pretentious nobody. It's an easy place to be impressed by. Still dining on the glamour of Brigitte Bardot's 1956 film '*Et Dieu crea la femme*', its simple

10

fishing lifestyle had been transformed into the epitome of chic, where a rum and coke in the trendy hangouts of Café' Du Paris, Bar Du Port or the Tsar Lounge would cost you a day's wage. On the way to the welcome humidity of the beer tent I'd passed aesthetically enhanced husband hunters drawn here to lure one of the plentiful Lamborghini driving prey into financially rewarding matrimony by wearing false smiles, Louboutin heels and the finest clothes other people's money could buy; the shallowness of their pursuit matched only by the middle-aged men happy to take another trophy wife until boredom would cost them a sizeable fortune in divorce payments.

Marco shouted from across the busy beer pumps, "Dom, I need a word."

It's usually a positive when a super yacht captain wants your ear. Before I could respond, my phone rang. Simon. When he rang I always picked up, whatever the circumstance.

"Hi Dom, what's your movements over the next couple of weeks?"

My reply was simple to anyone offering work, "I'm crewing a regatta in St Tropez for another week then I'm available."

"Can you get another two guys?"

"Sure, where's the gig?"

"Can't tell you. I'll send details when I have them."

Withholding information was never an issue in our world. It's closely guarded for a reason. But it didn't matter whether it was Manchester, Miami or Mogadishu. A gig was a gig. I called Nige. Fifteen years older than me, his body looked twenty years younger. We'd done a few tasks together providing armed protection for super yachts heading through the Indian Ocean. He was rock solid and

I trusted him implicitly. Like me, he was happy to do any job.

The second guy I called was the mysterious Frenchman, Philippe. I knew the canvas he painted on but not what paints he used. He'd operated all over the world in his past life. Nowhere was off limits.

As always, it was a waiting game to see if the job came off. It could have been worse; my personal waiting room was the Mediterranean off St Tropez. I had seven days to enjoy throwing Russian oligarchs around a racing yacht. I truly hoped they joined the America's Cup party. It would mean more work and I'd make sure my name topped their crew list when Misha and Olga invited me to lunch with the billionaires and Simon Le Bon at the iconic Le Club 55.

I surveyed the scene around me—the surprisingly rustic setting backed by a cerulean sky and an aquamarine bay supported a fleet of super yachts berthed after offloading their 24 carat passengers onto Club 55's jetty including the most beautiful woman I'd ever seen. After alighting a Russian super yacht she'd stepped off a magnificent 1950 Ariston Riva motor launch. With Sophia Lauren sophistication, she smiled gracefully to the gallery of lust as a queen would to her subjects. I could in that moment understand why the Berlin wall had been demolished—it was probably just so the West could see her.

I was possibly the only non-millionaire in the joint, yet felt at ease in the shade of subtle music and tamarisk trees. I could snort rum with the boys in the back street pubs of Plymouth or sip Perrier Jouet with the super rich overlooking this über exclusive corner of the Med. And that was part of the problem. Despite being a civilian for six years I felt a deep pang of guilt drinking champagne while many Royal Marines with whom I'd served were on pre-deployment training to slug it out with the Taliban in Afghanistan on Operation Herrick IX.

I'd reached the top of my game serving in Special Forces and was due to go on selection for a covert undercover unit when dawned an epiphany whilst sailing for the Royal Navy. We'd been invited on board billionaire Ernesto Bertarelli's super yacht *Vava* anchored off Porto Cervo, Sardinia, and while being pampered by his staff I concluded that after 15 years operational service there was a different world out there and perhaps this, yacht racing in the most beautiful parts of the world, was it. I wanted my life back and could only do that if I left the military. I promised myself that when a civilian I would never again wear a uniform and under no circumstances work in private security.

It was a big call leaving the Corps and as I walked out of the camp gates I was overwhelmed with instant regret. I felt like Judge Dredd taking the long walk into the Cursed Earth of 'Civvy Street'. The Royal Marines had been my family and had looked after me through my youth and into my adulthood, offering me advice whether I wanted it or not, and gave me the freedom to grow yet support me when I got it wrong. It had been a family that showed me the values of courage, determination, unselfishness and humour, yet exposed me to so many more under the advocacy of humility. It had introduced me to the true meaning of friendship, putting me together with strangers and turning them into brothers who were best friend to the good and a terrible enemy to the evil, and who accepted praise and ignorance in equal measure driven by those very values the Corps family had instilled upon me. Leaving my brothers in arms was the sadness that cut deepest.

13

In 'Civvy Street' I was alone and stumbled fairly early. After four months with little work, other than the odd yacht racing job, I'd headed optimistically to my local job centre assuming they'd be honoured that a highly qualified commando had graced their establishment. I foresaw a conundrum of which job I would choose—probably a management position with a decent salary. How wrong I was. I was offered a job emptying tampon bins from local pubs.

"Six pounds an hour," the job peddler concluded with a wink.

Reading a CV is one thing, understanding it another. I politely told him I'd think about it. No one cared about the title 'commando', they just thought 'ex-military' and pigeonholed me as someone who'd be on time, reliable and do as they were told. They assumed my skills irrelevant in this gentle world unless the local supermarket needed an assassin for shoplifters. It was a sharp but important lesson. I was nothing in Civvy Street.

The words of a close friend had echoed in my mind, "Never be afraid of coming back to the Corps, it's cold outside."

He was right. The long walk was getting longer. No one gave a shit about me on the outside and I roamed alone far from the pack looking for purpose. Taking self-elected exile, I walked only with my shadow. I wouldn't contact my brothers until I'd returned a success.

My subsequent journey that I named 'the wilderness years' took me twice to the high Arctic where I was nearly eaten by a predatory Polar Bear then attacked by a miserable Musk Ox. I'd been hit by a fishing trawler while rowing the Pacific and shipwrecked by hurricanes while kiting across the Atlantic surviving both by the skin of my teeth. Many people thought I was undertaking these adventures to be macho yet it couldn't have been further from the truth. I'd been trying to understand myself. If no longer a commando, who the hell was I? Being in the Corps had given life a meaning that I was now bereft of. I needed a reboot to make it through the Cursed Earth.

In contrast to the office-bound lobotomised process monkeys at the job centre, these entrepreneurial super-rich with whom I now shared my lunch were always very respectful towards my service. They loved to hear the stories of my time in the Corps and of my later adventures around the world. It was just a pity there weren't enough races to survive. I was living hand to mouth, and the only way to cover my mortgage arrears was to say 'yes' to any work being offered—If I was possibly the only non-millionaire in the joint I was definitely the only one about to lose their home.

Potential homelessness always creates a nicotine thirst, so I escaped outside to draw death into my needy lungs.

Marco, the super yacht captain appeared. "You're a hard man to catch, Dom."

"Sharks have to keep moving, Marco, or we die."

"You still doing the armed stuff?"

"Always." I'd escorted a few of his super yachts down to the Maldives and Seychelles. They weren't bad jobs— super yachts got the best berths, meaning a short walk to the nearest rum bar, highly beneficial when wobbling back.

"Great. Listen, I don't have much time as I'm flying out soon. I hope you don't mind but I passed your number to a crazy French chick. Her son is the skipper on a ship called *Star Clipper*, so if she calls, you know why. Got to run. Be lucky, my friend."

CHAPTER 2
Casablanca, Morocco
33'36N 07'28W

I was a stranger in a strange land. I'd bypassed the purgatory of border officialdom a few passengers before Philippe and many passengers behind Nige. We'd not so much as passed a glance to each other when waiting in our separate queues. We were jetsam floating in a sea of airline passengers with only invisible intent our common denominator. Simon; however, had been invited through doors marked *Privé* to answer whatever questions paranoid chain smokers dressed in Moroccan immigration uniforms thought necessary. If Simon was detained more than the pre-designated time we'd have to move hotels and sit tight until we received more information.

Simon and I had gone over the plan the night prior to flying out. He was now amongst the millionaire artisans of Swiss Cottage having downsized from circling with the multi-millionaire entrepreneurs of St Katherine's Dock after dissolving his old business.

I'd done a few jobs with Simon, and thankful he'd thrown me a lifeline when leaving the Royal Marines, sponsoring my Arctic expeditions. We enjoyed unwavering mutual trust and my discretion was always a high priority in his business. At 6'4" he was a giant of Hugh Grant floppy hair and Schwarzenegger muscle. He'd worked as a bodyguard for Robbie Williams before founding IDS specialising in maritime security. The decline of his once prosperous business would topple most, but not Simon. It's hard to extinguish the fire of someone so characterful and I could see his eyes burning bright at the thought of getting back out on the ground.

The brief was clear. Casablanca had suffered a spate of terrorist attacks aimed at tourists. Recently, an explosives laden suicide bomber would have boarded a tourist bus if not for the quick thinking of the driver. Suitably primed, the suicide bomber then detonated himself, killing one police officer and injuring many others. As no Westerner was killed it never made a column inch—that would be bad for business. With around 10% of Morocco's GDP depending on tourism, the government had tasked their security services to guarantee tourist safety; however, one cruise operator appeared nervous at the arrangement thus asked Simon to provide discreet overview to ensure the government offered appropriate security and to highlight other threats. Discretion was key.

"If compromised we're on our own. The cruise company don't want to ruin relations with the government."

If caught, our 'watching' of government security protocols would be redefined as 'spying', most certainly leading to a few years rotting in a Moroccan jail with espionage on our charge sheets. Now that *would* make the papers.

"Cover stories?" I asked.

"Of course." I could see Simon loved the high-risk element. He'd pushed a desk for far too long.

***

I pulled out a Marlboro. Even at 40°C, the open air is a welcome refuge to a cigarette worshipping pariah and my first long drag created the course for the first heavy bead of sweat to trickle down my face. I was on a job, yet my actions were the most natural in the world. I stubbed out the last of my cigarette into an overflowing bin before jumping in the next available taxi. Nige and Philippe were probably at different stages down the A7 by now.

Upon arrival at the hotel, I met up with Nige and an agitated Philippe. Having a team member stopped by immigration made him uncomfortable. He liked to be under the radar, on the move.

"Relax, mate, there's always some headache when you're moving our sort of kit." I offered a Marlboro to Nige. The sanctity of a smoking approved hotel room was my saviour when waiting.

Philippe's gesture indicated he wasn't reassured. It'd been a while since he'd last worked in Africa; I could understand his reaction—he'd operated in Algeria, Mali and Djibouti when things were extremely unpleasant. Clearly he carried baggage and both Nige and I recognised the demons that many of our cohort wrestled with.

"What's the story with the fifth member?" he said breaking his own silence. He was a man who rationed his words, meaning everything he said added value. Small talk wasn't in his vocabulary.

"All I know is she's someone Simon described as spending most of her life in a burqa," I replied.

"Ex military or intelligence?" Philippe still harboured suspicion.

"That's all I know. If Simon's asked her to come on board she must be pretty flash."

I looked forward to meeting her. Working with new operators always widened my knowledge base and everyone offered something different. Being already positioned in country she'd be invaluable, we needed as much local insight as possible, especially as we were back to basics with kit. We'd be even more basic if Simon was arrested. We needn't have worried. He finally arrived, sweating profusely but still exuding an air of cool.

"Drama with immigration," he said as he downed a condensation-wrapped bottle of water. "I told them I was doing a site recce for the new Monty Python film 'Life of Brian 2'."

"You're a very naughty boy," quipped Nige as sharp as a tack.

All but Philippe laughed. It was of no surprise. His life had been cast adrift from colonies of film watchers, instead offering himself to the business end as an intelligence agent for the controversial French organisation DGSE—*Direction Générale de la Sécurité Extériure*. The fact that they'd managed to infiltrate high echelons of American business told me they were a proficient set up. The fact their *'Opération Satanique'* sank the Green Peace ship *Rainbow Warrior* when berthed in New Zealand told me they'd go to any length to protect their interests overseas. A lifetime working undercover resulted in no relationship nor commonality to speak of. He was a real life Hauptmann Gerd Wiesler in the 'Life of Others'. The little I did know of him was that he understood mountains better than humans, maintaining sanity as a guide between security jobs. Somehow post-service he'd managed to re-engage with normality and married. Love, I believe, had saved his soul.

To preserve our covert nature, we were lodged in no frill accommodation off the beaten track. It's never easy being holed up in such a place, Nige and I found ourselves bunkered down in a Miami safe house on a surveillance operation earlier in the year and by the time we exited three months later we'd held the hand of madness. It was easy to see why Simon had picked this particular hotel. The top floor offered an amazing panoramic of the city— Satellite dishes Polka-dotted the flat roofs of crumbling buildings crammed together like a concrete crowd within the dirty white walls that gave the city its name. In the distance, over the shoulder of a five star hotel, infamous for its five star subterranean nightclub patronised by women offering themselves at five star prices, stood the King Hassan II Mosque, built in veneration of his predecessor King Mohammed V. Having the tallest minaret in the world, it's grandeur towered over the concentrate of poverty below. I loved such contrast—an instant caricature of humanity's inconsideration. It also gave us a perfect vista for orientating ourselves to key areas of the city.

Simon was already sat down with Catherine when we congregated for the brief. She immediately made a good impression. Short with mousy hair, wearing drab clothes that may have properly fitted her sometime ago she, like Philippe, appeared perfectly bland—an ideal in such a grey world.

Simon explained the task: The ship would dock in Casablanca's main terminal. Philippe and I would follow one group for a day trip around the city; Nige and Catherine would take overview of another excursion overnighting in Marrakesh. The ship would set sail the same evening for the southern port of Agadir picking up the Marrakesh group before enjoying a trip to the historical town of Taroudant with the remainder of the passengers. Should we fail to trail the coaches immediately from the port the mission would be jeopardised. We had two days before the ship arrived to get orientated.

"Nige and Catherine, your cover is as a married couple, so act accordingly," said Simon.

Nige and I exchanged comical glances. He seemed a magnet for short straws. On our last job, while Philippe and I were bugging houses and tailing fast cars around Europe, Nige sat embedded in a horsebox inside a stinking stable gathering intelligence with a female who he'd later refer to as the 'poison dwarf'. Hopefully for him, lightening wouldn't strike twice.

"Since some of the suicide bombers came from Sidi Moumen shall we go down there to gauge the mood?" I asked.

We'd all done our homework on the semantics of the city where tourists visited and where trouble brewed. Going blind into something like this was not only amateurish but life threatening.

"Sounds good, we can tie that in with the souk where one of the bombers tried to hit a tourist bus." The team nodded to Simon's suggestion. He turned to me. "But first we need to get you and Philippe your wheels."

***

"There you go," said Simon as proudly as the shop owner who grinned as if it was the finest motorbike ever assembled. Only it wasn't. It was possibly the worst motorbike in Africa. The only bike I'd seen in similar state of disrepair was the Honda step through I'd found on some waste ground when fourteen. I'd worked tirelessly to get it to start until my father had seen enough of oil stains being trawled through the house and insisted I take it to the scrapyard.

I shouldn't have been surprised. The area in which we now stood was a greasy throng of mechanical parts traders, welders and scavenging stray dogs. The owner, now stood over his pride and joy, offered us sweet tea.

I sat on it, curious if it would hold my weight let alone be my mode of transport. Scanning the squeaking hunk of metal it seemed built with plenty of resourcefulness but little skill—a Frankenstein motorbike reconstituted from various long deceased mechanical donors.

"Electric start, please test," the owner insisted.

The heat against my calves told me the bike had been recently fired up so it was no surprise it started first time, much to the mendacious pride of the smiling eyed owner. All I could do was reluctantly nod and thank him for having the most wonderful motorbike this side of the Atlas Mountains.

I rode it back to the hotel. It worked better than it looked, which was still terribly, but this was a low budget operation and besides, it wouldn't draw unnecessary attention.

∗∗∗

To avoid linking us to the hotel, we'd already changed taxis three times before entering the slum of Sidi Moumen. Even through the dusty window of a grinding taxi it was clear why here was a perfect hunting ground for jihadists to radicalise slum dwellers living from the scraps of a seemingly unjust society in their improvised huts fenced by rubbish dumps and an open sewer that made me gag. There was little need to import terror; there were plenty of home-grown volunteers for clerics to manipulate in the back street madrasses.

Rusting apartment balconies seconded as overspill living areas bedecked with beds and washing, leaned precariously from crumbling buildings that crashed the landscape. Music mutated into one long inharmonious drawl as we passed bedraggled street children and gesticulating hawkers. Plentiful also were the security forces. At least we were on the move. It's never a good thing to be held up in traffic when disaffected young men are throwing missiles at the security forces that, in response, slammed culprits against riot vans. We needed no further evidence that this place was a smouldering powder keg. Since the attacks, over 3000 suspected militants linked to Al Qaeda had been detained, many from 'Sidi'. It was certainly not a place to enter on foot. As our presence held no further benefit, we headed to safer pastures—the souk, and specifically the site where suicide bombers had laid up prior to attacking the tourist bus.

Back on foot, we pushed out in a fragmented diamond formation with Simon overseeing from a flank.

I received a text from Philippe, *'By the pool'*. It was safe to enter.

I followed Nige and Catherine to a dimly lit entrance. Inside, a labyrinth of tight cobbled passageways hid nooks and crannies that could spook the paranoid. This was a human rabbit warren where anything could happen and the tight meandering walls created a maze where disorientation became the norm rather than the exception. Life's enchantment played out on these grimy streets. Men stood on corners talking politics with their hands. Sweet apple and mint smoke emanated from inside cafés where tomb-toothed men simultaneously played *wari*, smoked hookah pipes and drank obsidian coffee; and young boys, wheeling pallets of scented goods, far too heavy to control, bullied everyone from their path. Souk life was exhilarating.

I then saw him—a man in his late twenties taking undue interest in Nige and Catherine. He could be a pickpocket, a mugger, or something far worse.

I texted Nige. *'Nice souvenirs'*. He now knew he had a tail.

I closed within striking distance. Nige casually locked on to the follower through the crowded street. The jostling of the crowd assisted Nige and Catherine in creating a moving barrier, and the narrow passageways greatly helped Simon who shoved past the follower enabling him to give a quick yet sufficient covert body search.

"He's carrying," whispered Simon as he passed me.

I texted, *'Bar time'*. When a possible gunman hunts you, it's time to go.

***

I returned last to the hotel. I'd followed the tail until he'd lost interest in Nige and Catherine getting into a taxi. It wasn't my remit to follow him and should his anti surveillance skills be better than his surveilling he may clock me as I had him.

"Interesting city," Simon mused as he sipped iced water. "Carry conceal under his jacket, possibly 9mm. Dom, you pinged him first, what do you reckon?"

"He didn't draw attention to himself, locals ignored him, even plain clothes are on the take here, right? So, maybe military?"

"*Direction Général de Surveillance du Térritoire Maroc,*" said Philippe quietly from left field, his French accent as thick as the coffee I now drank.

He recognised the silence. "DST to you English. They used to train with us in the 1980s but after they abducted a political opponent in Paris we cut ties. They were linked to organised crime in France along with a host of dirty cops. We really don't want to get picked up by these guys."

"Why's that?" asked Catherine. She'd already asked questions that one wouldn't expect of a seasoned professional and from someone currently embedded, it raised eyebrows. It was a question she didn't want answered.

"They torture people," said Philippe softly. "There's a secret facility in Temara just up the coast. It's not a nice place. The last I heard, CIA were using it to question suspects they'd picked up in Afghanistan."

Simon and I simultaneously smiled. Both of us had been trained as interrogators when serving in the intelligence cell of the Special Boat Service, so the word 'questioning' was recognisable as lipstick smeared on far less attractive undertakings. It confirmed; however, that we needed to be even more low key.

***

Philippe and I left early the next morning to find a suitable vantage point to observe the port. The only information yet received was that the ship would dock at the harbour's northern jetty. The Ship's Security Officer (SSO) hadn't replied to Simon's many emails. SSOs can be territorial, seeing outside security as a threat to their position and, in some cases, are blind to threats reasoning they have it all under control. Evidently we were to accomplish this gig blind.

We hoped the unkempt back streets adjacent to the port would provide an ideal surveillance location. After pounding miles of dusty lanes we noted an area of rundown buildings. We didn't know if the place had been half built or half destroyed.

As a local walked by we became navigationally challenged tourists looking at our maps noting escape routes and choke points should we be compromised. Construction trucks thundered by, gluing dust to my sweaty back, as we noticed a potential building. Six storeys high, it boasted a perfect vista, no security, and seemingly unoccupied; a shell that had been forgotten and left as a monument of bankruptcy from someone's pipe dream. There were too many eyes for us to scale it in the daytime. We'd have to return that evening.

The nearby Sofitel had already been earmarked as an option, standing as it did at the port gates. After four hours trapped in the sun kissed maze of the back streets, an ice cold drink would be most welcome. The international hotel guest caste system means Westerners can usually enter anywhere so we walked straight to the bar and found it an ideal spot. A hotel room overlooking the port would be low risk and offer a perfect control point for the operation. I phoned Simon to ask if we could move hotels.

"What did he say?" asked Philippe bluntly.

"No go. There isn't the budget to stay here."

"No budget for a decent hotel? What sort of job is this?"

It was a fair point. However, there was something satisfying in doing things low budget. And this job was about as low as it could get. The only other option here was to access the roof space, preferably without getting arrested.

Philippe hit the elevator button to take us to the roof entrance on the 24th floor. On exiting, we saw no CCTV. I took a right and Philippe peeled left. The corridor suffered the malaise of a generation without upgrade, threadbare carpets on a floor tired of being stomped on by amorous couples, and scratched walls from heavy suitcases and unwieldy porters. I soon located the access door to the roof and checked it for alarms. Surprisingly, there was no indicator and even more astonishingly it was unlocked. I covered Philippe from the corridor as he stepped onto the rooftop to recce a potential site for his solo observation. He returned and took more photographs of the lock and access door before exiting.

"How's the roof?" I asked, as we sat amongst the throng of dockworkers, being belt fed mint tea by over-worked waiters. It was the first we'd discussed the rooftop. We'd never debrief on site as we never knew who might be listening.

"Not good. Someone else has been running an op from here fairly recently. I saw bipod leg indents in the dirt along with empty water bottles and food wrappers. They were sloppy whoever they were."

Sharing a site was a problem we didn't need. Our mission could be compromised and we could end up in a world of pain, especially if we impacted on a DST operation. We'd have to return to the backstreet shell later that night.

CHAPTER 3
Casablanca, Morocco
33'35N 07'35W

Darkness cloaked the silent street; no one in their right mind would walk down here unless they wanted to turn an ankle on the many invisible potholes. The bikes were doing the basics of getting Philippe and I from A to B and their lights were the only ones working in the area.

Climbing through a hole in the chain link fence, we studied the building. With no stairs yet constructed the rickety bamboo scaffolding, clumsily anchored by rusty nails, would be our only means to ascend.

Philippe was a skilled mountaineer. I wasn't. He scaled like a mountain goat whereas I struggled to mount bouncing beams and shaking cross poles. The whole structure seemed ready for collapse. My heart jumped into my mouth. I daren't look down. In the Royal Marines, I'd rappelled from buildings, climbed cliffs and parachuted from planes, all while being terrified of heights. The only thing worse than fear was letting your mates down. It was the only motor that moved my arms and legs as I now scaled this creaking monstrosity. The breeze did nothing to quell my angst as I reached the final beam; indeed it worsened. The scaffolding wasn't anchored at the top so required a six feet jump to reach the rooftop. When you're 100 feet above a hard landing and scared of heights it looks like six fucking miles. The scaffolding whistled and swayed as I tried to steady myself for the leap across.

"Hurry Dom," whispered Philippe, oblivious to my terror.

It would have been easy to close my eyes and let fate take me, but I leapt with the imps of fear biting my ankles. Feeling the scaffolding give way behind me, I hit the edge of the rooftop with a winding blow. Philippe grabbed my belt and hauled me to solid concrete. The scaffolding flexed and clucked begrudgingly. It still stood. Thankfully.

The building was perfect. It commanded a perfect view of the port area and not a soul was seen in our three hours watch. Undoubtedly it was forgotten.

Descending this stack of matchsticks was far easier once we anchored the scaffolding at the top with building materials found on the roof. It would also make it easier for Philippe when he returned in darkness the next morning.

***

The plan had changed. As the SSO still hadn't replied, Nige and Catherine stayed to offer greater flexibility. I met Nige in the hotel cafe after escorting Philippe to his observation post. I needed coffee. 4am starts are most disagreeable in any climate.

"We haven't a clue where these buses are going. Simon has pushed the client but no joy."

"Looks like another cuff job," I replied. "Best get to the port early."

Catherine waited in the car with the driver. Nige and I had been sat at a café opposite the port drinking our body weight in coffee watching the night slowly turn to day and cold-blooded workers using the sun to guide them to work. We again studied the roads we'd already assessed as likely bus routes. In a perfect world we'd have already driven them. This was not a perfect world.

My phone rang. Philippe. "Dom, I'm compromised. Many construction workers have turned up on site."

"Sit tight, I'm on my way." I quickly explained the situation to Nige.

"Of all the buildings in all the world, you had to pick that one," he quipped. He was a hard man to panic.

"It is Casablanca, mate."

Extracting Philippe was hardly the covert operation we'd intended. Armed with a map, two packets of Marlboro and $30 worth of Moroccan Dirham, I approached a group of builders stood around a concrete mixer drinking tea. "Ada'tu tareequi." *I am lost.* I carried on in Arabic, "who wants a cigarette?"

The international currency of Marlboro is strong on the baksheesh stock exchange and has helped me from clearing body armour through Khartoum customs to getting super yachts through the Suez Canal. Soon everyone gathered around, conversing in Arabic.

"Hal beemkanek mosa' adati?" I asked handing out cigarettes as they pointed at the map answering my request for directions to the Grand Mosque, hoping it would distract them from Philippe descending the deadly scaffolding.

Once informed I was English, they reverted to the international language of football, something I knew little about, but took up the necessary time while Philippe neared the ground.

"David Beckham, Bobby Charlton, Brian Rooney," I reeled off names of footballers whose interest had passed me by.

One of the builders then spotted Philippe. This could turn nasty.

"It's OK he's with me. He's an Arsenal Rovers supporter trying to see where the Mosque is."

While conversation was convivial, time was not on our side. If we couldn't get Philippe into an observation position the whole op could fail.

"Al maghrib baladun jamee, shokran," said Philippe in perfect Arabic. It did the trick. Waving goodbye we sped off as fast as our mean machines would take us to the Sofitel.

We zig zagged through steadily building traffic down narrow streets festooned with debris and garbage dodging potholes that made perfect motorbike traps, pushing the coughing engines as hard as we dared in between impatient honks and crash test pedestrians.

Pulling outside the Sofitel, we immediately hit the lifts. As we approached the 24th floor I tried some humour. "The way this morning has gone, DST are probably already there and you'll be shot."

Philippe didn't respond in kind, instead his attention diverted to more serious matters. "The door is locked."

Locks are not my area of expertise. Philippe pulled out a Leatherman Wingman and another tool. Within seconds the lock sprang open, the sun hitting us with a welcome punch. The rooftop stood empty as we scanned the port where the cruise ship's deckhands were busy throwing lines to the Moroccan stevedores on the dock. We were back in business.

"Back on. Philippe will call when they're unloading passengers." I'd returned to sit with Nige now surrounded by empty coffee cups and an overflowing ashtray. With my strawberry face sweating from the morning's unexpected exertions, I pulled out a Marlboro and tried to gain the attention of the nimble waiter.

"Still no word on which buses are going where," Nige said.

"Roger, we'll go firm on you tailing the buses that go straight on. I'll take the ones going either left or right. If they all go the same way we can work it out en route." My attention was smashed by the voice on the pavement.

"What's going on? I've been sat in that car for two hours," Catherine shouted, her face red with anger.

The silence of those around told me our covert presence was no more.

"Sit the fuck down," I seethed under my breath.

Catherine slumped into the aluminium chair like a surly teenager.

"What was the brief?"

"Wait in the car until Nige reports in," she answered.

"Correct, so I guess you should be waiting in the car until Nige reports in, and not drawing attention to us in a fucking café." I cut her short as she tried to respond. "Get back in the car, pretty please."

"Bit harsh, Dom," smiled Nige as she stormed back to the vehicle.

'Day trip.' Philippe's text told us it was time to get in position and await the loaded buses.

Four coaches screamed from the port gates and turned right. I picked up their tail but struggled as the drivers hurtled at breakneck speed throwing up a peppering of coarse dust that gradually abraded my face.

I tried to call Philippe, he should be joining me on the tail. No answer. That was bad news. Worse still, my bike cut out. I'd lost the tail. "Shit."

The phone rang. "Dom, I couldn't take your call, the maintenance team came onto the rooftop I had to take evasive action. Where do you need me?"

"I've broken down. Just head to the Grand Mosque, it's got to be where they're heading."

Having pulled over I needed someone to repair this piece of shit I rode on. I pushed the bike down a back street to look for a mechanic's shack. A scruffy little urchin with a face of an angel joined me. In Arabic I explained I needed to get the bike fixed.

"Come, come," he waved, leading me down a rabbit warren into a ramshackle quarter. This could go two ways. I could find a mechanic or a gang of thieves.

"Baba mikaniki" smiled the boy.

His dad a mechanic, my luck had finally changed. The boy's father quickly set to work. Within twenty minutes the dead bike had been resurrected, once more purring like a chain-smoking cat. I gave him $20. His eyes lit up before vigorously shaking my hand. I patted the angel on the head and rode to the Grand Mosque where the coaches had already parked, Philippe already sat inside keeping an overview of the tourists.

The mosque stood awe-inspiring. Cleverly built by architects with Allah as their inspiration, heat as their guide, the alcoves allowed air to circulate, a welcome relief when running around all morning like an idiot. I took some surveillance photos disguised as holiday snaps then casually engaged in conversation with a section of cruise passengers, obvious from their stickers, to see where they were next headed.

I felt more relaxed; we were now back in control after an inauspicious morning and we'd managed to blend in with the tourists enough for them to offer us all the information we needed.

After a restaurant stop, we headed to Quartier Habous, a toy town version of a traditional medina. It seemed ideal for tourists; however, the bus driver decided not to follow the most obvious route. Something was wrong.

I pulled next to Philippe. "Where are they going?" I shouted over the drone of our motorbikes.

He responded with a Gallic shrug.

It then became clear. We were heading to the souk where DST had possibly tailed Nige on the first night.

Philippe also recognised the danger. "I don't like this."

We were approaching the area where the bus attack happened. I would have expected them to alter their routes. To my horror, the buses pulled over exactly where the suicide bomber had detonated. We stopped by a small park to observe what was going on. The buses decanted their occupants at the massive souvenir shop that evidently handed out huge commissions to the drivers, irrespective of it being a suicide bomber hot spot.

Despite the recent atrocities, this part of Casablanca didn't possess the febrile air of Sidi Mouman, rather it seemed to be burying its head. Maybe that was the idea— allow people the freedom of ambivalence rather than the worry of an unfolding story. That was the security services job—take the burden of an impending tragedy and strike it from the page before it hit the headlines.

It was easy to see why the bomber chose here. It was a target rich environment—four huge coaches bottlenecked into a busy narrow street with tourists crammed into a three storey Aladdin's cave of tacky trinkets. If a bomber initiated, the body count would be massive. In such a place, where locals filled the streets, it was impossible to distinguish between killer and victim.

Philippe disappeared into the crowd. I took a high vantage point to see what security the government provided in this area subjected to a bomb only a month earlier. There were no visible police, just a security guard on the shop door wearing an old 9mm pistol in a cracked leather holster. The local threat analysis seemed to be more concerned with shoplifters than jihadists.

As reward for surviving a bombsite, the buses loaded back up and drove to Quartier Habous. We followed. My motorbike started to cough and splutter more than usual.

As Philippe shot ahead to cover the coaches arrival, I peeled off to a parking spot ideal to watch disembarking passengers. As I accelerated, the motorbike's exhaust fell off. The bike erupted with an un-muffled roar, amplified a thousand times by the alcoves. I'd gone from covert operator to the Crazy Frog on a mosque tannoy. A police officer reached for his holster and locals were transfixed as I passed louder than a low flying Cessna. It would be best to quell the enmity of those whose tranquillity I'd disturbed by turning off the engine, but to my horror the bike's vibration had caused the ignition key to fall out. I echoed angrily through the quartier as the passengers disembarked, bewildered by the deafening noise of my overgrown hairdryer. I jumped into the nearest shop adorned with rugs and tourist tat, knocking over a teapot and a hookah pipe. I ran directly into the shopkeeper.

"Do you have key?" I asked in pidgin English

"Yes, of course. Please sit." Clapping his hands, he shouted to a boy, "Atay."

"No, not tea, a key."

I wasn't alleviating the owner's confusion, garbling in my haste to silence the mean machine still roaring outside and now the number one attraction.

We continued a Monty Python sketch where my Moroccan Arabic sign language seemed to be a Bulgarian phrasebook to the shop owner, all the while being deafened by the mechanical clodhopper outside. Finally getting a key, I silenced the crippled machine under the hostile glare of deafened shopkeepers.

I withdrew to the back streets and phoned Philippe. "I'll do a perimeter here but I'm off task after that. My bike has finally died. You'll have to cover the return to the ship."

In all the years of knowing Philippe, I'd never known him to even raise a smile. But now back at the hotel lobby, with mint tea in hand as I recounted the comical events at the Quartier Habous, he sat bent double with laughter.

We returned the bikes in the dead of night to avoid confrontation. They were junk when collected, they were even worse when returned. Thankfully we wouldn't be using them en route to Agadir.

***

Simon now possessed an itinerary. Agadir had been a far easier task and it was good to meet with Nige who'd eventually followed the Marrakesh tour parties.

"How did it go with Catherine?" I asked.

"Well, she blew our cover as she asked for a separate room, she then went out on the piss and got hammered. To make it worse, she ended up sleeping with the Police Chief in charge of looking after the ship."

"Wow, you really do know how to impress the ladies. I'll sit on it for now, let's just get the last phase done." I certainly didn't mention it to Philippe he may have taken her out. And I don't mean to lunch.

Quiet trips out to the beautiful medieval city of Taroudant that appears from the dirty scrub like a mirage, and watching the cliff-hanging goats eat the fruit of the Argania trees that sprout horizontally from vertical outcrops made the job far easier. While we'd never let our guard down, securing a rural area was far easier than zooming through feral city streets. It also seemed that security had been beefed up. Maybe Catherine's pillow talk with the Police Chief had been more calculated than envisaged.

At the ancient gates of Taroudant, my phone rang. Number withheld. I asked Nige to cover me as it could be more work. The caller spoke with what I called a 'cocktail' accent, one where the original speech had been diluted then mixed with a host of others—a sure sign of a worldly-wise traveller laying their hat wherever money took them. He asked about getting security for his ship passing through the Gulf of Aden. I explained how it worked and what I could offer to secure his vessel. He wanted more detail than I wanted to give over the phone, plus I was on task. He agreed to call me back the following week.

I asked what company he represented so I knew who he was.

"Star Clipper."

CHAPTER 4
London, UK
51'30N 00'12W

The tube was packed with head-phoned passengers wishing they were anywhere else, with only James Blunt, Beyonce or Wagner to side-saddle their I-imagination. The doors opened and I followed the colony of ants surging for the surface. The rarity of a really hot English September day always makes it feel warmer, so with the delays encountered on the Circle Line I was eager to reach street level and breathe city air. My heavy winter pin stripe suit designed for conditions the exact opposite of what I was encountering smudged the outward coolness I wanted to portray.

I'd just finished a meeting with a small war risk insurance underwriter. They'd seen an article published by Yachting World about me protecting super yachts in the Indian Ocean and had asked me to give a presentation outlining the general threat to shipping. Things had become spicy with the number of ship hijackings doubling that year. I gave them fair warning that this was only the tip of the iceberg and the situation would only worsen. I felt they'd not taken me seriously. They'd soon understand the reality when a foul mouth Somali thug, high on khat screamed down the phone demanding $20 million.

As I walked to my destination, I cast my eye over the mighty Thames. I knew every bend and eddy of this most famous waterway, having two years before rowed from London to Paris. I'd also managed to win the biggest river race in Europe—The aptly named 'Great River Race'—a 22-mile sprint along the Thames from Richmond to Greenwich. We'd taken five trophies, including overall winner. It seemed a lifetime ago.

I reached the Tattershall Castle. Despite its grand name, it's actually an old 1934 Humber ferry, delivered to the Thames in 1975, then converted into a floating bar where it has remained, becoming somewhat of a landmark. I sat facing the entrance, as I always did, and waited for Peter.

Peter Charles was a civil servant who worked for a secret intelligence organisation where even working in the shadows could compromise you. Seventeen years had passed since first meeting him after I'd returned from Northern Iraq. As part of 40 Commando's intelligence cell I'd been loaned to a top-secret intelligence unit from Defence Intelligence Staff for the last two months of Operation Provide Comfort to secure the safety of Iraq's Kurds. The unit was made up of operators whose intelligence on Saddam Hussein's nuclear, biological and chemical programmes would be the foundation for 'Operation Rockingham'—the UN inspection headed by Hans Blix. I'd been assigned to assist in their protection, as many of their human intelligence sources were located behind Iraqi lines. It was my first taste of real intelligence work and I felt hugely privileged to be an integral part of this unique unit.

Hezo, our Kurdish interpreter, had been displaced along with thousands of others after the Iraqi army launched a genocidal offensive on the Kurdish enclave. He was a fearless, intelligent man, with genuine warmth easy to befriend. I'd hoped that the kind word I'd put in for him had, in some small way, assisted him being granted asylum in the UK. Hezo had stayed at my house in England for a few months before studying in London. It stuck in my craw that these brave guys, who'd risked everything to assist the coalition, were often ignored in their attempts to escape tyranny. If his asylum claim had been rejected he would have been savagely tortured before being executed by the Mukhabarat Iraqi intelligence service.

I'd received a phone call from Hezo eighteen months later. He sounded frightened and asked to meet in London. He looked great, dressed smartly in a suit while working in the small computer shop he'd opened, but behind his business façade I could see the paranoia of a man who could not totally cover his tracks, never sure of who may be watching him.

He'd recently attended his nephew's wedding in Iraq. Recognising the obvious dangers, his brother, a commander in the Kurdish Peshmerga militia, had guaranteed his safety. Before returning to London, Hezo's brother had woken him in the night, and thrust sheets of paper into his hand with an instruction to hand them over to someone trustworthy in London. Hezo had been petrified of these mysterious papers being found in his possession when leaving Iraq. Without any further instructions on what to do, he'd called me.

He'd nervously unfolded a piece of paper and whispered to me, "This is a list of high ranking Ba'ath Party members and military leaders prepared to overthrow Saddam."

Stunned was an understatement, but my poker face prevented him from further distress.

"I just want this out of my hands, I have started a new life here, I don't want any trouble."

"OK," I said putting a comforting hand on his shoulder. "I'll take care of it. Just don't tell anyone."

This was strategic intelligence, way above my pay grade, and needed pushing into the right hands without delay. I decided to bypass my chain of command at 40 Commando, preferring instead to contact Major John, who'd been part of the 'Rockingham Cell'. I organised a trip to visit the Royal Engineers Map and Chart Depot under the pretence of collecting maps. Major John was a real gentleman and it had been a pleasure to work for him in Iraq. I explained what I held and asked for his advice.

"Well first things first, we need to translate this list into English."

Major John spoke five Middle Eastern languages and the senior instructor teaching languages to every arm of the military when not assigned to various intelligence operations as a linguist. I felt excited to be in the possession of such revelatory information on senior Iraqi leaders. He methodically scrutinised the list of 52 names. Here we were in possession of a document that could influence global politics, yet my prying eye focussed on the banal items found in any dreary office: a stapler, a dishevelled IN tray, and a half drunk cup of coffee.

"Dom, this is pretty important. I need to speak to someone on how to proceed," he said before disappearing.

I was offered tea by one of his staff, curious to why a scruffy arsed Royal Marine was getting the VIP treatment.

Major John returned ten minutes later with instructions to call the number written down on a scrap of paper to arrange an appointment the following week. "When they ask you who you are, just say you work for me."

A perfectly elocutionary voice had answered the phone and asked me to report to his office in London the following Wednesday. Luckily my boss was on a course so I'd be able to sneak away.

In my early twenties with an address for a Whitehall office to discuss matter of national importance, I'd been overflowing with anticipation. Expecting it to be the highest security building in London, the address was hidden away, a   discreet barnacle within the annals of power. I knocked on the door. An elderly security guard answered. I informed him I was expected at room 12. He let me in without even giving me a security pass, which I'd found odd at the time. I wandered along the jaded second floor, only the massive oak doors that lined the landings didn't require repair. The silence was agitating. I stopped outside number 12. Composing myself, I knocked at the huge door. It echoed like Black Rod had smashed it.

"Come." The voice rang with a headmaster's tone.

I entered nervously.

"Ah come in, young man. It's our Royal Marine with his interesting list."

I walked into the office seemingly untouched since the 70's. The most modern item visible was a golf ball typewriter sat on a teak bureau. I could have been in a time warp. The man I now know as Peter sat at his desk, dressed sharply in a pinstriped suit with a slightly younger man to his right. They both offered a reassuring handshake. I handed over the information and sat patiently.

"Where did you get this list?' asked Peter.

"Northern Iraq. The source is reliable."

The younger man offered me a plate of biscuits. On inspection, I identified them as fruit biscuits from a 24-hour ration pack. I declined. He must have been of that ilk that thought Royal Marines only ate military rations in between killing.

Peter finally looked up after intensely studying the list of names. "Have you informed your commanding officer about this?"

"No, only Major John."

"Good, let's keep it that way. If you hear anything else regarding this list call me directly. There's no need to burden your chain of command, you've done the right thing bringing it here," he smiled cunningly, like a Somerset fox.

My mind was brought to the present by my phone ringing. As if he'd tapped into my thoughts. Peter. "Dom, I'm frightfully sorry, old chap, I can't make today's meeting I've been summoned to number two. I'm sending Trevor over, you don't know him but tell him what you need and I'll action it."

Peter was one of those characters you'd only come across once in a lifetime, a man the country required only when things got really dirty. I never imagined I would ever see or hear from him again. How wrong could I be?

As is often the case in London, I became distracted as two beautiful girls walked up the gangway and stepped onto the deck of the old ferry. They both wore dizzyingly high heels that complemented their long tanned legs rising up to short black miniskirts. They walked onto the upper deck confident that all eyes were upon them. I caught the eye of the taller girl. She smiled through glossed pouting lips. She was stunning. As I imagined joining them for a boozy lunch, a sweaty dishevelled man in a cheap suit appeared, looking lost.

That'll be Trevor. I thought. I signalled him over. He looked exactly how someone on a Ministry of Defence's MIDIT (Means of Identifying and Developing Internal Talent) scheme should—overworked with little time for personal appearance. The girls ignored him as he sat down.

I explained my concerns on Casablanca before handing over our written report. I wanted Peter to make sure it got to the Foreign Office via M16.

43

"That's it? You've come all this way just to issue warnings to tourists?"

"I was a bootneck, Trevor."

"Bootneck?"

"Royal Marine. And we tend to have a conscience. A few hours spared to spare a life? I don't think that's too much trouble."

"No, of course, thank you. I'll make sure this gets the attention it needs at Vauxhall. I'm fairly new to this department. May I ask what favour Sir Peter owes you? He mentioned something about Iraq."

"It doesn't matter, Trevor, it didn't make a difference for Iraq. No one is interested in the truth anymore, that's why I'm out of the circus."

He seemed uncomfortable at my dissonance. "OK," he stated with a pause. "Well, take my number, if there's anything you need just let me know."

I thanked him and shook his hand firmly, grateful that he too gripped with confidence before I headed off leaving the tab for Trevor to pay.

***

Stockholm, Sweden
59'39N 17'55E

I waited outside Arlanda airport, my cigarette smoke contaminating the crisp, distilled air. I watched many cars pass, hoping one was to be Hasse Moller's. All had dirty rims, it seemed car cleaning wasn't high on life's priorities at this time of year. Even in late autumn, the roads were lined with banks of soiled snow.

I was here due to the Star Clipper call I'd received while in Taroudant. The mysterious caller was revealed as Mikael Krafft, an extraordinary Swede and confidante of King Carl XVI Gustaf, who'd fulfilled a lifelong dream of reviving the golden age of tall ships. He operated three beautiful sailing vessels—the world's largest square rigger in service, *Royal Clipper*, the 170 passenger *Star Flyer*, and her four-masted sister ship *Star Clipper*.

Star Clipper was heading for Thailand from the Suez Canal. The voyage had been a disaster from a security standpoint, and after a major struggle, a German warship had escorted *Star Clipper* through 'Pirate Alley'. The ship was due to return to Suez in six months time and Mikael needed a solution in place. The immovable German captain, who flatly refused any weapons on his ship, had dashed all options.

"Dom, if you get an escort vessel to protect *Star Clipper* for the return voyage I'll give you the contract and you can name your price."

I accepted immediately, relishing the challenge, despite not having met Mikael. I didn't even bother with a contract. We were both men of integrity. In this gentleman's agreement I'd have to purchase, fit out and pilot a patrol craft 10,000 nautical miles to make the rendezvous with *Star Clipper* in less than five months. The fact I had no money to finance such a project mattered little.

Through an old acquaintance, Hasse Moller, Mikael had seen an old patrol boat in Sweden that he thought may be suitable and advised me to take a look.

Hasse arrived at the airport and welcomed me with a good firm handshake. Sometimes you meet certain people that give you the feeling that in another life you were close friends. I felt this warmth the minute I saw his smiling face, rubicund from years of enjoying sailing and alcohol. We jumped into his Volvo and headed to his boatyard on Hogmarso Island located in the Stockholm archipelago, arriving there by a small ferry hand built by Hasse. The fields were patchy with stubborn snow and muddy brown grass framed by a dull grey sky, a few weatherboard houses were the only indications that anyone inhabited the area. We drove down the only small track big enough for a Volvo to connect the southern part of the island. I smiled at the bleak beauty of my surroundings that could only be truly appreciated by these hardy people.

Hasse's boatyard was a collection of draughty boatsheds and small houses. The jetty space was around 300 metres long with an odd farrago of boats either at various stages of refit or sadly abandoned to slowly rot on rickety finger pontoons. I even spotted an old decrepit submarine. I loved the place. We walked until we reached *Combat Boat 234*, the vessel he wanted to show me. In Swedish naval circles, her class was known as the S200. Commissioned into the Swedish Navy in 1963, she was powered by two Volvo TMD 400HP engines that gave her a top speed just shy of 20 knots. At 22 metres, she was a good length, her armoured bridge, mounted just behind the bow section gave her the look of a waterborne tank. Originally designed to transport Swedish marines to defend the Swedish archipelago if the Soviet Baltic Fleet made a Cold War move, after 45 years of being knocked around, she was a prime candidate for Scrap Heap Challenge. Her structure was a neglected paint job of dirty white bows and blue patched sides half completed with greys then forgotten in the realisation that it was pointless. Pretty she was not, but character she possessed in spades; if Mad Max had been sent to ride the ocean he'd have picked her. Any pirate seeing this brute zoom over the horizon armed to the teeth would realise they could end up in a world of pain.

Hasse and I headed back to the yard office to talk business over a shot of *akvavit* that, as intended, burned the belly with friendship. I was honest with Hasse and explained that I had no money but some upcoming meetings to secure funding. He seemed supportive and unashamedly excited, as *234* would be the first private anti-piracy boat to enter the region with the noble mission to protect fellow mariners.

I needed to spend time alone with *234* to get a feel for her. I wandered around on deck careful not to bang into the array of protruding air intakes, hatches and lagged pipes that led to mysterious systems below. I entered the sanctum of the bridge more akin to a tank turret, awkwardly twisting my large frame to gain access to the cramped compartment. I sat on the captain's chair—a hybrid of a spring-loaded office chair melded with a barstool. It felt good with a beer in my hand sitting behind the small ship's wheel and massive throttles seemingly sized to boost the ego when pushed. A strange periscope in front of the steering position displayed the heading of the compass mounted on the bridge roof. A basic panel of ancient truck dials showed engine temperature, revs and starting switches. My 1975 Mini Cooper displayed more information. The small bulletproof windows gave a limited view but by standing on the chair and opening the hatch above I had a great vantage point and left me feeling like a tank commander. It was beautifully simple.

Time stood still in the space below deck. Only the yellow trails of rust staining the cold white bulkheads had changed in 45 years. Even the air felt old. If it wasn't for the rows of wooden benches, where marines once patiently waited ready to charge from the bow doors to attack their imaginary Baltic rivals, it could easily be mistaken for a tomb—a grim prophecy should things go wrong at sea. Trying not to bang my head both on entering and exiting, I failed both times.

The marvel of military boats is that they are over-engineered, built to withstand adrenalin fuelled young men defending them as hard as possible against equally supercharged young men trying their best to destroy them. *234* was rock solid and, despite her age and scrappy appearance, had plenty more sea miles ahead in the right hands. I entered the heart of the vessel—the engine room. Two big Volvo engines, made to last like the Swedish car, dominated the space. With the added bonus of 40 years in production, I'd easily be able to acquire parts from the back streets of Alexandria to the souks of Zanzibar. With the complexity of the anti-piracy operation working from remote areas, simplicity and reliability were the keys to success. I felt comfortable with *234* and as I'd be her first captain in the high-risk area, this was important for the safety of my crew. Once I had a crew, that is.

I returned to Hasse and held out my hand. "Do we have a deal?"

He didn't hesitate and firmly shook my hand. Trust is a maligned characteristic in the modern litigious world that I abhor, so my heart boomed with excitement as we agreed on a deal based on instinct of the other's eyes.

With no money to speak of, we spent the rest of the evening without a care in the world talking about our passion for boats.

***

West Buckland, UK
50'58N 03'10W

The clock ticked. I quickly needed cash. With the banks making a hash of things, the private investment market was on the rise. My black book overflowed with entrepreneurs, adventurers and oddballs, yet my plan appeared too rock 'n' roll for even the wildest card. I eventually tried my bank. Behind on a financially crippling mortgage, I approached them resigned to my proposal being an exercise in optimism. Of course, they declined. Misha and Olga offered to help but pulled out after taking a huge hit when the world banking system flat lined.

I called my old buddy Barry Roche who'd just sold his carpet cleaning business, so flush with cash. It was too risky for him to invest but as he loved the idea, he knew some people that might be interested. He introduced me to Chris Moore, a great big teddy bear and one of the nicest guys you could meet. He was willing to invest but needed a few people to help. We worked on a business plan before arranging a meeting in the mundane surroundings of a nondescript industrial complex on the outskirts of town. I was introduced to an interesting collection of potential investors that I'd never have associated with being interested in a maritime security company: owners of a construction materials business, a murder squad detective with the local Constabulary, and Andy Lynes, an unemployed former financial director. We conducted the meeting like an episode of Dragon's Den, just with less attractive investors. They wanted 49% for a £175,000 investment. I agreed as long as Andy worked as the Financial Director. This reassured them, as their mate would control the cash flow leaving me to focus on winning business and delivering it by fighting pirates.

Immediately after the meeting I rang Adrian 'Titch' Wibrew. He and I had become good friends while serving with 40 Commando in Belfast during the troubles. Fate dictated that we'd followed each other around the different units of the Royal Marines until we left the Corps within six months of each other. As he'd been the project manager for my solo kayaking expedition through

Canada's North West passage, I knew how Titch worked and trusted he could deliver.

"T, what are you up to?" I boomed excitedly down the phone.

"Could be better, mate. I quit my job at the real estate agents. It wasn't me to be honest, so I'm back instructing at the drop zone." Titch was one of life's optimists so I was surprised he sounded so low.

"I guess in between jumping out of planes you can work for me? Ring Ang and get a desk sorted out in the office."

"Roger that," his tone already improved. "What are we doing?"

"No time to explain, but believe me, it's the best one yet. Get hold of Bob Day and Killer. Oh, and get as many bootneck CV's as you can."

***

Hogmarso Island, Sweden
59'39N 18'51E

Hogmarso's snow capped tranquillity was destroyed with the growl of angle grinders and dancing sparks from welders feverishly working on patrol boat *234*. As a half finished project she looked even unhealthier than when I'd first fallen in love with her.

I knew Bob Day from working together on the Royal Navy offshore yacht racing team. Well versed in similar projects, he'd been in location for the last six weeks working on the boat and would be part of crew to Djibouti. *234* wasn't designed for such a long journey so modifications included adding bunks, constructing a galley that could provision for a fortnight and extra fuel tanks. Preparation was slower than hoped. Heavy snowfall hadn't helped, especially as I'd brought the departure date forward three weeks. Some years before, I'd sailed from Southampton to Qatar on Tracy Edwards's recording breaking catamaran *Maiden Two*. The voyage was to have taken around six weeks but after hitting a force 10 in the Bay of Biscay and ferocious winds in the Mediterranean, the voyage had turned into a hard fought battle to win every mile. The voyage had been in the autumn; *234* would be attempting a similar voyage in the depths of winter. We needed lots of snag time, for when the big storms rolled across the Atlantic the team could be held up in port for weeks waiting for the weather to clear. I couldn't afford delays of this nature. I needed to send my secret weapon—Mark 'Killer' Cowell.

No one really knew why he was called 'Killer', but he was a Royal Marines legend. He'd just returned from travelling around Europe in his beloved VW campervan; however, his marriage was not in good shape. His wife had given him an ultimatum: "The van or me."

She'd gone, leaving Killer to join me on yet another adventure. It was ironic that I was sending Killer to Scandinavia, as it was where we'd first met during arctic warfare training in northern Norway. My BV205 over snow vehicle had broken down. In the midst of a blizzard, all I could do was wait for recovery. The temperature had dropped to -35°C; even with my arctic clothing I'd felt dangerously cold. Mesmerised by the blinding whiteout outside, a man dressed in arctic white camouflage and snow goggles banged on my cab window.

"Hello Royal, I'm Killer. My cab's working, join me and get warmed up."

This random act of kindness was the catalyst for a lifetime of friendship.

Killer knew how to gets things done. When put on a straight line to an objective he was unstoppable. I needed his commitment and bulldozing brute force to get the boat to Djibouti on time; a challenge he savoured and a welcome distraction from matrimonial woes. Killer would also be on the delivery crew. He didn't know much about boats nor how to navigate them, and after the first day Bob phoned me to ask the purpose of Killer's arrival.

"What's he achieved today?" I asked.

"He's made bacon sandwiches, a few cups of tea and told some jokes."

"Well if he wasn't there you wouldn't have had those, would you?"

***

Bergen, Norway
60'23N 05'19E

It was raining, but it always rained in Bergen, even the ducks got trench foot. I sat outside the Metro nightclub under a canopy fitted with heating lamps that did nothing but warm pigeons cowering for shelter above.

It would be easy to bask in the sweet sunshine of securing the *Star Clipper* contract, yet I could see this as a conduit to a wider scope of work. Patrol boat escorts were innovative and may seem a little too left field for many companies but it gave me a foundation to go back to what I knew—onboard escorting of ships where I knew work would soon be plentiful.

Seizing upon any opportunity, a close friend and mutual acquaintance of Mikael Krafft, Stein Åre had kindly organised for me to give a presentation on the piracy situation in the Indian Ocean at the Norwegian Hull Club—a reputable and proactive organisation, insuring around a thousand ships, including *Star Clipper*. Through Stein I also managed to secure a business presentation with Jo Tankers—a big player in shipping with a large tanker fleet specialising in transporting chemicals. To maximise my opportunity, I brought Nige to Bergen. With twenty years of commercial security experience, he was a calming and reassuring influence in the boardroom. The *Star Clipper* contract gave us gravitas we could deliver a service to Jo Tankers.

I felt less nervous than expected when led into the plush Jo Tankers boardroom where sat a room of critical eyes surrounding the large oval table. From the outset, I took a confrontational stance to current security protocols. I spoke confidently on how we'd do business and to show we were different.

There'd been a recent incident in the Gulf of Aden that, on the face it, made the security industry look a bit of a shambles. MV *Biscaglia* had been en route to Suez loaded with palm oil when she came under attack from six armed pirates. The company had employed a security company to protect the vessel. The security team were unarmed but had utilised a LRAD acoustic device that emitted a supposedly unbearable noise to ward off potential pirates. After being pointed at the pirates for forty minutes it was clearly not an effective tool. After a sustained attack, the pirates had boarded *Biscaglia* forcing the security team to dive overboard. The pirates had then tried to shoot them in the water once they had control of the bridge and taken the crew hostage. The security team was only spared when a German Navy helicopter had arrived on scene to rescue them. I openly expressed my annoyance at the incident.

The meeting was going well. We were up against G4S, the world's biggest security company and a whole host of other organisations claiming they knew about maritime security through flow charts and financial reports. We had to impress. Nige and I fielded questions.

"Are you going to jump overboard when the pirates show up?" piped up one starch-collared board member with a rather condescending tone.

"I'll initially be on the ships myself and I can tell you 100% the pirates are not getting on board." I met his stare until he blinked.

Another man sat next to his doubting colleague asked, "How can you make such guarantees?"

It was a fair question, yet in these days of corporate double meanings, caveats and small print subterfuge, only straight talking would separate us from the rest. "I'm a man of my word. If I say they're not getting on board then it's not going to happen. Some pirates may die in the process. These are the new rules."

The board fell silent, wide-eyed glances exchanged; the room temperature had risen. It seemed a good time to break for lunch.

The cold fresh air was blessed relief to the compressing air of a highly charged boardroom. Nige and I discussed our feelings over a cigarette on how I had gone all in. Telling them we were prepared to kill for their company was a massive risk. I'd worn my heart on my sleeve and left them in no doubt I was not there to pussy foot around.

I really needed Nige if we won this contract, but he was about to leave for Iraq on a contract to secure the oil fields off Basra and the volatile Shatt al Arab waterway. He assured me that once the Iraq project was over he'd be there to join the team for the *Star Clipper* task.

We headed back in. Johan Odfjell, a senior member of the company, invited us into his office. It was brief and simple.

"Thank you for coming to Bergen to see us. I'm happy to inform you the board has unanimously voted for you to take care of our onboard security in the Indian Ocean."

I tried to play it cool despite welling excitement. "We're honoured that you've chosen us. Thank you."

After working on the upcoming vessel schedule, Johan escorted us to our waiting taxi. "If I could have your company information and banking details so we can put you on the system."

"Of course, I'll get the company secretary to sort it out upon my return," I said rather grandly as I shook his hand before jumping in the cab.

I looked at Nige. "I suppose I better get a bank account."

I'd only registered the company a couple of days before. I named it Protection Vessels International (PVI) with little thought in a dull thud of haste— we nearly owned a patrol boat that could be described as a 'protection vessel', and 'international' as it sounded flash.

In this moment it didn't matter. I hugged Nige. We were in business.

CHAPTER 5
Colombo, Sri Lanka
07'10N 79'52E

I watched intrigued by the flight plan on the screen of our Boeing 777. The plane approached Sri Lanka, giving a wide berth to the island's north where the government was in the midst of a huge offensive against Liberation Tigers of Tamil Eelam (LTTE), a fanatical terrorist group that had waged war against the Sri Lanka leadership for 25 years. They were known in the West as the Tamil Tigers and the group used suicide bombings, assassinations and child soldiers in their aim to have an independent state. The government had been secretly growing their military over two years and were now entrenched in a bitter fight to unseat the resilient Tigers from their northern stronghold.

Tension was palpable as passengers exited the aircraft—an attack here on Air Lanka flight 512 had left 21 Western tourists dead. More recently, the LTTE had launched vicious airstrikes against the airport and a ground assault by Black Tigers suicide squad had destroyed many aircraft.

Carrying body armour, radios and a whole host of military style equipment didn't quell my apprehension. Being detained at the airport is never a great start but an occupational hazard in our line of work. Our flight was under particular scrutiny; the government fearing the Tamil diaspora living in the UK would try and enter the country to launch attacks on the capital. I noticed to the right of the overzealous customs officer a kind looking local holding a board bearing my name. He introduced himself as Anil De Alwis from Sri Lanka Shipping Company. He quickly escorted me and my eight-man team to the front of the queue. After a momentary protest from the customs officer, our passports were stamped and we were whisked to the waiting minibuses.

Dave 'The Seat' Seaton smiled at me. "That was easier than expected."

"Indeed, now we just have to get to our hotel without getting blown up."

With a civil war raging just 100 kilometres to the north, Colombo was on high alert. The previous week, a female suicide bomber had detonated a device in the city centre killing two airmen and injuring 36 civilians. We slowly entered the outer limits of the capital, traffic moved at a snail's pace not only due to congestion, but by endless checkpoints manned by nervous, trigger happy young soldiers, creating a ring of steel to prevent attacks. The scene was chaotic as tuk tuk's weaved in and out of traffic and overloaded motorbikes wobbled along the pavement in the brutal midday heat.

Philippe watched the hive of traffic. "I'm glad we're not chasing buses on mopeds here."

"I thought you'd be happy to be back with suicide bombers."

Our first Jo Tankers job was to protect three of their ships: *Jo Oak* and the *Jo Brevik* out of Colombo, and *Jo Betula* from Durban, South Africa already heading north on task with the security team disembarking in Djibouti—the smallest of enclaves perched on the Horn of Africa

I sat with Anil to get an update on the ships' estimated times of arrival to Colombo outer port limits (OPL). Anil warned that with the tight security it could take three hours to pass through the port. My ship, *Jo Oak*, wasn't due in for another day, but Dave's ship, *Jo Brevik*, would be available to board in four hours.

I'd never served with Dave but he was highly respected within the Royal Marines and I liked him from the minute we met. Having already completed many maritime transits in the region, he seemed the ideal choice to be the Team Leader of lads who were complete strangers with only commonality of operational scars and military humour to bond them for the weeks of potential conflict ahead. Mark Rippin had been working out in Iraq for three years when I'd called him. He signed up and left Iraq a week later. It was a good time to go. His team lost two guys on the next rotation. It could have been him. John Rhodes had not been so lucky. The company he worked for were cutting safety to make more money. His frustrations had boiled over when his warnings that one route to Baghdad airport was being overused were ignored. With a week left before he finished his rotation, his vehicle was hit by an IED. He lost his whole team. These events never made the news. They weren't celebrities regurgitating stage-managed drivel on irrelevant issues. Apart from their families and the brothers with whom they served, no one cared.

Setting off 24 hours ahead, Dave and his team would check in with me daily to warn of any trouble before disembarking in Djibouti. Although *Jo Betula* had already set off, watching the lads prepare for their departure from Colombo filled me with pride. These guys, a few of whom I'd never met before, were my trusted steeds going to battle, so the hug I gave them prior to boarding the vessel was one of trust that they would do the business.

"Keep safe, brothers." It was all I could say. The rest was up to them.

***

After clearing customs, via five equally fastidious offices, we finally arrived at our transfer vessel on the dock. Anil came to wave us off.

"Thanks, Anil. I hope the war finishes soon, my friend," I said truthfully.

"Pray for us." His smile couldn't hide his sadness.

With that, the lines were taken on board and we headed for the OPL. The port closed at night due to the threat from Sea Tigers the LTTE maritime wing that used explosive-laden suicide boats to attack naval and civilian vessels. Already having been delayed two hours for us to board, the *Jo Oak* captain would obviously be nervous waiting too long in these deadly waters. This apprehension would not be eased by the Napoleonic defence system with naval detachments deployed on individual jetties and concrete gun positions all wanting to check us. All requested the same forms, all noted our body armour with the same suspicion and all asked the same questions. All were answered identically.

Jo Oak appeared on the horizon. At 175 metres, her red hull and white superstructure made her look like a dirty Polish flag. We boarded the vessel by pilot ladder, our welcome a direct question from an unsmiling Filipino crewmember asking if we had weapons. "This is not Subic Bay," he warned.

Already fully laden with palm oil bound for Port Sudan, the captain put the tanker underway, keen to get as far away from Sri Lanka as possible. Our destination was hardly a tourism hotspot either—Sudan had been crippled by sanctions imposed by the USA after the guided missile destroyer USS *Cole* was bombed while refuelling in the Yemeni port of Aden. Seventeen sailors were killed as the crew ate in the galley. Al-Qaeda had taken responsibility for the bombing, but a US judge ruled that Sudan was

59

liable for the attack and froze $13 million of Sudanese assets that were later paid to the victims of the attack.

Before we became reliant on expensive satellite comms, I gave Titch one last phone call to update him on our situation and to ask if everything else was going to plan.

Now heading up the operations and logistics for both the deployed PVI onboard security teams and the patrol boat project, Titch knew *DM234* needed to get a wriggle on if it were to make the RV with *Star Clipper* in April. Hasse Moller, although a man who I'd witnessed accepting trust as sacrosanct, rightly asked for payment for the work so far completed, but Titch kept getting stalled by Andy Lynes from our small admin office in Hatfield. Something wasn't right.

I couldn't dwell on problems I couldn't solve, so sat down in the captain's cabin, gratefully accepting his simple hospitality. He confirmed the requested stores had arrived, but the company could only procure barbed wire not razor wire, and the flares, while plentiful, were woefully outdated. It was hardly reassuring. With little of the stores required to properly prepare the vessel for a safe passage through the pirate-infested waters of the Indian Ocean, resourcefulness, I would often realise, became an increasingly important business attribute and 'cuffing it'— the military term for imaginative improvisation on the go—was a delicious contrast to the confined corporate world I viewed with disdain.

I briefed my team on the 'Macgyver' task ahead, one they undertook with relish. I was lucky to have a former Special Forces communication specialist to locate any radio blind spots and a former Royal Marine Landing Craft coxswain to survey potential boarding points on the stern. Philippe and I headed down to the deck level to work out how to secure the accommodation block if we failed to repel the pirates and were boarded.

The ship was an older vessel in the Jo Tankers' fleet and due to be scrapped later in the year. On the plus side, she carried plenty of spares and offered an extensive workshop where we could manufacture improvised weapons and defence systems. If, in the unlikely event we were overrun, we would cut all power to disable the ship and muster in the ship's citadel—an area where we could safely bunker down until the navy arrived. We had two days to convert her from a jaded old tanker to a medieval super fortress of the seas.

After working around the clock, we practised emergency drills with the captain and crew including calling the UKMTO. The United Kingdom Maritime Trade Operations connects merchant vessels around the world to military forces in the region. This safety protocol is supposed to speed up communication with nearby warships when a vessel is attacked, though the results don't always live up to expectation. With this in mind we hoped we'd never have to call them.

At last I stood in the comfort of the sea—my womb where I felt at one with the world—my men already primed for a war yet to begin. I could stand on the bridge wings, breathe in sea air and look to the horizon. Beyond where the sun sat on the sea I knew predators were hunting ships. If pirates wanted us, they better be prepared to die for their spoils. PVI was ready for business.

***

North of Socotra, Gulf of Aden
13'22N 53'14E

Already one could smell the ocean chill that hid behind the late afternoon heat. I joined Philippe on *Jo Oak's* bridge wings speckled with rust blisters from elongated inattention; maintenance budgets for soon-to-be scrapped ships weren't massive. It was sunset, my favourite time of day at sea. The molten deity Ra dipped below the iridium metal horizon setting the sky ablaze. Despite the serenity, we knew from reports over the satellite system that there'd been a number of attacks in the area. Titch relayed updates of other emerging threats, but in that moment, with tea and binoculars to hand as we drifted along at 13 knots, calmness was the order of the day.

Container ships were passing to starboard heading at full speed to make the northbound convoy at Suez. In twelve hours we'd reach the illegal crossing between Yemen and Somalia.

The intense street fighting in Mogadishu between the American backed Transitional Federal Government (TFG) and the radical groups Hizbul Islam and Al Shabaab had triggered an exodus of war-weary families to leave the besieged city. The desperate diaspora, under the absurd notion of buying a passage to freedom, headed to the northern Somali port of Bosaso where unscrupulous people traffickers waited to profit from their misery. Happily taking the last of their money or possessions in return for a boat ride to the Promised Land, the traffickers would tell the families that once they landed in Yemen they could easily cross the mountains to the north to reach Dubai's gold-paved streets. In reality, few would make it to dry land. The people traffickers would, in many cases, fire their AK47's into the air upon seeing the Yemeni coast, forcing their fearful cargo of women and children overboard to swim for shore. Most never made it. The beach at Wadi Al-Barak would bear witness when the sea released the bodies of these poor unfortunate souls. While Mexicans crossed into California or Eastern Europeans hid under trucks to enter the UK, African corpses rotting in the Middle East were swept under a Western media rug.

The few that made it ashore would be become official refugees at the UN camp at Mayfa Hajar; Dubai's 6 star hotels an unreachable mirage of unfulfilled dreams. The brutal traffickers would then return to Bosaso and try and hijack a ship en route. I hated these cowardly scumbags with a passion.

"Do you know much about the individual pirates out here?" Philippe's question caught me off guard.

"As much as there is to know I guess. I've heard a lot of chatter about Garaad Mohamed who is making a big name for himself as a successful hijacker."

It was patently clear that Garaad Mohamed exuded confidence. He 'd risen to the top in this new era of piracy, revelling in his own myth. Unrecognisable to anyone outside of his pirate crews, his elusiveness magnified the legend he'd carved as 'Carlos The Jackal'. Rumours abound of him serving in the British Army, and while false, he *had* been trained by British Army officers and by a British security company contracted by the then Puntland President Abullahi Yusuf when forming the new Puntland Coast Guard. Sadly, it was another example of Western interference coming back to bite it on the arse.

Garaad had been one of 70 trained in boarding techniques, ship security, weapons training, and seamanship, all skills that would become useful later in life. The unit proved to be an efficient force, arresting many trawlers fishing illegally in Somali waters, but like many success stories in Somalia, it was short-lived. As warring factions in Puntland took part in the cultural pastime of mutual murder, chaos ensued, forcing the British security company to withdraw. The contract was renegotiated and bizarrely given to an opportunist Somali whose only training in conflict was kicking out drunken passengers as a Toronto taxi cab driver. The Somali Canadian Coast Guard (SOMCAN) was formed and quickly grew into a force of 400 marines backed up by six patrol boats. Three years later, the president disbanded the force due to some rogue units hijacking a Thai fishing vessel asking for an $800,000 ransom. It's not known whether Garaad was responsible, but now unemployed he'd decided it an opportune time to carve a lucrative career as a pirate.

It was also an ideal opportunity for former civil servant and entrepreneur Mohamed Abdi Hassan, also known as 'Afweyne'—translated as 'Big Mouth'—to turn his local clan Hoybo fishermen into an exceptionally hardcore group calling themselves 'Somali Marines', operating from Harardhere. Supposedly they were the most organised of all pirate groups, trained by Garaad whose initial pirate faction had already seen fantastic financial returns on their pirate ventures.

Never one to sit under anyone's command, Garaad soon formed the National Volunteer Coast Guard, a rather official name for his exceptionally well-trained bandits who ran from the Southern port of Kismayo. Rather than become each other's adversary, bloodlines as well as business acumen resulted in Big Mouth financing Garaad's operations—an alliance that made them the number one pirate business on the market with reach as far as Haradhere and Hoybo.

Although successful, they weren't the only ones trading in lucrative misery. There were a number of traffickers and opportunist pirates working out of Bosaso commanded and financed by the fierce Farah Hirsi Kulan, known as 'Boyah', a man who masqueraded himself as a businessman, yet like many of the country's rich, he ran his business through unethical accountants and savage enforcers. It may not be the West's idea of business, but in the mayhem of a fractured society, the most common negotiation tool is an AK47.

Other groups operating from the mid-coast towns of Garacad and Eyl were mainly used as reinforcements when hijacked ships came to anchor in the area to await ransom payment. After four to six pirates hijacked a ship, thirty or more would arrive at the main pirate anchorage to protect her, ironically from other pirates. There was no honour in this modern criminal world.

It'd been over a year since I last passed through this troubled waterway. It felt good to be back. Work here had dried up two years before when the Islamic Courts Union (ICU) had seized power. Their decree that piracy was against the teaching of Islam and punishable by death seemed, on the face of it, to bring a semblance of law and order to a chaotic Somalia and a welcome break for many Somalis after years of fighting.

The US administration; however, had feared the birth of an Islamic terrorist state, so backed the Ethiopian Army to invade and assist in putting someone they could deal with back on the throne in Mogadishu.

The inevitable fall into anarchy ensued as the US backed TFG, controlling just a few suburbs of the capital, declared itself as the Somali Government. The Ethiopian troops, bogged down and caught in the cross fire, decided it an ideal time to return home and let the country slide into its normal state of turmoil.

In the power vacuum left by the fallen ICU, the pirates were back in the game. Business boomed. Piracy had not been so profitable since Captain Kidd and all the other pirates sacked from the Caribbean headed to a new hunting ground of the Indian Ocean between 1680-1730.

Like a ghost from the past, we were entering a new golden age of piracy.

"Dom, skiffs up ahead," said Joe Jones, an ex-paratrooper who'd made an unlikely leap from land to sea.

I threw on my body armour and entered the bridge. The captain looked nervous. Joe pointed out the potential threat—two skiffs about a mile ahead. Neither moved.

"I've sounded the alarm. The crew are in the galley all accounted for."

"Thank you, Captain. It's probably nothing, but we need to be ready," I smiled as if I did this every day, but my heart sparked with eagerness.

I asked the captain to increase to top speed, adjusting the course to 5° starboard then another 5° to put further distance between the skiffs and us.

The key was to maintain good speed if attacked. Should the captain make a big turn we'd lose speed, allowing the pirates better opportunity to board.

My team positioned themselves as drilled. With both bridge wings covered, Philippe stood on the stern ready to fire our rocket tubes. I stood shoulder to shoulder with the captain to control security and calmly offered reassurance even if adrenaline coursed through my pulsing veins.

The ship's fire hoses were activated, high-powered water sprayed out along both sides of the vessel to make boarding harder. It also notified the skiffs' occupants that we were prepared should they try to take us on. The skiffs remained static standing off at around 500 metres as we passed. This could quickly change if they decided to go for it—they'd be on us in five minutes.

Both skiffs contained four men. I couldn't see any weapons or ladders but they watched us closely. The second mate picked up a static dhow three miles out. This could be their mother ship. Pirates had adopted this tactic to enable them to stay at sea for longer periods. A hijacked fishing vessel could launch skiffs to attack merchant ships. This *modus operandi* offered them greater range and had yielded much success.

The skiffs chose not to attack and drifted away to our stern, yet this gave no reason to relax. It would be easier for them to try a weaker ship, and there were plenty of those rolling through the Indian Ocean. Many ship owners and captains were oblivious to the pirate problem and did nothing to protect their ships. I found this approach a lack of a duty of care and totally reckless.

I stood my team down after two hours at defence watches, but remained vigilant. This group could communicate our position to a larger pirate group ahead. Looking at our course and speed we'd thankfully pass through the narrows of Babel Mandab at night. This choke point separating the Gulf of Aden from the Red Sea is only ten miles across, and a place where pirates are guaranteed to find ships.

***

Port Sudan, Sudan
19'35N 37'16E

After turning the ship into a fortress, we now dismantled all our defences to ready the ship for entering port—harbour authorities don't appreciate barbed wire. The deck became a flurry of activity as the crew prepared the cargo ready for discharge. Palm oil solidifies in a ship's tanks, so at the base of these huge tanks sit industrial elements that slowly heat the oil in what could be considered the world's biggest kettles to make the oil flow through the outlet pipes. As our job finished, the crew's main purpose began.

The ship was delayed due to no berth being available. We weren't alone, the OPL teemed with waiting ships. This gave me a chance to check in with Titch and Killer, as our patrol boat should now be on its way heading south. It wasn't. Titch explained that Hasse still hadn't been paid, and Andy hadn't explained why. I couldn't hide my frustration. I'd done the deal with the shareholders, yet they clearly didn't understand the big picture. I thought maybe they'd got cold feet.

Being stuck at sea didn't help. I'd given my word to Hasse and Mikael—my personal bond that I feared had been abused. I rang Hasse to apologise. Having spent most of his life at sea he knew the complexity of boat owners and late payments so sympathetic to my issues. I reassured him if they didn't pay I'd leave the investors behind and personally cover the cost from the Jo Tankers job.

Titch relayed some other chilling information. An Israeli airstrike had recently hit Port Sudan in an attempt to intercept an arms convoy heading to the port with rockets bound for Gaza. Great, after passing through a seaborne threat we were now in an airstrike zone.

I love entering a new port—the expectation of exotica, the people and the food always makes my hairs stand to attention. The first noticeable difference here were the masses of UN vehicles and containers stacked high on the sun-bleached concrete. The UN was intensifying one of its largest missions to protect civilians in Darfur located along the border with Chad. The war had claimed over 300,000 lives and displaced 2.5 million. Later that year, the International Criminal Courts would indict President Omar al-Bashir for war crimes.

Jo Oak approached the berth, nudged along by two invalided tugs, much to the irritation of the captain. The long dock was electric with ships unloading as quickly as possible. As fast as our mooring lines hit the bollards, discharge tubes were connected, and palm oil immediately sucked from *Jo Oak's* massive hull into huge landside storage tanks.

I said my farewell to the captain who seemed extremely impressed by our service. Such recognition always gave me a wonderful feeling of satisfaction. The fact that our job was protecting people only made it greater.

We climbed the steps of the Sudan Airways 737 for our flight to Khartoum. Sudanese women clumsily carried an assortment of large colourful bags that would never fit in the overhead lockers but no one cared. I was keen to get the flight over with as soon as possible, this flight route didn't have a great safety record—five years before, Flight 139 had crashed killing 116 passengers and crew, remarkably a three year old boy survived. More recently, flight 109 had crashed killing thirty after being diverted to Port Sudan in bad weather. With the added danger of Israeli jets flying covert airstrikes, it was time to go home.

CHAPTER 6
Roville-devant-Bayon, France
48'28N 06'18E

Through the squeaking wiper that smeared February sleet across the windshield I could just make out the French customs official aggressively pointing me into the search bay. Having previously declared my firearm to British customs before boarding the *Pride of Canterbury* ferry, I readied my firearms licence for inspection. My main worry was what the surly customs agent would think of the four General Purpose Machine Gun mounts squeezed into my Saab 900 convertible.

He looked at me with Gallic disdain in his neatly pressed blue blouson and his perfectly aligned kepi hat. "What is the purpose of your visit to France?" he asked, as though I had 20kgs of cocaine stashed under the hood.

"Wild Boar hunting," I said with a Roger Moore tone.

He inspected my military style Franchi SPAS semi-automatic 12-gauge shotgun. He seemed happy with the explanation despite the weapon looking better suited to robbing banks than shooting boar.

My trusty, rusty old Saab, as draughty as a barn on the Nebraska plains, rattled along the French highway towards Roville-devant-Bayon, a pretty nondescript town on the French canal system where Killer had organised us to meet so I could drop off the shotgun and machine gun mounts for the patrol boat, newly named *DM234*, now finished, but still not paid for. The shotgun was for the crew's protection once they got to the southern part of the Red Sea where pirates had recently been hunting.

This was not the original plan. *DM234* was meant to motor through the canals to Rotterdam then head south across the Bay of Biscay and enter the Mediterranean via

Gibraltar. After doing some research, Hasse believed that the boat could make it to the Med through the canal system via Germany and France. It was quicker but a major gamble. If the boat didn't fit through a lock somewhere en route, we would not make the RV with *Star Clipper* in time. With time running out, it was the better of the two options.

I reached the towpath and for the first time saw the newly refitted *DM234*. I glowed with pride. She was back to her former glory painted in a battleship grey—a dour colour that strikes menace on the high seas. I took the boys out for dinner with a mandatory large side order of rum. Due to his alcoholic overindulgence, Bob, failed to negotiate the *DM234*'s narrow walkway and fell overboard, losing his phone in the process. He had been officially 'Dommed'—a rite of passage all my friends must go through. I love rum and drink it like a pirate. The irony isn't lost on me.

Still tight on time, it was frustrating that no vessels were allowed to navigate at night, and with the canal frozen, *DM234* had to break the ice all the way through France. I hoped her reinforced bows would take the punishment.

Mikael Krafft called me weekly for updates, clearly nervous we wouldn't make the RV. He had 170 passengers' lives to think about. I reassured him that we would be there even if I had to swim with a towline in my teeth. I refrained from mentioning the 160 canal locks we had to pass through before we hit the open sea, I didn't want him panicking further. Killer, one of life's problem solvers, bought a bike and cycled ahead of DM234 to open the lock gates ahead of the boat to save time. He did this the whole length of France. Killer got things done.

***

DM234 arrived victoriously in St Louis, Napoleon after an epic voyage from the Baltic. Finally setting eyes on the Mediterranean, the crew of *DM234* had succeeded by the skin of their chattering teeth. The following day, the last lock of the canal was to be closed for four weeks maintenance. If the admirably generous Hasse hadn't released *DM234* due to not yet receiving a cent for the boat or subsequent work, PVI as a business would have folded at this final lock gate and with a reputation in tatters I'd struggle to find security work again.

The customs officers were especially interested in this reconditioned military boat and a team of officials were soon crawling over every inch of her. They found my shotgun along with a copy of my licence but confiscated it, insisting that the owner had to be present. The four GPMG mounts, Russian night sight and the host of military equipment raised even more attention.

The Customs Inspector asked in failed English, "Are you Missionaries?"

Never one to miss a punch line, Killer replied with a deadpan face, "Yes we are delivering bibles to Djibouti."

Despite having served over twenty years in the Royal Marines, Killer showed scant regard for authority. On one occasion in his distant and eventful past, he worked as a radio operator on the Amphibious Assault ship HMS *Intrepid*, when the First Sea Lord—the figurehead of the Royal Navy—boarded the ship for his inspection with his usual entourage of officers. For the ship's captain, failure to give a good impression could result in a major slowdown of promotion, so all visits were micro-managed to ensure that any crewmember present had an officer close by to stage manage behaviour. The herd of officers piled into 45 Commando's operation room and, after small talk with other marines, approached Killer to the dismay of the Zulu Company Sergeant Major who knew him as a wild card.

The First Sea Lord leaned forward to Killer. "Marine Cowell is it? What's your impression of HMS *Intrepid*?"

"Sorry, Sir, I don't normally do impressions; however, seeing as though it's you…" With that he leapt from his chair, and wobbling on his right leg pointed to his left now horizontal in the air. "This," he said, pointing to the outstretched leg; "this is the stern…"

The dropping pin was deafening.

"…And this," he added to the astonished crowd, nodding to his outstretched right arm; "this is the bow, which is the front bit, just in case you didn't know. My head is the funnel, toot toot!"

The entourage stared in disbelieve. The Admiral smirked, then chuckled, then burst into raucous laughter, the catalyst for a chorus of sycophantic guffawing from the junior officers keen not to be left out. The sergeant major didn't laugh, and Killer spent an eternity on punishment duties.

The team in St Louis needed to lift *DM234* to check for any hull damage from breaking the ice. The propellers were broken but everything else remained workable. Hasse had already dispatched the new replacement propellers from Sweden and would arrive the following day. I truly appreciated Hasse's support. Without his benevolence our adventure would never have worked.

I also had to replace the temporary Swedish crew who were required home to re-join their ship, so contacted super yacht captain Bill Lawrence, affectionately referred to as 'Mr Bill', to see if he knew someone to deliver *DM234*. I'd worked with him on board the super yacht *Hetairos*, racing in the 'Maxi World championship regatta'. He was at a loose end so volunteered himself and 'Taff'

Falvey. Mr Bill soon took charge and prepared the boat for sea.

The voyage across the Mediterranean hit problems immediately, as bad weather, a big swell and 45kn winds slammed *DM234*. One of the bow doors failed, causing a huge intake of water just as the bilge pumps failed. To avoid sinking, the crew sought refuge in the nearest port of Toulon to make rudimentary repairs using door sealant and car body filler. The choice of going via the canals had been a good call, if this situation had happened in the unpredictable seas of the Bay of Biscay, the boat and crew could have been lost.

***

Port Said, Egypt
31'15N 31'18E

The entrance to the Suez Canal is always an over-zealous throng of boats offering the best in Egyptian tat. *DM234* appeared an obvious target as she entered port. This would be the start of lies and confusion by the masters of baksheesh.

Egypt's disorder masquerades as its working system. The country runs on the fabric of imagination, masked by official ministries that issue rubber stamps of fantasy to those happy to offer something in return. In essence, Egyptian officials are pantomime actors who make up rules as they go along and charge for imaginary services.

Karim was the first cast member to arrive on the dock. He carried an old worn out tape, more useful for a tailor than a waterway, and grandly declared himself 'The Official Measurer Of The Suez Canal'. In fairness, he played the role extremely well, writing down in-depth, but incorrect, measurements of the vessel in his note pad, just to sprinkle a dash of authenticity to his charade.

Sayeed, the agent, then came on board carrying a red spined ledger that gave the impression of authority without really fooling anyone. He declared the ship's papers fake, as they displayed no stamp. Killer jumped down below and immediately fashioned his own crude replica from a potato embossed with the letters 'PVI' then covered it in broken pen ink to stamp all the boat's paperwork. It was truly the work of a kindergarten arts class, but upon his return Sayeed declared his delight that Killer had found the official stamp to clear customs.

Amidst this farce, *DM234* ran the gauntlet of rank and file seaborne hawkers slugging it out to catch the crew's ambivalence, all begging with their well rehearsed sales pitch stuck on repeat. Their plan was simple: wear you down so you would eventually pay. They all held a MBA in irritating and a PhD in unhelpfulness. In contrast, the local bank manager kindly allowed Killer to draw unpaid funds, as long as Killer then paid for the manager's yearly gym membership. I could only imagine the quizzical look on our Financial Director's face when reconciling increasingly bizarre receipts.

DM234 finally received permission to be released from the greasy paws of the canal after an American warship passed through and more importantly, Killer's payment of two of cans of ice cold Coca Cola and 200 Marlboro cigarettes. Now they could enjoy the calmer Gulf of Suez heading south into the Red Sea.

After five days steaming through the deep blue waters of the Red Sea, they sighted the Hanish Islands as a low flying USAF F16 tipped its wings to say 'Hi' before playfully swooping them in a fly by. A number of warships loomed on the horizon as they approached the high-risk area. A Royal Navy Lynx helicopter buzzed *DM234*, asking for the ship's peculiars, watched closely by a Royal Marine sniper from the side door.

It was one of those days where the weather sought approval, light winds hushed away the sun's kisses, a mirrored sea only too happy to absorb the dappled shadows of the perfect cotton ball clouds, yet the crew knew they were entering a war zone. *DM234* passed through the dangerous straits of Bab el Mandab bearing to starboard into the Gulf of Tadjoura. For some of the crew, this would mark the end of their adventure. For the rest, it was just the beginning.

***

Djibouti
11'36N 43'08E

As the Qatar Airways Boeing 777 came into land, I caught sight of the tail section of a MQ1 Predator being hastily pushed into its hanger away from prying eyes. These pilotless aircraft were the latest arsenal available to the CIA in East Africa to kill Al-Qaida suspects operating in Yemen.

This lucky glimpse hadn't been the only unusual occurrence on my journey. The previous day I'd been detained by customs in Qatar for carrying *DM234's* body armour, night observation scopes, combat helmets and radios.

The Qatari customs officer had seen me pushing my excess baggage to the nothing to declare exit so directed me to the x-ray machine. Clearly my cargo was not that of a tourist and it wasn't long before I was surrounded by a gaggle of customs officials. It is always wise in such a situation to listen and not speak. From the little Arabic I understood, it emerged that my equipment wasn't welcome in downtown Doha before my onward flight to Djibouti.

A senior customs officer had arrived to translate and take charge of the situation. "Why are you carrying this equipment, are you military?"

Upon leaving the Royal Marines I'd illegally kept my military ID card for the sole reason of retaining a serving member discount at a London hotel. This act of penny pitching could save the day. The SAS motto *Who Dares Wins* was quickly becoming my business model and cuffing it now second nature. The downside being if I was rumbled I'd likely be arrested.

I pulled out my expired ID card. "I'm serving with the Royal Navy and joining my ship in Djibouti. These are ship stores," I said with conviction. The art of lying is to really believe what you're saying.

His mood immediately changed. "We will keep your stores in the airport and return them before your onward flight."

I thanked him as he'd actually saved me a rather sweaty job of lugging all this kit into Doha, so had headed downtown hoping they wouldn't run a check on my service number.

The noxious hairdryer of Djiboutian air hit me as I walked down the aircraft steps. An assortment of old Russian cargo planes littered the hard stand. My fellow travellers charged towards the ramshackle arrivals building ignoring a man dressed in a quirky medical outfit optimistically trying to stick an otoscope into arriving passengers' ears to make sure they weren't importing foreign infections to add to their domestic ones.

It soon became clear why the plane's occupants had stampeded to the airport building. The visa section was a first-come-first-serve scrum. I decided to deploy the

British reserve and wait till the kerfuffle subsided. The immigration counter welcomed passengers with a tired old fan that re-circulated hot air, and nicotine stained walls unpainted since the French ran the show. Beyond, lay a noisy baggage belt where scuffed cases were thrown roughly from the beaten up cargo truck parked at the mysterious side of dirty rubber flaps.

After finally collecting my visa, I received the unnecessarily large page-filling passport stamp from the disinterested immigration official. A large sign behind the counter read '*No Kha't*'. Kha't, khat or qaat depending on where you're from, is a flowering evergreen shrub native to East Africa. The plant contains two alkaloids that act as stimulants. Users simply chew the green leaves, keeping a ball of partially chewed leaves against the inside cheek, similar to chewing tobacco. Legal in most east African countries, it has been classed as a substance of abuse by the Western led World Health Organization, ignoring cultural heritage. Some side effects have been described as manic and delusional behaviour, suicidal depression, hallucinations and paranoia. Pirates love the stuff and are often armed under the influence of this ancient high.

No one batted an eyelid at my body armour and equipment. This was a frontier town surrounded by instability. On its southern border, Somalia, to the west and north, Ethiopia and Eritrea respectively, where recent border clashes created simmering hostility.

I'd arranged to be picked up by a man called Bruno, a local fixer who'd take me to *DM234's* crew and could organise the necessary permits to sail from Djibouti. He was also the point of contact for certain business items I badly needed—weapons.

The key factor in selecting weapons for onboard security teams was range. Any long barrelled 7.62mm full metal jacket, or Winchester .308 would easily out range the Kalashnikov and from a ship's stable platform could direct more accurate fire at any potential hijacker. It was simple. UKMTO wouldn't agree, of course, but it's hard to comprehend realities when an odious silver spooned clown sat in the safety of an air-conditioned office in Dubai, their biggest danger a lip burn from an overly-hot takeaway coffee.

The smell of a new country always revives my intrinsic love of travel. Here, the first sniff of Djibouti told me it was dangerous, exotic, exciting—a place where a stare could get you sex, violence, or both.

I pulled out a Marlboro and stood under a tree to get some shade; here, even in late March, a waning sun could drill through my skull and boil my brain.

Airports are havens for jackals waiting to take advantage of the tired and disorientated. A scruffy young guy, languorous with unkempt long hair approached me. "Hey you, are you from PVI?" he asked in a surly French accent.

"Who's asking?" My glare indicating I didn't appreciate his salutation.

"Bruno sent me."

I threw him one of my bags and jumped inside his dilapidated 4x4 that bore all the mechanical hallmarks of my motorbike in Casablanca.

DM234 was already in port. Titch had arranged for the crew to spend two well-deserved nights in the plush Kempinski hotel after the long, cramped voyage from Sweden. Taff had pulled the short straw and stayed on the boat, where a pair of opportunist thieves had relinquished him of his mobile phone and wallet. Thankfully, this haul was satisfactory enough for them to steal back into the darkness and hide under the rock from which they'd crawled.

I walked into the Kempinski bar, already surrounded by a gathering of Spanish Navy personnel and some American naval officers who sat talking politics. All were in uniform, something I found strange, as in my former service life all I wanted to do was jump into my civilian clothes to blend in and relax.

Whiling away the time, I watched a grey haired guy dressed smartly in a dinner jacket playing a parlour grand piano accompanied by a similarly aged singer dressed in a figure hugging black dress that complemented her seductive curves. She radiated class and her soft voice massaged the room. I guessed they'd been in the entertainment business most of their lives. They took a break and the pianist approached the bar. I bought him a drink in appreciation. He introduced himself as Maurice Hope, a familiar name that I couldn't quite place. We talked for a while, he explaining that he and his wife mainly worked on the cruise line circuit. He mentioned he'd worked on the *Oceanos* cruise ship.

"The *Oceanos*?" I interrupted, just to confirm I'd heard correctly.

"Yes, but it was a long time ago."

The penny dropped, I now knew why I recognised the name. I bought him another drink and vigorously shook his hand.

In 1991, the *Oceanos* embarked on a voyage from East London, South Africa to Durban carrying 571 passengers when she hit bad weather. The ship hadn't received a proper refit in years and a multitude of defects would collaborate into a disaster as 9-metre swells smashed the ship. Passengers trying to eat in the main dining area were thrown across the floor as waiters fell with full trays of food while the storm violently rocked the ship. A muffled explosion had vibrated through the ship from the engine room before the ship lost all power. As the captain hadn't made an announcement to say otherwise, passengers calmly returned to their cabins assuming things were under control. The lower deck passengers first noted signs of impending doom when their cabins flooded. Knee deep in seawater, some headed to the bridge to inform the captain. To their horror the bridge was empty. The captain and ship's crew had abandoned ship without issuing the order to passengers. They were alone.

One of the ship's entertainers, Maurice Hope, on finding the bridge empty, used the ship's radio to broadcast a mayday until another ship responded. With the stricken ship now listing heavily in the wild ocean, Maurice took charge and, assisted by the cabaret, organised an orderly evacuation as rescue helicopters arrived. Maurice and his wife Tracy were the last to be rescued, an action normally undertaken by the Master, but Captain Yiannis Avaranas, like Captain Francesco Schettino of *Costa Concordia*, was a coward.

Before he returned to play, I again shook Maurice's hand; this time with such gusto he feared I'd end his piano career. I was honoured to meet him.

The *DM234* crew walked into the bar. I was relieved that they'd arrived on time and I knew it was partly down to Mr Bill's considerable experience. I stared at Killer's feet. He was wearing the hotel's complimentary slippers.

"Don't ask," he said, knowing that was exactly what I wanted to do. "I've lost my shoes and my flip flops went overboard on the way down."

I can unequivocally say that the only solution when temporarily shoeless is a cold beer.

DM234 was berthed alongside a livestock ship on which camels were being hauled aboard by crane. There seemed no order to this process as 500 or so camels comically ran around the port, their spindly legs dodging potential captors. They had every reason to. Their journey to the markets of Saudi Arabia would see the Bishareen breed being selected for brutal racing or the Rashaidi for meat. Neither option was favourable. Camel shipping is a prosperous business in Djibouti, caravans historically driven down from South Sudan by the sand blasted Kababish nomads. These particular camels hadn't travelled so far. They were courtesy of the Haud Plateau pastoralists from Somalia's Sanaag region. The herders, grazing on khat, watched us intensely from the shade. No doubt the pirates would hear of a new boat in town.

Bruno and Hassan Said Khaireh, the Head of National Security and the Djibouti Navy, wished to inspect *DM234*. Waiting for them was unbearable. Like a mad dog, I was an Englishman stood in 48°C heat dressed in my signature beige suit and pink shirt with matching handkerchief—the camouflage to conceal my status on planet earth. I dressed smartly but gave little away, never wearing a tie, nor expensive watch or jewellery, creating an uncertainty in those I met rather than immediate judgement.

Our distinguished guests were highly impressed with our tour of *DM234*. Bruno and I arranged to meet later at the Kempinski to talk business.

I first heard about Bruno from Mr Bill who'd met him when previously transiting through on a super yacht, describing him as the port's main fixer. Mr Bill had called Bruno from Alexandria to enquire about weapons for *DM234*. Bruno said he could organise this without a problem. It wasn't the first time I'd heard a fixer boasting of what he could accomplish. Bruno's company 'Dolphin Marine Services' advertised itself as a tourist boat for whale watchers and divers trips. It didn't look right, so I sent Harry as a solo advance party to undertake some due diligence. After a career as a SBS communications specialist, Harry had been my support when I'd attempted to row across the Pacific. He was totally trustworthy and as a short, softly spoken grey man he could mingle as if invisible, so perfect for the job. Within 24 hours he was in Djibouti to check out Bruno and get the full schematic of the former French colony. Harry had concurred with Mr Bill's information that Bruno was the man to deal with.

I walked into the hotel café and immediately spotted Bruno shouting into his phone to look important. Everything about Bruno made me think he totally bluffed everything. I liked him. We were around the same age but he purveyed the air of a rich kid with a charmed life, and the epitome of conspicuous consumption. Handsome with black hair so slicked back it looked like painted tar, he oozed a callous charm that I imagined wooed local women impressed by tailored suits and razor sharp compliments. The fact he may be out of his depth didn't bother me. He'd managed to corner the market working as the interface between maritime security companies and the government.

He finished his call. "Good news, the government is happy to support your operation," he smiled, pulling out some certification paperwork. I made sure it was stamped.

"And weapons?" I asked.

"Of course, I can get you anything if you're having trouble. Let's finish our coffee then Hassan and I will take you to the armoury," he replied softly before shouting down the phone to answer the new caller.

Without even a cursory look, the bored sentry waved us through the navy base gates, the surrounding weariness suggesting a military reliant on foreigners to do its dirty work. The commanding officer, a dandy clotheshorse of tawdry gold braid, was clearly astute, recognising the personal benefits, so offered his full support.

We walked upon cracked concrete, havens for weeds evidently too hardy for sailors to pull up, and passed embalmed buildings bleached from years under an unrelenting sun. A small, motionless radar perched precariously on a metal pole was the base's first line of defence, should it have worked. A collection of patrol craft all bobbed in the paint of milky dock water, their bow ropes creaking to be set free. They were the neatest things I'd yet seen, probably due to the gelatinous kelp on the hulls indicating that these boats rarely went to sea.

The ear-piercing screech of the small side door mirrored the neglect of the small square armoury, the familiar smell of oiled metal touched my past. Bruno turned on a dusty, single bulb to dimly reveal an Aladdin's cave of post-Soviet hardware. My eyes lit up as if I had just rubbed the lamp myself. A rack of rocket propelled grenade launders (RPGs) caught my attention.

Bruno noticed my gaze. "Those are not for rent."

I hardly paid attention, my eyes feasted on the arsenal: AK47's, AKM's, Dragunov sniper rifles, grenades and, in the corner, four belt fed PK Machine guns that fired at a rate of 650 rounds per minute. They were perfect for *DM234*.

"I'll take those four in the corner," I said as if picking dining chairs.

We were now ready to dash across the Gulf of Aden and fulfil my side of the gentleman's agreement with Mikael.

CHAPTER 7
Djibouti
11'33N 43'09E

Killer and I headed to the airport to meet the new crew. Apart from Joe Jones, the ex paratrooper, I didn't know any of them. To say this was, as yet, PVI's most important mission, I hoped they'd uphold the standard of the Royal Marines, my baseline for initial recruitment. I saw big Joe looking over the heads of the surrounding crowd, and warmly shook his hand. He was the only man I knew with bigger hands than me. I introduced myself to the weary faces before helping with their bags.

Ryan Tipping, a qualified RIB coxswain, had just left the Royal Marines when he received my call, so recruited as the stern gunner. Nige had recommended 'Smudge' nicknamed as such due to Smith being his surname, but like all called 'Smudge' 'Dinger' and 'Buster' we would never know his real name. Irrespective of the mystery he would be starboard gunner and by the way he spoke—chief swearer.

Mr Bill and Bob Day had already flown back, leaving Taff to remain as the boat engineer, which was pretty handy—most of us didn't have a clue about engines. He welcomed us all aboard *DM234*, now moored in the safer fishing harbour of Port de Pesh and crawling with welders lead by Enzo, an Italian guy rumoured to be on the Italian mafia hit list. We kept a close eye on all the workmen, not only for security, but because the electrician blew himself up and the workers seemed curious of how to use their tools.

The meagre budget didn't stretch to another hotel, so we'd live on board until completing the *Star Clipper* job. Below deck was a sparse claustrophobic tube of narrow bunks and a basic galley of metal racks crammed with dried food. Two of the three hit their heads on the overhead beams as they descended.

"Welcome to your home for the next fortnight," I said with a grin. It wasn't returned, yet we all knew that such stifling intimacy expedited brotherhood.

I hoped the onboard BBQ and a barrel full of chilled beers would give us an opportunity to get to know each other, often through the medium of ribbing, and to talk about the job. As his first commercial gig, Ryan kept a low profile. I instantly liked him, he exuded an honest, hardworking air. Smudge was a little older and it was clear he'd keep morale alive.

Djibouti, already a city that satiated the wayward desires of foreign troops, had become a boomtown for former soldiers offering their niche services. Old French colonial buildings, crumbling like a cheap mille-feuille, surrounded Place Menelik, the main square. Dim neon lights emanating from Arab inspired arches tried to tempt groups of salacious drunks moving unsteadily between seedy bars. The town was Africa's Tombstone, with gunslingers from around the world looking for post-service trigger time—US Green Berets, Ukrainian Spetsnaz, French Foreign Legion and British army paratroopers, but not many former Royal Marines.

"What's going on?" I scowled.

"Djibouti is full of pongos," Killer said using our term for army personnel. "Apparently it's been like this the whole time."

"Are you fucking serious?" added Smudge.

"Yeah, army guys on nautical missions? What's that all about?"

I took a big swig of St George beer and shook my head. "OK. We've got to change that, shippers."

"You're not wrong there, and you're the man to do it."

Little did I know how fast we'd change it. A year later it would be all Royal Marines down here—as it should be. 'Royals' know about ships. We've been protecting them for over 350 years. We know how ships work, how to interact with captains. Special Forces and paratroopers are not maritime. This shit belonged to us bootnecks. The way I saw it, we were taking back our territory; this was our turf.

It would have been rude to boast about changing life here and not tame Djibouti's infamous nightlife. Outside a sleazy joint called Planet Hollywood, two large Russian paratroopers, one wearing a facial scar to suggest he'd lost a fight with a machete, shared their vodka with a couple of satin-clad hustlers no doubt trying to tempt them back to their dodgy pay-by-hour flophouse for services not normally offered by hotels. We dived into La Chaumiere, one of the few bars with air conditioning. Killer headed off to get some footwear, if things turned nasty, his fluffy hotel slippers were no use in a scrap.

After a few beers we headed to the late night bar called Menelik, our outdoor entertainment on the dimly lit steps, two blood soaked giants tumbling out from the piss-encrusted entrance in a ball of flying fists and torn clothing. Casual apathy borne from years of similar sights meant we ignored their brawl to enter the den of iniquity.

Acrid perspiration overwhelmed the senses as we pushed through the beaded curtain entrance into the cigarette fog of the crowded bar stuffed cheek by jowl with scammers, working girls and men who preferred to view life through a sniper scope. Bent wobbly chairs surrounded the small dance floor below a mirrored disco ball that reflected the cheap lighting onto the entangled sea of sweaty pheromones and illicit congress. It was as if Doc and McFly had transported us back to 1975, free from the stifling rules and regulations of modern society. It was my kind of place.

Beautiful ebony skinned Ethiopian girls with big ivory smiles greeted us at the bar. All asked for a drink. News travels fast in the world of vice, whether it's in the back room of Kabul's Chinese restaurants, the business glitz of Dubai's hotels or here in the flea infested bars of backwater Djibouti; gunslingers with money and low morals were prime candidates for business and if the girls got really lucky, a visa to the promised land of Europe or the USA.

The French guy who'd picked me up from the airport staggered across the bar. He'd been an arrogant prick when sober. Drink made him much worse. After absorbing a barrage of personal insults, I felt manners needed to be addressed. The crew didn't need a crystal ball to see the immediate future. I put a friendly arm around him, then crushed it around his neck. Poor lighting and sexy girls are great camouflage when choking somebody out. When his legs gave way, I released my grip. It was a move I'd perfected over the years.

Gagging as his windpipe came back to life, I picked him up and hissed in his ear, "We're former Royal Marines, old chap, we expect a degree of decorum." I then bought him a beer. I wanted the word to get round that we were in town.

Out of the corner of my eye I saw Taff disappearing beyond the bead curtain with an Ethiopian princess resplendent in cheap jewellery and sweat rivulets. He had an air of the British comedy actor Terry Thomas, renowned for portraying disreputable cads and not one to shy away from female company, and here, draped with brazen promiscuity, Taff was impeccable in the role, albeit without an upper class English accent. Wherever he was headed, it would be a damn sight more comfortable than *DM234*.

***

Gulf of Aden
11'49N 43'37E

The sea retained a welcome calm as we headed east steady at 12 knots. Without a cloud to accompany us, the brilliance of a blue April sky emphasised the clarity of the day. In the distance I observed a container ship heading west to Suez. 90% of the world's trade is moved by sea, and where we now sailed remained a crucial passage for the movement of cargo. Piracy in these waters impacted the global economy in one way or the other—from squeezing the oil price to the delayed delivery of a washing machine destined for a Western kitchen.

Killer was in the galley keeping morale high with lunch and laughs while the gun crews rested. With the bridge to myself, I opened the roof hatch and stood on the captain's chair steering the wheel with my feet. I felt like a floating George Patton Jnr. I checked in with Mike Broughton—my go-to man in the UK for weather and without peer at understanding the maritime environment. We could expect light wind conditions for the next 10 days. This was good for our passage plan but equally convenient weather for pirates. We were around 24 hours ahead of schedule to meet with *Star Clipper*; I wouldn't take any chances. Nige was en route to India to liaise with her in Goa and prepare the vessel before we met 150 nautical miles east of Salalah, Oman.

I was blissfully happy to be back at sea. The ocean was my sanctuary. It simplified the complexities of the life

I'd chosen. I left home at 17 to join the Royal Marines. At 18 I sailed across the Atlantic on a warship bound for the Caribbean stuffed into a cramped mess deck with drunken sailors and future mates. My mum did similar, working on cruise liners as a medical officer much to the protest of my Grandmother. I learned to sail in the services and represented the Royal Navy in offshore yacht racing before going professional after leaving the Corps. Here, where land seemed a distant memory, the bright day was my pathetic fallacy, where contentment overwhelmed me as I inhaled briny air.

Taff appeared on deck from the engine room dripping with sweat, wearing only steel toe capped boots and his oily white Y-fronts. It wasn't a pleasant sight, but it mattered not, we were on a workboat not a super yacht where, ironically, I'd first met Taff.

I'd raced on a 67-metre super yacht *Hetairos* owned by German industrialist Otto Happel. I joined the boat in Porto Cervo, Sardinia to compete in the Super Yacht Cup. Mr Bill had taken over as temporary captain as the last one had unexpectedly died. He'd brought Taff along to help out and join the race crew. Mr Bill always looked out for Taff and he jokingly remarked in Djibouti that Taff was now my property. Taff hadn't made a good first impression with the *Hetairos* crew. On the first night he'd hit the booze hard in the Clipper Bar. The next morning, all the crew reported for work, except Taff. He eventually turned up at lunchtime, still drunk and covered in blood after falling down a hillside of cactus bushes. We had two days to get the boat ready for racing as Otto would be arriving on race day. If the boat wasn't ship shape, the entire crew would be fired. So with everybody's jobs on the line, Taff had been viewed as a liability they didn't need. The chief engineer had reported bad news. The

Volkswagen engines wouldn't start due to a complex fault that required stripping of the engines—a job impossible to do alone.

Taff had jumped to his feet, still stinking of rum. "I'll help you. I may be a dick in a bar but I know what I'm doing in an engine room."

No one argued. Taff and the Chief Engineer worked solid for two days, taking naps in the engine room. The engines were still getting worked on even as Otto arrived at the airport. As news filtered in of Otto's chauffeur driven Mercedes arriving at the marina, the chief engineer attempted to turn the engines over. Nothing. As Otto pulled up alongside the yacht, on the second attempt, the four Volkswagen Marine TDI engines fired into life. Otto walked straight on board, put the throttles forward and left the dock. Taff had gone from zero to hero.

"Good to be under the red duster again, Dom," Taff bellowed, referring to the British Red Ensign. The old salt had spent most of his life on boats as a sea gypsy. "It's the only roof I've had over my head for many years."

"Apart from last night," I smiled, referring to his early escape with an escort. "Good night was it?"

"Oh yeah, you know me; I can't resist the skinny ones. I love a bony ride."

I laughed. At sixty he retained the libido of a man half his age and lived in a world far removed from his peers. He was, in many ways, a kindred soul, more at home here in the middle of nowhere than the town of his upbringing.

The sat phone rang. Nige. "Dom, I'm being deported from India."

I unhooked the phone from the bridge, moved to the main deck and fired up a Marlboro while I did time calculations in my head. We'd be off Salalah in 40 hours. "When you get back to Heathrow, get on board the next

91

flight to Muscat, then an internal to Salalah. I'll make sure Captain Siad meets you at the airport."

I called Titch to bollock him for not sorting out Nige's visa. I then briefed him on the new plan.

***

12 nautical miles off Salalah, Oman
16'57N 54'08E

Ryan's sharp eyes were the first to spot the small grey Omani Coastguard launch on the horizon. Hung off Omani territorial waters as we were not permitted to enter armed, I'd pulled a favour with my good Omani friend, Captain Siad from Dhofar Shipping. As always, he delivered. I hadn't seen Nige since winning the Jo Tankers contract in Norway. He'd kept his promise to be here for *Star Clipper*. I hauled him aboard and gave him a big hug. It was the first time he'd set eyes on my new anti-piracy machine even though he'd suggested the name *DM234*.

My happiness in things finally going to plan was heightened as I spotted a pod of sperm whales. I loved their majesty and many times had been privileged to be up close and personal with these magnificent animals. With a crew of hot, sweaty lads, I switched off the engines, and in the beautiful silence of the sea called 'hands to bathe'—a naval tradition of jumping from a vessel to swim. We had a job to do, but such a morale boost as swimming with sperm whales could only energise the crew. I smiled as they cavorted with these gentle monsters of the sea, and all jumped back on board mesmerised by the experience.

Star Clipper's topsails came over the horizon. I watched in awe as the magnificent barquentine gracefully approached, the most beautiful homage to the grand age of sailing, her white hull giving her the look of a majestic swan.

Cruising alongside this beautiful sailing ship I couldn't help but feel we were adding to the fascinating history of the Indian Ocean. We were the first privately owned anti-piracy ship to enter the region since the golden age of sail, when the East India Company patrols would protect ships laden with Indian spices and gems from pirates operating out of Madagascar.

***

Approaching Point A on the IRTC
12'13N 44'56E

In response to the deteriorating security situation, NATO and the European Union had tasked their navies to tackle pirates. Under control of the European Union Naval Force (EUNAVFOR) and Combined Task Force 151 (CTF151) commanded by US Rear Admiral McKnight, Operation Atalanta created a safe transit corridor for ships. Point A was south of Aden and point B southwest of Salalah. This corridor was called the International Recommended Transit Corridor (IRTC). It managed to curb some pirate activity, but ships were regularly taken in this presumed area of safety.

Killer climbed up from the galley to the bridge carrying a mug of steaming tea, *DM234* as hot as a bread oven motoring over a flat calm sea. Swedish marines didn't need air conditioning in the Cold War, and all we had to keep cool was a small individual fan clipped to each bunk. The bridge now popular as the only comfortable place on the boat, I basked in the tranquil sea air that swaddled the nearby *Star Clipper* into contentment.

"Mayday, Mayday, Mayday. MV *Anatolia*, I'm under attack from pirates."

Killer wrote down the position from the VHF radio report. "That's only seven miles away."

"Mayday, Mayday, Mayday. Please help we are being shot at by automatic fire and rockets. Warship help, help. MV *Anatolia*."

I looked through the binoculars at Spanish Warship F332, a mile to starboard. Her helicopter sat in the hanger with no activity on the flight deck. The warship sat just six miles away with her helicopter the only hope for MV *Anatolia* whose crew would be desperately trying to repel gunmen.

The whole crew joined us on the bridge to listen intently to the desperate captain on VHF. The bulk carrier was taking bullets into the bridge and superstructure. They then reported an RPG rocket had blown a hole in the captain's cabin. As former marines, every fibre in our body wanted to go to their aid, but our job was to protect *Star Clipper* and her passengers.

"Get the helo in the air for God's sake," I willed, my stare constant.

Killer felt the same anger. "So much for the cavalry."

The *Anatolia* crew fought off the pirates with fire hoses and continued their voyage with an unexploded grenade in the captain's cabin. Their only assistance from the UKMTO was insipid advice not to touch the RPG warhead as it may explode. No shit, Sherlock.

We were now on high alert. Pirates were nearby hunting for ships just like ours. We knew they were working from a mother ship and would attack with one to three skiffs. Usually armed with AK47's and RPG launchers they weren't afraid to throw down plenty of firepower to 'encourage' ships to stop. Any hijacked crew would be then held in appalling conditions until the company paid a ransom to free the ship, with negotiations taking from three months to a year.

The good weather would mean a spike in attacks. Less than 100 miles behind us, MV *Panama Anna* was attacked but the attack repelled. US owned Tug *Buccaneer* was not so lucky. Towing two barges, she was a sitting duck. The pirates easily hijacked the vessel and already heading to the pirate anchorage, along with her crew of sixteen. Both incidents happened in the 'safety' of the IRTC. Witnessing the infuriating inaction of the Spanish warship, it was not hard to understand why.

The spectacular sunset now finished, the cloaking darkness reminded us that out here everything was transient and peace could be shattered at any moment. Both *DM234* and *Star Clipper* were at darkened ships, a basic defense measure in these dangerous waters. It assisted our night vision tremendously.

Nige called on VHF from *Star Clipper*, "We have an engine problem. The captain is going to have to shut down the engines for the chief engineer to fix it."

From a maritime security perspective, she was limp prey, and we had pirates nearby. With *Star Clipper* static, we slowly motored around her to enforce a 100-metre security zone, not just for security but also for safety, to avoid a collision as the west bound ships were stacking up.

My bridge radio boomed. "Dom, target two miles out, inbound 20 knots."

I checked the radar; ships were everywhere. "It's a busy night in the Gulf of Aden." I said to myself. I locked the radar on the unidentified radar target.

"Dom, one mile out. The captain is getting nervous," Nige continued.

"Roger that."

As instructed, the gun crews stood to. Donning body armour and helmets, they took their positions behind the guns. I gave a hasty set of orders.

"Dom, half a mile, still on a intercept course with *Star Clipper.*" I could hear the agitation in Nige's voice

"Chill Nige, I'm on it." I shouted into the intercom, "Taff, I need full power."

I pushed *DM234*'s throttles to the limit. The Volvo engines gallantly responded, the large propellers firmly gripping the water raising the bow as we accelerated to 20 knots. I stared through the bridge windows obscured by the sea spray that tasted of excitement. Exhilaration joined adrenalin as we tore through the darkness looking for our opponent.

"Make ready."

As drilled, the crew cocked their machine guns ready to fire. I locked on to the target guided by my radar and headed straight for the tiny blip on my screen. I felt calm but my pulse elevated as we raced through the black oil of a dark sea to the unknown threat ahead. I positioned *DM234* to approach from behind to give all my guns a clear shot at the other vessel. In the olden days they called it a 'Broadside'. I'm pretty old fashioned.

As we neared the vessel, I turned *DM234* hard to starboard. On final approach, Killer hit the searchlight.

"Stop, it's military," Ryan shouted.

"Concurred military, it's armed to the hilt," Killer confirmed.

"Shit." I locked the wheel hard over and disengaged our attack.

In these lawless seas anything could happen—even a major gunfight with the Yemeni Coast Guard. It had also been undertaking escort duties for the nearby *MV Stolt Pond.* Neither vessel had answered any calls on CH16 until after our stand off. It was clear the Alphabetti Spaghetti of CTF, EUNAVFOR and UKMTO needed to improve their co-ordination or there was potential for friendly fire incidents. There's only one thing worse than being killed by your enemy—being killed by your friend, and in these early days, there was a high chance of both.

The *Star Clipper* captain had set the time perfectly to pass through Bab el Mandab at night. I was keen to get them in a safe area. Just on this short journey the Red Sea had seen five ships attacked, including the hijacking of the Maersk *Alabama*, released when Seal Team 6 shot and killed the pirates. It may seem gung-ho when watching 'Captain Phillips'—the movie recounting the hijacking— but when sailing the same waters where it's happening, it's a sobering situation.

Garaad, who organised the hijack of the *Alabama*, announced all American ships would be attacked in retaliation for the killing of his friends. The pirate response came within 48 hours. One of Garaad's teams ferociously attacked the American Flagged MV *Liberty Sun* delivering food aid; however, French Warship *Nivose* captured all eleven pirates. Garaad had raised the stakes in a game that was only going to get worse.

French Yacht *Tanit* had also been hijacked with the crew of two married couples and a three year old boy. French Hubert Commandos were scrambled from their base in Brittany and flown to Djibouti before parachuting into the sea to join a French Frigate monitoring the yacht. The commandos hastily assaulted as the pirates threatened to execute the crew. They attacked in two RIBs and retook the yacht, killing two pirates and capturing three. In the fire-fight, Florent Lemacon, a 28 year old father, was killed. This was the third French yacht to be hijacked in the area. The navy still defended their statement discouraging vessels to arm. This would only lead to the piracy problem spiralling out of control.

CHAPTER 8
Red Sea
14'12N 42'09E

We bid farewell to *Star Clipper* at the pre-designated point in the Red Sea and headed south to our new home of Djibouti. Killer cooked a celebratory meal of steak with all the trimmings including his signature coleslaw that made a daily appearance. With plenty of fuel, we put the hammer down. It was time for a beer on a job well done.

Over breakfast, I briefed the crew on their next tasks although Nige was offline needed, as he was, in Iraq. Taff and Killer would remain in Djibouti to look after *DM234*. Joe would head straight to South Africa to join the tanker *Jo Cedar* bound for Jordan, and Ryan would escort a tug through the IRTC. His jaw dropped. Tug transits were the most dangerous, highlighted by the two hijackings the previous week. Ryan was hardly overjoyed to leave our heavily armed patrol boat to instead stand on a floating target armed with nothing more than flares, but in this game if you turned down a job you didn't get asked again.

"Wanna swap, Joe?" asked Ryan hopefully.

"Ha, not a chance, I'm happy with *Jo Cedar*," replied Joe. He knew the risks.

The last thing was for me to give a hug to each one of the crew. In our world, things were always uncertain. I always did proper farewells.

I headed south to meet another weapon supplier.

***

Durban, South Africa
29'49S 31'01E

It balanced well in my hands, the pistol grip comfortable. As the iron sights aligned with the target, I steadily controlled the rise and fall of my breathing; exhaling halfway, I paused momentarily to gently squeeze the trigger in one fluid moment. I fired five rounds into the target 30 metres away. I unloaded the magazine and cleared the action before laying the SAR M14 Dashprod safely on the firing point. I noted for the first time the demarcation of my pale palm against my tanned knuckles that blanched as I gripped the weapon. The sun had become my closest friend of late. I twisted my ear defenders horizontally above my ears and reeled in the target to check my grouping.

"Nice shooting, " Derek complimented.

"Nice weapon," I replied.

Derek Coetzee was an ex-Chief Petty Officer in the South African Navy. His cropped hair and hard eyes made him look a thug yet he was anything but. We'd encountered a fair amount of trouble boarding from Durban on our last transit and Titch found that Derek could help, not only with boarding, but also supplying equipment such as body armour, radios and weapons if required. Richards Bay and Durban were key ports trading chemicals between Africa and the Middle East and the Jo Tankers contract relied on us overcoming these many obstacles.

My phone rang. Nic the Greek. "Hey Dom, did you hear about the Maersk *Alabama*?"

"How could I not? It was world news. Sterling work by your boys."

"Yep, those SEAL guys did good. Hey look, I need to get weapons on the *Alabama*. Can you help me out, mate?" He always used 'mate' when talking to Brits.

I owed Nic a favour. When I'd been on the Miami job, a close childhood friend and intelligence expert, Roman Cioma, had told me if I required anything in the

States call Nic the Greek. We required a wide array of surveillance equipment so Nic, having a private investigator's licence, did our shopping. Nothing seemed too much trouble and he'd moved heaven and earth to support us. He was now heavily involved in the maritime security business, and even as a competitor, I was happy to help.

"Have you spoken to Bruno in Djibouti?" I asked.

'That guy's a weasel; he's all about the money. I can't deal with him."

I smiled. The French and Americans were equally hard negotiators and sometimes stubbornness dissolved amicable solutions.

"Don't worry Nic, I'll sort you out."

I rang Bruno and asked for four AK47s, telling him I'd picked up a new contract and needed them loading on a ship. He wouldn't allow it without an escort. I called Taff and put him on a notice to move. By the sultry groans in the background, he seemed to be already moving on an Ethiopian.

Taff would board the Maersk *California* and head south through the Red Sea to Salalah where he'd cross deck onto the Maersk *Alabama*, currently on her return journey from Mombasa under US naval escort after her high profile hijack. Some former US Navy SEALS had just won the contract and were en route to the *Alabama* to take over the security with the weapons supplied by us.

"You're a busy man, Dom," Derek commented.

"Sorry mate, it's a bit crazy at the moment." It was. I seemed to be spending most of my time with my phone strapped to my ear.

Derek introduced me to his business partner Kerk, a huge Afrikaans who once worked on Nelson Mandela's close protection team. We dined amicably but Kerk troubled me. My instincts would prove to be correct.

***

Frankfurt Airport, Germany
50'01N 8'33E

I love Frankfurt Airport, it's a bastion of liberated efficiency, You can smoke in the transit area and it even boasts a sex shop should you wish to buy a loved one the latest in German fetishes—an eye opening alternative to a duty free bottle of perfume. I entered a smoking pod. There's always affinity between us social pariahs irrespective of culture—a quick nod through the fug, accepting each other an outcast.

After suitably satisfying my lungs, I turned on my phone, dreading any disasters befalling us in the twelve hours since leaving Johannesburg. The tirade of beeps and alerts suggested plenty. Twenty missed calls, ten texts, twenty five emails. Before I had a chance to prioritise, my phone rang. Titch. "Dom, *Jo Cedar* is under attack."

Acid filled my stomach but I resisted the urge to gag. "Any details?"

"No, ongoing. They've contacted UKMTO. That's all I know at this stage."

"Roger, keep me updated." I hung up. *Shit, shit, shit.*

The stakes couldn't be higher. The PVI team would be up against khat-crazed gunmen hell bent on taking the ship. If the attackers boarded and hijacked the ship, my guys would be executed.

In a crisis like this, we needed someone like Livy, the PVI team leader. I held every confidence in him and the team, but a chill still ran through me. No matter their skills and bravery, they were alone, unarmed and fighting pirates.

***

MV *JO CEDAR*
07'56N 56'44E

Livy, still wet from his shower, heard static screeching from his handheld radio. Joe Jones. "Three unmarked skiffs 500 metres off port, inbound."

"Roger that." Livy hurriedly threw on shorts, t-shirt and body armor taking the six stairs to the bridge in two leaps.

Now in charge, he directed the crew to emergency muster in the deck above the engine room and two PVI team members to their defense stations: big Ted Butcher on the starboard bridge wing, Joe Jones on port.

Livy instructed the watch officer to sound the alarm and call UKMTO.

The captain had already ordered starboard 20° to course away from the pirate skiffs. The 183-metre tanker began to slow down. Such a deep turn costs the ship too much speed, making it easier for pirates to gain ground. The second mate quickly put the ship amidships and her speed picked up again.

Too late. A skiff had already pulled alongside. Four occupants, each with a back-slung AK47, were preparing to board. Joe noted that the two occupants preparing the steel ladder to hook on were juveniles, no more than 16 years old yet already proficient in piracy. The first crack and thump of high velocity rounds passed Joe's ear. Ducking behind the bulkhead he picked up a bucket of scrap metal. Popping up quickly he threw the metal onto the skiff. He hit a target. Screams heard, the skiff pulled off, more rounds splashed above Joe's head.

"Two more skiffs fast approaching port side, five in each. All armed," shouted Livy.

Rounds pinged metal as the pirates opened fire. Joe moved behind the bridge wings popping his head up to try and keep their aim wayward and, most importantly, avoid being shot.

Now under siege, these weren't local fisherman playing pirate with makeshift ammunition. Bullets breached through the four-inch reinforced steel bulkheads into the cabins of the Chief Engineer and Steward—clearly armour piercing (AP) rounds—if Joe took a hit, he'd be turned inside out.

The watch officer finally managed to reach the UKMTO. "Mayday, Mayday, Mayday. This is MV *Jo Cedar* under pirate attack. Shots fired." he shouted as an AP round smashed through the bulkhead embedding itself into the bridge ceiling.

The UKMTO Naval reservist sounded worried. "Are you armed?"

"No, we're not armed,"

"That's good," the officer said with relief. "Having guns would only put you in more danger."

Livy and the captain exchanged glances, both found it equally stupid.

"Port five degrees," shouted the second mate, careful to keep the ship above 16 knots.

The skiff alongside was shoved away by the three-story wall of steel.

"Starboard five Degrees."

With every course change, the ship created space to prevent boarding.

At the higher speed, only one skiff managed to stay close. Two other skiff pilots appeared to be inexperienced unable to ride the ship's wake. Still dangerous, they fired further shots into the bridge hoping luck was on their side.

The tenacious skiff, its pilot more competent, kept the threat alive.

"Five degrees port," instructed the second mate again.

The ship barged the skiff once more. This time no shots were fired. Instead, they waved their weapons aggressively. No matter how aggressive you look, a weapon without bullets isn't a threat. The skiff broke off and headed back to the skiffs lagging behind.

"Casualty report," asked Livy over the radio.

No physical injuries were sustained, but everyone took a mental hit. At least on the bridge one had sight of events unfolding even if target practice for maniacs; however, the Filipino crew down below were blind to the developing situation. Hearing gunfire was terrifying and not knowing whether or not they'd been boarded meant prayers were offered to ask that they'd see their families again. They were initially suspicious when the captain asked them to report to the mess after the attack—could he be asking with a pirate gun at his head? It took 40 minutes to coerce them from the engine room. While Livy had risked his life to save the crew, he ensured they felt part of the success and congratulated the crowd of relieved faces on their actions. He'd never felt so humbled by their simple gratitude of buying him a beer upon arrival in Mombasa.

***

I remained in the airport's smoking pod sucking on tobacco like a man about to face the gallows. The phone rang. *Jo Cedar* Satphone. Pausing to gather myself, I picked up.

"Dom, it's Livy." His soft Scottish brogue had never sounded so welcome. "We're all OK mate and the captain's happy. Joe took a fair bit of incoming. He wants a word."

"Hey Dom, I've found out that pirates don't care much for me throwing scrap metal at them. They replied with a full magazine." Joe was clearly still high on adrenaline.

Livy debriefed me on the events adding that the pirates carried an RPG but hadn't fired it, possibly uncertain whether firing it at a chemical tanker would blow everyone sky high.

"Great job, lads. When you get into Aqaba the bar bill is on me. It better be a fucking big one," I said, my dread replaced with relieved pride.

I read my emails and saw that not far from *Jo Cedar* the US flagged cargo ship MV *Harriette* had also just been attacked. Garaad Mohamed and his men seemed to be winning the war on the high seas and we were right in the middle.

*** *

Alone in his job, Titch had been a star keeping resolutely calm throughout the *Jo Cedar* incident. I hugged him upon my return and invited Andy to join us for a pub lunch and to update us on the financials.

As I liked to treat everyone, we all sat down for ham, eggs and chips at my local pub, the White Horse. Andy was very happy indeed. If Andy was happy, so was I. *Star Clipper* and the other transits we were making good money for our start-up that had just celebrated its first year in business. Our reputable service delivery put us on the map with the insurance industry who now started to see us a serious player and a worthy competitor to the big established security companies such as G4S, MAST and the controversial American security company Blackwater whose reputation had been significantly tarnished after 17 civilians were killed by their contractors in Iraq. European ship owners didn't want such problems for their fleets, and gave the navies more ammunition in labelling us all mercenaries, a term I deeply resented. We were men of honour, there to protect lives and assets; not guns for hire with only the amount of money the negotiation point. That would make us no better than the pirates.

To redeem itself, Blackwater undertook a huge PR campaign and bought the ex US Survey ship MV *MacArthur*, claiming it would protect all shipping. I studied their grand plan. For me, it was utterly fantastical. They seemed to think that shipping companies had money to burn. The founder, former SEAL Eric Prince, had been accustomed to utilizing huge resources. He would have had at his disposal attack helicopters, F16's and the whole host of the US military might for operations. MV *MacArthur* was a high maintenance and expensive asset. It never did a transit.

By contrast, I'd spent the majority of my service in a British commando unit where resources were, at times, none existent. We read waterproof maps and carried everything on our backs. Helicopter lifts were as regular as birthdays and fast air rarely available. If things got really bad, we'd be reliant on our in-house mortar section to get us out of Dodge City. This lack of assets often allowed the Brits to get lots done with little. I mirrored this austerity in the business world—*DM234* was cheap, functional and run off her feet with work.

I never really bothered about the competition. I knew where we stood in the big picture, so I focused all my energy in supporting my guys on the high seas as they were my best sales people. Captains would sing our praises, which in turn, got us more work. I could never understand why corporations tried to complicate matters. Running a business is pretty straightforward when you break it down—gain trust from clients and employees and you'll get the best from both. No one in the security industry saw us coming. I kept my operation low key and my clients appreciated my discretion. We knew business would boom as another high profile attack had just happened.

BW Lion was huge. At 470 metres, she was 21 metres longer than the Empire State Building high. As a Very Large Crude Carrier (VLCC), laden with 281,390 metric tonnes of crude oil, her freeboards were low in the water.

VLCCs carry most crude oil shipments around the world, but are excruciatingly slow making them vulnerable to attack. What they gain in size, they lose in manoeuvrability, especially when fully laden.

A VLCC has blind spots. The radar blanks out completely astern, obstructed by the massive funnel. The captain can't see the stern at all from the bridge, so a knowledgeable skiff pilot can creep up on a VLCC undetected. A small crew and a highly flammable cargo make any pirate attack even more dangerous.

On a moderate sea with low swell, two white skiffs approached the *BW Lion* at 25 knots from the port bow; no way could the tanker outrun them.

Pirates sprayed the ship with AK47 automatic fire, peppering the bridge wings, the crew quarters and emergency room with rounds. One rocket propelled grenade crashed through the bridge to take out the bridge team. Another blasted into the Master's cabin, starting a fire, but didn't explode. A third shot through the wheelhouse ceiling and out the other side exploded on the small upper bridge, known as a monkey island. The final grenade just missed the bridge, ripping a hole in the black-and-gold, '*BW Lion*' name placard, before plummeting into the sea.

The Master, Captain Sunil Fredrick Mani, a seasoned mariner with more than 12 years experience on VLCCs, knew the ship's limits.

Throughout the attacks, Captain Mani turned the ship hard to each side to keep the skiffs off-balance making it impossible for pirates to board. Unable to maintain the 18.3 knots that Captain Mani pushed the tanker to, the skiffs finally gave up the chase. While relieved, the crew remained alert. There was no guarantee that they wouldn't be hit again as it was common for a ship to be hit twice on the same voyage—pirates, like burglars, returned to the scene of their crime knowing the target's weak spots.

The ship had motored far into the ocean hoping to out range the pirates, only to find themselves miles away from any sign of help instead. Here sat an unprotected $350 million VLCC on its own in the middle of nowhere—1700 miles from the coast of Somalia.

It was a wake up call, not only for ship owners, but also for military fleets and the UMKTO, who only received information after the event.

With a less skilled captain or less courageous crew, *BW Lion* would have been boarded by pirates, yet even after surviving such an attack the willingness of crew to sail again would be surely in question. If pirate attacks were increasing, ship owners may struggle to hire crews. Merchant sailors weren't trained in the brutality of combat and moreover, they shouldn't be expected to.

The attack on the *BW Lion* painted a vivid picture to ship owners that they needed to provide their people with well-armed, professional protection. It was a total sea change.

I assessed the number of sales enquiries for patrol boats. We needed another vessel. I rang Hasse and bought another S200. This time we would bring the boat to be named in the heart of London and invite Lloyds underwriters and shipping companies to reinforce we were the go-to guys for protecting their ships. I would call the new vessel *AM230*, in honour of my wife Angela. It was a final gesture to thank her for a marriage now coming to an end. We were both unhappy, our relationship rocky since I'd left the Royal Marines. Instead of sanctuary, home now became the battleground for domestic conflict. The upside of working away was I rarely stayed home, which suited us both. In our marriage absence didn't make the heart grow fonder, it made life bearable.

I'd met Angela while I was a Royal Marines recruit based at Commando Training Centre near the sleepy village of Lympstone in the South West of England. Ten years older than me, Ang owned a fast car and had swept me away with her stunning good looks. I first met her on a night out in Exeter, and after dating for a while love cemented our relationship. I used to break out of the base at night—not an easy task as a recruit—to meet Angela who'd wait for me in her car to whisk me away for the weekend. Ironically, the Royal Marines taught me all these commando skills, I just practiced them off duty.

We secretly married two years later, eloping to the small Scottish village of Gretna Green, famous for illicit weddings—a quaint British version of Las Vegas, just with less neon and more rain. My mother never forgave me, but aged nineteen it seemed just another exciting adventure to add to my list.

The years had taken their toll. Fifteen years in the Royal Marines she waited for my safe return from conflict zones around the world. She was the perfect service wife, always accepting of me doing my duty. Military wives always bore the worst of service life; while we were running around doing exciting things they battled

109

loneliness afraid of bad news knocking at their door. Things went downhill when I left the Corps. I stayed at home more in the first few years. Adjusting to this period of re-entry, I tried to slot back into the rhythm of home life, never seamless when trying to embrace the mundane and interrupting Ange's routine. It wasn't long before we started to drift apart. I married too young and now, nearing forty, my perspective had also shifted. Angela and I both knew the early fire of our marriage had been dowsed years ago and any embers of reconciliation had turned cold. It was easier just to bury our heads in the sand. It's never the solution.

***

London, UK
51'30N 00'08W

I arrived late, not because I was particularly unpunctual, but because I hated conferences. Three pretty conference girls, surrounded by unnecessary Christmas tinsel, manned the desk with false smiles and a table full of name badges. I was shown to the Castle Suite to join those already seated listening to a representative from the Baltic and International Maritime Council (BIMCO). After listening to him for thirty minutes it was clear the guy didn't understand the situation on the ground. A maritime lawyer stood up next with pretty much the same line as the BIMCO guy—*'If you turn up with guns the pirates will bring bigger guns. Weapons on ships will only escalate the situation, making it more dangerous for crews.'*

The keynote speaker was a Royal Navy Commander, recently returned from a tour of duty in the region on his frigate. Understandably, ship owners were keen to hear his viewpoint—mine being that the Royal Navy and EUNAVFOR had employed a facile policy of catch and release. When pirates were caught red handed their weapons would be confiscated but the navy would give them enough fuel to get back to Somalia, a country hardly short of weaponry.

The commander reverted to stereotype—a typically pompous blue-blooded bellowing buffoon boasting about the number of weapons confiscated by his ship and the great achievements of Operation Atalanta. It reminded me of wartime arrogance that it would be over by Christmas. He too stated that arming ships would escalate the violence against ships. Maybe he was experiencing some cognitive dissonance of the realities on the ocean or maybe he was a spineless 'yes' man keen to feather his nest with his politically aligned bosses by being contrary to popular opinions of the knowledgeable people around him. I guessed it most likely the latter.

"What about using private security?" asked someone in the audience.

"Good luck with that. If you want untrained cowboys who are probably more danger to your crew than the pirates then that's your look out."

My blood boiled. I thought of my guys on the front line. It was time to plaster some brutal truths onto this wall of politically motivated misinformation.

We were given the opportunity to ask questions to these so-called experts. Angered, I needed to remain a beacon of calm when floating in this sea of potential clients. "I'd like to ask the panel their opinions of the recent attack on the *BW Lion*?"

The BIMCO guy was the first to respond to my question, eager to peacock to a thirsty audience. "The *BW Lion* was not hijacked, the crew evaded the pirates," he offered lamely.

It was time to ruffle his feathers. "The vessel was 1700 miles from Somalia and was attacked for two hours, hit by nearly 1000 AK47 rounds and 3-4 RPG grenades fired at the bridge and accommodation block. May I ask the panel how much more violence could be escalated in this attack?"

"It was an isolated incident. It can't be classed as the norm."

"Not yet." Everyone in the room recognised the lawyer's bullshit. I turned to the audience. "If this level of violence continues unabated none of you will have crews willing to sail. It's unacceptable to put your crews through this kind of ordeal. I provide professional armed protection using only former Royal Marines," I turned to the commander to emphasise his bullshit, "respected men who, as the Commander will know, are trained to be anything but cowboys." I turned back to the crowd with my legs still shaking in anger. "We'll stand up to thugs on the water and protect your crews. We have the resources and we have the experience. None of our vessels have yet been taken. Nor will they ever." I sat down. I needed a cigarette.

The coffee break told its own story. The speakers stood alone by a Christmas tree in the corner, ship owners surrounded me like Christmas presents. Like their captains and crews, they'd endured enough toothless politics and military bluster; they wanted to take action. I'd honour my claim that no ship would be hijacked on my watch.

Garaad and his pirate group would soon feel the winds of change.

CHAPTER 9
Southeast, Three Foot Rock, Red Sea
13'37N 42'46E

The engine growled as I slowly pushed the throttles of *DM234*. With no moon to compromise us, we skated stealthily under a pitch sky. We were nigh invisible. So were they. I gazed at the skiffs on my radar—three tiny dots of terror.

I instructed the cable laying ship to shut off their navigation lights, the onboard security team already keeping their own noise levels to a minimum. We'd encountered many fishing boats so far, mainly grouped in twenty or more. These three green dots were alone, miles from the main fishing fleets.

Silent. Watching. We were in hunting mode. The crew made ready their weapons. Killer, laying hidden on the bow, cradled the PK machine gun butt in his shoulder with his night sight locked on the target. Once comfortable with a range where he could take out all skiffs in one long burst, he would give the signal to hit the searchlight.

He tapped his helmet. I lit up the sea with three million candela. Startled men, snapped from their khat-induced delirium, jumped half blinded in panic and feverishly tried to start their outboard engines. Soaked in cold condensation, the engines spluttered in defiance. I moved swiftly up through the bridge hatch into a fire position to cover Killer. I switched off my AR10 safety catch and scanned for weapons, my vortex red dot following the erratic movements of the stunned skiff crew. If I sighted one weapon, they would be cut to pieces, ribbons of meat in their floating abattoir.

The men fell over their cargo of white wrapped bundles.

"Khat smugglers. Probably unarmed," whispered Nadheer.

'Probably' wasn't quite confirmatory enough to stand the lads down. In this sea, the threats were many. Gun smugglers, people traffickers, Al Qaeda, and pirates all sailed these routes. Khat smugglers were the least of our worries...

The skiffs finally made a run for it. As a member of the Yemen Navy, Nadheer would contact his comrades based on Hanish Islands and vector the smugglers in to intercept. They could sort them out.

Nadheer was our onboard advisor, as the cable layer we were escorting would soon enter Yemeni territorial waters. He was an agreeable man with Arabid almond eyes and an aquiline nose as hooked as the blade of a traditional *jambiya* knife suggesting North Yemeni heritage. He spoke perfect English and drank lots of tea, possibly a throwback from his time training at the Britannia Royal Naval College in Dartmouth, England.

The cable laying operation was part of a region-wide project to connect Africa to the super highway of fast internet access, a godsend to many countries racked with infrastructure problems. This connectivity would mean internet accessibility for most—in theory. The cable layer appeared to be a pirates' dream—a painfully slow moving target that glided at 1.5 knots to allow her massive reel to unwind the fibre-optic snake onto the seabed with centimetre accuracy guided by giant onboard computers. It was a high risk but crucial contract. Many companies had turned it down claiming it too dangerous. I stood by my edict we could go anywhere implementing the correct security posture.

We worked around the clock. Night times were a fractious mystery of a latent enemy, daytimes were often brutally hot and any perusing of passing skiffs would mean us being stood to. Sleep was taken when necessary, in between maintenance, eating and watches, yet we as a crew upheld military tradition of being able to switch instantly between rest and kill mode.

Taff sweated in the engine room while Killer sweated in the galley preparing breakfast for the guys sweating up on deck.

"Fast moving target. Two miles out, traveling at 25 knots," Leon Green shouted from the bridge.

Through my binoculars I watched a battleship grey vessel at full speed heading north. The vessel then stopped abruptly. *DM234*, similarly painted with all her mounted machine guns on glorious display, readied for action. The cutter in my sights sped off again but changed course and was now heading directly for us. I watched intensely to ascertain her intentions. The covers of her 12.7mm *Dushka* heavy machine guns were being removed. Two crewmembers on the bow uncovered a larger main gun. *Shit.*

"Where's Nadheer?" I shouted.

"He's sleeping," Killer responded from the galley.

"Get him up here at the rush, before we start headbutting *Dushka* rounds."

Nadheer stumbled confused on deck. I asked him to raise the ship on VHF.

"Stand down from the weapons and no sudden movements, fellas," I shouted. This could go horribly wrong if our actions were misinterpreted.

The vessel stopped 150 metres off our port side, her guns trained on us. They were taking no chances.

Nadheer, despite his many calls on channel 16, received no response from the cutter. I wandered on deck and waved like a friendly tourist to the ship in a lame attempt to look less threatening. The ship edged forward until she floated so close I could look down the barrel of their 20mm cannon. It's never a good place to be.

Nadheer joined me. The captain of the naval vessel came out from the bridge dressed in camp Hawaiian shorts and a Manchester United football shirt. I stared in disbelief. He must have seen my reaction so leaned into the bridge to quickly don his Yemen Navy baseball cap, as if to add authority to his ridiculous garb. "Who are you?" he shouted across the divide in Arabic.

"British security on escort duties, Sir," Nadheer responded in kind.

On hearing we were British, the captain smiled and pointed to his non-issue football shirt. With that, he waved before turning his vessel around to proceed back on patrol. Once again, the international language of football had saved my turkey bacon.

At the straits of Bab el Mandab, the cable layer dropped the cable's end onto the sea floor to be connected to another cable being laid through the Gulf of Aden. This was a complex process, taking a couple of hours. If this wasn't hazardous enough, the drop location was right in the middle of the narrowest point of the straights' shipping lanes. At night. As a storm brewed.

The wind strengthened by the hour. Massive ships approached. None took any notice of the exclusion zone we'd enforced to protect the cable layer. All barged through at full speed, knocking us around the confused sea like an errant cork. They were never going to hang around in 'Pirate Alley'. The bow of *DM234* dug into the waves, torrent after torrent of black water engulfing the entire vessel. The bridge windows became completely submerged making visibility impossible. We knew danger lay ahead—we just couldn't see where.

Five more ships approached as a squall smashed us with the force of a freight train. The blinding rain and constant barrage of seawater washed over *DM234*, driving us off course into the northbound shipping lane. Another big wave hit as we punched through the other side. As the foaming sea cleared from the bridge windows, I caught a glimpse of a light that vanished in the spray. I looked again. A huge tanker bore down on us. *Shit.*

I hauled the wheel hard to port and pushed the throttles for full power to escape. Too late, we would soon be on the seabed to join the cable we were trying to protect. The tanker missed us by two feet.

Taff came on the bridge carrying a thermal travel mug of tea as if he were on a Caribbean cruise. I cherished his company, protecting the crew from near death is a heavy burden when alone.

"This weather has picked up," he said casually.

"It's pretty hairy. We have ships everywhere. I'm not risking it. We'll head back to the cable layer and sit this out on her leeside." I hoped I hid my fear.

DM234 was designed for the inshore waters of the Swedish archipelago. No matter her hardiness, she wasn't made for this. It was the first time I'd experienced heavy weather in her, and my nerves weren't helped by the fact that, with the exception of Taff and Killer, my crew had amassed little sea time.

The layer finally dropped the cable. Our task would finish upon us escorting her back to the Yemeni port of Aden, if we got there—the swell in the Gulf of Aden deepened and the wind started to whistle. I called Mike

Broughton my weather guru. I needed more information for a safe passage.

"It's due to get worse further east you go. It's going to hit the top end of a force 8 gusting to force 9." He'd given me grave news many times before, and always managed to offer it with a calming tone.

The ocean, unforgiving as she always is, pounded us evermore. The bow doors were now leaking, flooding the sauna-like compartment.

'We should be OK," said Taff casually, although I didn't like the word 'should'. "The bilge pumps are handling the water coming through."

We ploughed through another big wave. Taff had been through similarly heavy weather on the boat when they'd nearly sunk in the Mediterranean.

"What do you think?" I hoped Taff's opinion would quell my concerns.

He must have sensed my uncommon angst. "Always looks bigger at night. I'll get the kettle on." Tea solves many problems on the high seas.

The tempest rode the monstrous waves like an apocalyptic horseman. Battered like submerged flotsam by high rollers, *DM234* shuddered as waves crashed higher over her deck. I'd been through much worse weather. I'd endured three typhoons while rowing across the Pacific and five hurricanes while kiting solo across the Atlantic in a 4-metre dinghy and my yachting career had seen me hit some extremely worrying weather. Yet this storm rattled me. Being the only member on *DM234* who'd been shipwrecked, dark memories came flooding back as we continued through the wild night. Here, the burden of responsibility for everyone on board hung heavy. I re-checked all safety equipment and continued my masquerade of calm for the sake of the crew.

I tried to sleep while Taff took the wheel. My tired eyes closed easily but my mind stayed alive, taking me back to the Grand Banks in the Atlantic where I'd clung to life, attached to the wreckage of my tiny boat in 70 knot winds and 60-foot waves. Huge vertical walls of the demonic north Atlantic broke into my dreams, tossing me onto the deck. I woke startled in a cold sweat thinking *DM234* had capsized.

Sleep was not an option. I needed to stay prepared should something go wrong. I climbed onto the bridge. Taff stood alone. "Where's your partner?"

"He's on the open deck. He won't stay on the bridge and I can't leave the helm in this gale." I could see his frustration. He could see my anger.

I stepped on deck, my eyes peppered by sea spray, my breath stolen by the deafening wind. Gaz crouched on deck soaking wet with his lifejacket donned and safety line hooked onto the boat.

"Gaz, what the fuck are you doing?" Over the throaty keening of a banshee wind, I had to shout to be heard even as I stood directly over him.

"We're going to sink."

"Get on the bridge and do your watch or I'll feed you to the fucking sharks." I raged like Melville's Old Thunder.

The sea is an unforgiving place, especially hungry for the souls of the weak. We couldn't afford passengers in these conditions, every man did his duty, no matter how furious Neptune became.

The conditions suggested that the chance of the cable layer being attacked by pirates was zero. The chance of us sinking was 50:50. It was time to cut and run for Djibouti, but with a beam-on sea, it would be extremely uncomfortable. The sea would hit us side on and cause horrible rolling, and subsequently raise the risk of capsize.

Noise has its own rules at night where loud bangs shook the core and even small squeaks, scratches and bumps gave rise to inquisitive alarm of their origin. Wave after wave towered above the boat, yet whatever unrelenting tumult the sea offered, *DM234* took it on the chin. She was a great boat.

The angry ocean had cheered considerably as if happy to see the sun peek over the horizon. I stuck my head out of the bridge hatch to see the new day and sucked in the fresh wind that now eased to a light 10 knots. No matter how long I spend at sea, the first glimpse of a morning ocean always enchants. Plateau du Heron could be seen rising from the horizon as we entered the Gulf of Tadjoura. Djibouti was not perfect but after narrowly surviving the night, I was glad to see lights in the distance.

The climate had been brutally hot during our voyage. Even with 45 knots of wind in my face, I had sweated heavily on deck during the night. The claustrophobic belly of *DM234* smelled of hot diesel, of rationed dried food and the farts of people eating it. At a steady 50°C, a pitiless heat rash had spread around the crew. It was not the place for the weak. Gaz would not see her again.

With a few hours to spare before Hassan could open the armoury to return our weapons, I headed for the small Moucha Islands to anchor and call hands to bathe. After being cooked in a salty bread oven for the last ten days, a swim was always good for morale even if the Gulf of Aden teemed with aggressive Tiger Sharks that patrolled the mysterious depths of Pirate Alley. Many of the livestock ships that visited Djibouti's port contained an onboard butchering shop to prepare the meat prior to offloading. These cruising blood banks would usually have

120

a procession of stygian-eyed killers following. No one dare swim while they were alongside. The AR10 remained on deck, just in case.

As we entered Port de Peche, I saw *AM230* alongside. It was satisfying to see the fruits of our labour in the form of another S200. Now with our new vessel, we could combine tasks with *DM234* enabling us to widen our scope.

Les Page stuck his head out of *AM230*'s bridge, "Alright lads, it was a bit breezy last night. How was the trip?"

"Fucking hot," I quickly returned with a smile.

Les would Skipper *AM230*. As another S200, the many lessons learned through mistakes on *DM234* were implemented on her in Hasse Moller's boatyard. The bow doors had been replaced with welded steel to make her watertight and a wave breaker installed on the bow to give the captain a fighting chance against bad weather, an improvement reinforced by our recent transit.

"How's *AM230*? Ready for the big voyage?" I asked.

"She's in great shape, good to go," Les replied.

Satisfied, I turned to Karl Stott stood with Les. He'd skipper *DM234* on her next trip to Tanzania. "The downside is that *DM234* is far from ready. We need to get the welders down and start work today. She's leaking everywhere."

Karl was one of my newly appointed captains. The son of a bootneck, Karl was a member of the Royal National Lifeboat Institute (RNLI) working on the Exmouth Lifeboat. While bootneck coxswains were undoubtedly skilled, not many possessed the necessary experience of operating in storm force conditions—a key attribute when optimising the safety of my crew.

The dock bristled with onlookers curious to see who we were. We appeared military, but our casual clothing, salted with dried sweat patches, suggested we weren't. We were the new breed of privateers.

A century had passed since the region had seen people like us. Unlike our forefathers of the old 'John Company', no Royal Charter protected us, but most of us had been Marines before the mast and our moral compass pointed true.

***

Killer had been working on the patrol boats since leaving Sweden over a year ago and had a great knack of getting to know people. Having spent a lifetime travelling he could hook you up with anyone from Mongolia to Manhattan. He was a good hand and never complained. He needed a private word. Something troubled him. It would be good to check under his bonnet, so we arranged to meet later in La Chaumière, where he usually did the accounts. As a popular bar for foreigners it was of little surprise when, a couple of years later, a man and a veiled woman walked in and detonated themselves killing three patrons and injuring fifteen more.

I walked through the bare brick arches and saw Killer sat near La Chaumière's well-stocked bar chatting with three characters as if he'd known them forever. He introduced me to each: Vincente, an Italian who married an Ethiopian girl and had briefly owned a bar on Mickey Leland Street in Addis Ababa before losing it in a game of cards. The big French guy named Arroussi, recently released from prison after serving a 25-year sentence for murder, and Banu, an Iranian artist with no art. Eritrean soldiers had confiscated it as he attempted to cross into Djibouti via the fragile Ras Doumeira region, recently the backdrop for a build up of forces from both countries. He seemed more Nathan Hale than Picasso but his inept ruse had luckily fooled the Eritrean border guards, if it hadn't, instead of sitting here he'd now be bleached bones past consideration of carrion scavengers.

I bought the table a round of St George beers and invited Killer to a corner to chat privately.

"Straight to the chase, Dom. I need some time back in the UK."

He still hadn't sorted out his divorce. I felt a pang of guilt. We'd all been so busy I forgot that anyone had a life outside of my world. He'd been away from home for twelve months without a break and needed shore time. He knew the region and all the key players, so perfect for the newly invented position of UK Head of Operations. This would allow Titch to concentrate on heading logistics.

He accepted my offer immediately. We could sort out the details over a beer. PVI was growing. We needed to. Things were getting spicy on the high seas.

CHAPTER 10
London, UK
51'29N 00'10W

On December 28th, a bitter Arctic frost swept across the British Isles. As the coldest December in 100 years the media called it 'The Big Freeze'. They would. We British are obsessed with the weather.

At home, Phil Shaw took a welcome sip of Scotch before joining his wife, Sarah and two daughters, Mary and Emma, by the hearth. As the Company Security Officer (CSO) of Zodiac Maritime, one of the world's largest privately owned shipping fleets; it was rare to find a day quiet enough to enjoy family life.

His mobile phone rang. He moved into another room to keep his business from intruding upon festive spirit. It was the Greek Coast Guard.

"Mr Shaw, we've received a distress message via the satellite Mini C system regarding MV *St. James Park*."

Phil wasn't immediately worried. The satellite system was sometimes activated by a clumsy move by one of the crew leaning on the red distress button. He'd received such a call the previous week. "What's her position?"

An alert via text from the *St. James Park's* security alarm system (SSAS) interrupted him: *The ship is under attack*.

Phil quickly opened his laptop to check the position of *St. James Park*. Everything seemed fine. She remained on course—headed due east in the IRTC, yet the odds of a false alarm from both the Mini C and the SSAS were nil.

He called Zodiac to tell them they'd potentially lost a ship to pirates.

Kissing his family goodbye, Phil headed out into the bitter frost, mobilising the company's emergency response team on the way. All team members made it through the snow in less than thirty minutes. None had ever experienced a ship hijacking.

"We haven't yet made contact with the captain," Phil announced. "When last I checked, the vessel was in the IRTC headed east. Jacob, can you confirm?"

The safety officer pulled up the satellite transmission and squinted at the flashing dots on the Indian Ocean. Zodiac had over 100 ships currently at sea.

Jacob blinked as he identified *St. James Park*, "They've changed course."

"Where are they headed?" Phil asked.

"Somalia."

It punched him in the gut. Phil had spent eleven years with Zodiac and this was the day he had dreaded since day one. No one would blame him personally for a hijacking, but ships safety was his responsibility. If the hijacking turned nasty, men could die.

"Looking at their log they passed a warship an hour ago," interrupted Julian the operations manager, pointing at his computer screen. "The ship's helicopter can be there in 15 minutes."

"I'll call the UKMTO." Phil's phone hadn't left his hand since he'd heard from the Greek Coast Guard. Now he put an urgent call into the UKMTO. They could dispatch any warships in the region to assist *St. James Park* before it reached Somalia. Hope still remained.

The tone of the UKMTO trade officer's dashed his optimism. "Your vessel has been pirated. When the pirates call, you'll have to pay a ransom for the release of ship and crew. We advise you to employ a hostage negotiation team."

"You're the liaison to the military," Phil shouted. "There's a warship not 25 nautical miles northwest. Can you not engage that ship to intervene?"

"That's not how it works," the officer sniffed. "Your vessel is now in the hands of the pirates. There's nothing we can do."

Phil felt the eyes of the room upon him, all waiting on his every word. "We're on our own."

With lives at stake and millions of dollars to negotiate, they turned to Google. Jacob typed 'Maritime Hostage Negotiators'. The first Monday after Christmas is always the worst time to try and contact people, but Phil spoke to a handful of reputable negotiators and scheduled immediate interviews.

Terror can spread through a fleet like wildfire when a sister ship is hijacked. Morale is shot and captains do their best to keep crews calm. Whether unspoken or not, everyone at sea knows that if a sister ship is hijacked, so could they. Phil needed to implement tangible protection to restore confidence or he risked losing crews.

A few minor players in the shipping world had plucked up the courage to recruit armed guards, but none of the largest companies had yet done so. The prevailing wisdom still advocated that using guns against pirates only escalated the violence. Phil had been stationed on an unarmed supply ship during the final battle of the Falklands War. He'd borne witness that it was better to have a weapon and never use it than not have a weapon when needing one. It sickened him to think that his crews could experience the helplessness he'd felt on that day in San Carlos Sound. He knew a hijacking might well be worse.

Despite the frantic activity in the office, one fact niggled like meat stuck in his molar. He'd received no word from *St. James Park*. Displayed all around the tanker were big red signs stating IN AN EMERGENCY CALL COMPANY SECURITY OFFICER PHIL SHAW with his mobile and home phone numbers clearly emblazoned beneath. Yet no one had called. Phil wondered whether they were already dead. It was 2am. Sleep was the last thing on his mind.

Fatigue had finally taken its toll and he was asleep when Sarah picked up the phone.

"I am the pirate. I have your ship. I kill your crew. I want money."

She struggled to understand his thick accent. "Sorry, but…"

"…I am the pirate. I have your ship. I kill your crew. I want money," he repeated as if working from a script of a story he didn't really understand.

Again he regurgitated his rehearsed lines. "Excuse me," she shouted over him; "but I don't know who you are but I can't help you, you need…"

"…Give me money! I am the pirate! I kill your captain!"

"No, you don't understand…"

Worried by the sound of her mum's voice, Emma approached.

"What is it, Mum?" she said softly, hugging her mother's trembling arm.

Sarah mustered only a whisper, "A pirate."

Emma's eye lit up.

Sarah gathered her thoughts. "You're speaking to the wrong person, I can give you the number of the person you need to speak to."

"If you lie, I kill your crew. Give me number."

Sarah's head was a fog of panic, of confusion, of fear. Shaken, she couldn't remember Phil's mobile number, one she could normally recite easily. "One moment, please," she said, searching frantically for the family address book directly in front of her. She needed both hands to find the right page. She handed the phone to Emma, not realising how eager a child is to talk to a pirate.

"Do you know Johnny Depp?" asked Emma excitedly, hoping he wore an eye patch as well.

Horrified, Sarah grabbed the phone. She gave the pirate Paul's cell number and hung up.

Even by just being on the phone, the pirate had invaded the sanctity of his home, an oasis of calm away from his frenetic work life; they may as well be on his doorstep. His phone rang. Blocked. He nervously pressed the receive button.

"I am the pirate. Give me money or I sink your ship. I kill your captain..."

***

PVI Headquarters, Tiverton, UK
50'54N 03'21W

I felt fairly relaxed. Business seemed to be doing well and we'd received nothing but praise for the jobs so far completed. With our fleet of fast gunboats armed to the teeth, each with PK machine guns and assorted assault rifles manned by highly trained former commandos, we were an attractive option for shipping companies wanting protection—the pirates would be foolish to take on the speed and firepower we displayed out on the water.

I couldn't say the same for my unarmed teams deployed on board tankers; they were a constant worry. Killer and I had worked over Christmas. We noted we'd worked every day of the year; the stakes were just too high to close the door and go home. I never forgot that my men's lives were consistently on the line, so a 9 to 5 routine remained a pipe dream. To raise the stakes further, the pirates vowed to execute all security teams found on any hijacked vessel.

I looked at the board. We'd grown to around forty operators rotating constantly under the PVI flag. We had four tankers in transit: *Jo Oak* in the Gulf of Aden heading to Suez, *Jo Betula* boarding in Richards Bay, SA heading to Aqaba, Jordan with two others just embarked from Djibouti.

I had two gunboats escorting cable layer *Nexans Skagarak* from Pemba Island in Tanzania to Suez. Our patrol boats, *AM230* and *DM234* had escorted her down from Djibouti and were now on the way back. I called *AM230*, to check in and give them a piracy update. "Hey Sharky, what's your lat and long?"

"5° 18'19"N and 50° 00'06"E. We're sailing about 150 miles east of the Somali coast, all the way up. The captain's a proper ninja."

We both laughed. It was a bold move, but further reinforced our profile that the *Skagarak's* captain felt so confident under our protection.

The vessel I felt most concerned for was Tug *Topez* towing an accommodation barge through the Gulf of Aden. Travelling at 3 knots she was a highly vulnerable target. I'd handpicked a team of hard core door kickers for the job. I knew if the pirates managed to board, some would be killed. The team knew what they'd be up against and were willing to go the full distance to protect the tug. As I saw potential in the rising star Ryan, it seemed an ideal job for him to hone his skills.

I studied the IMB reports closely. *St. James Park* had been hijacked at 14:49 UTC on the 28th December. Four hours later, the Greek bulk carrier, *Navios Apollon*, was seized in the Gulf of Aden. MV *Al Mahmoud II*, a Yemeni cargo ship, was hijacked the same day. The hijacking of the fishing vessel *Shahzaib* caught my attention. It could be utilized as a pirate mother ship.

Killer walked into my office, "Busy day at sea, shippers, three hijacks."

"I can see. We have to arm the onboard teams, things are getting out of control. Do you have any pictures of that fishing vessel taken?" Such information was vital intelligence for our teams on the ground.

"No, she looks like a ghost ship," he replied with a frustrated look.

Already having read my mind, Killer handed me a dossier on the ship. The *Shahzaib* had been registered in Jiwani, a small town in the Gwadar district on the extreme southwest of the Pakistani coastline. She was an illegal fishing vessel hauling sharks with 29 Pakistani crew onboard. When hijacked, the spotlight fell on the owner. It transpired the vessel's real name was *Shah Zeb*. Illegal fishing was rife on the Indian Ocean and many analysts contributed the rise of piracy as a reaction to illegal fishing depleting stocks and the dumping of toxic waste in Somali waters. In pirate hands, the crew of *Shah Zeb* faced an uncertain future.

Titch ran into the office. "*Jo Betula* is under attack."

"Roger that. Who's the TL and where's the ship?" I asked calmly.

"Livy and she's in the GOA."

"Livy again? He's a shit magnet," Killer butted in.

I immediately stepped outside and fired up a Marlboro. Livy had managed to evade capture last time, but we were pushing things too far.

My phone finally rang. *Jo Betula* Satphone.

"Hi big man. All boarders repelled," Livy said joyfully as if talking about rugby, another area where he excelled having been one of the first players ever to reach 100 caps for the Royal Navy.

I could have kissed him down the phone.

His tone turned serious. "One skiff, six men, all wearing black fatigues, they were noticcably better equipped and well drilled. We fought them off using flares, but to be honest we only just got away with not being boarded. Bottom line is we need to be armed or we may not be so lucky next time."

"I hear you, brother. We are working on it. Bar bill on me again, you're costing me a fortune. See you soon."

I rang my contacts both at the Norwegian Hull Club and Jo Tankers and explained that Norwegian flagged ships needed to look at allowing weapons onboard. The fact that my teams had just saved them millions of dollars in ransom payments gave me some leverage.

***

MV *ASIAN GLORY*
12' 16N 43'46E

Captain Veliko Velikov stood on the bridge with his first officer at the chart table plotting their new course. He'd already received the news of the hijack of *St. James Park* so doubled his crew watches to keep a look out for potential pirates. The hijacking had rattled the nerves of every Zodiac captain. He had less to be worried about. His ship, *Asian Glory,* was 184 metres long and five stories high with plenty of horsepower. Car carriers were strange looking ocean travellers, resembling a huge top-heavy box possessing no aerodynamic efficiency yet seemingly vulnerable in a hurricane. A host of self-proclaimed experts suggested that she was a fortress that even the most skilled climber would falter trying to scale. The sheer walls of the ship made many believe that car carriers were impossible to hijack. They had clearly forgotten about the low freeboard of the stern ramp and underestimated the pirates' knowledge of ships.

Captain Velikov checked the Automatic Identification System (AIS)—a marine version of air traffic control. It was clear ahead as they approached the narrows of Bab-el-Mandeb. He asked the chief engineer for full speed, keen to reach Point A just over ninety miles away where warships were positioned.

"Captain, we have a small vessel one mile ahead, Sir," reported the sailor fixing his glare to the radar.

"What is her closest point of approach?" the captain requested.

"0.1 mile, Sir."

The captain left the chart table to assume command of his bridge. The radar operator reported another larger vessel three miles off, probably a dhow. The captain calculated his next move.

"Skiff approaching high speed," the starboard watch reported.

The first burst of bullets hit the upper part of the ship with a resounding crack. Captain Velikov hauled the controls sending the ship hard over, trying to use the ship as a hulking bull to shake off a cowboy. He could hear the gunfire intensify, the watchmen now within the bridge to avoid the lead hornets now strafing the ship.

"Where are they?" the captain yelled.

Before anyone could answer, a young Somali stood at the bridge door brandishing an AK47. Bullets split open the glass sending shards and bridge crew scattering to the floor. Four more armed pirates boarded and ran down below to grab the rest of the crew.

Captain Velikov tried to remain calm, hard to do while being dragged outside with a gun to his head. A pirate fired a flare out to sea. Such an action would normally be used to signal a ship in distress. It confused him, *why would they do this?*

All became clear when a fishing vessel approached. He could see more armed men on board- –it was a pirate mother ship. He saw her name. *Shah Zeb.*

CHAPTER 11
Zodiac HQ, London
51'30N 00'06W

Phil and his team at Zodiac HQ had hired Neil Young Associates (NYA) to negotiate payment for the release of *St James Park*. Business for NYA was booming. When the company started, hostage negotiation was a rarefied field, but that year there had been 700 hostages being held by Somali pirates. Hostage negotiators were now in high demand. Because they kept the tricks of their trade secret, people started calling hostage negotiation the 'black arts'.

Phil carefully monitored the Zodiac vessels in the Gulf of Aden, happy that all container ships and oil tankers remained on course. The car carriers, MV *Triumph* and *Asian Glory*, were safely on their way down the Red Sea.

It seemed strange that *Asian Glory* had made a sudden loop just outside the straits of Bab-el-Mandeb.

"Jacob, take a look at this," he said. "*Asian Glory* just did a complete 360."

"That's odd." Jacob skated his chair over to Phil. "Steering failure?"

Phil's phone rang. He could hear screaming in the background—the sound of bullets unmistakable.

The voice on the phone trembled, "I'm a steward on *Asian Glory*. We've been pirated heading for Somalia. Help us please."

Blood drained from Phil's face. *No, not again.*

Losing one ship was bad enough; losing another within a week would shake the company to the roots. It was time to dig deep for the sake of the Zodiac crews, hard to do when he felt himself falling apart.

Since the *St. James Park* hijacking, NYA were permanently on site to advise on what actions to take, yet the pirates would only speak to the man in charge—Phil. The success or failure of any negotiation hinged on him and the burden hung heavy for a man with so little experience in these matters. Alex and Cameron, the NYA negotiators, signalled to him to put the call on speaker.

Seconds later, the pirate leader crackled down the line. "Your ship is mine, Phil Shaw," he crowed. "Your captain and your crew will die, unless you do everything I say. Do you understand me?"

"What's your name?" Phil demanded. He was quickly learning to convey and outward firmness and authority, no matter the inner turmoil.

"Carlos." The line went dead.

Alex stroked his jowls and Cameron exhaled deeply. Phil's concerns grew.

"If he *is* Carlos," Cameron said; "things just got far more complicated."

"Go on, hit me," said Phil as if things couldn't get any worse.

"Carlos The Jackal is one of the world's most wanted pirate leaders, possible real name Garaad Mohamed but also called Abdi Garad amongst others. Some reckon he commands 800 pirates operating under 13 separate groups."

"He's aligned with a guy called 'Big Mouth' who finances a lot of what we see," Cameron added. "Garaad's like a Bond villain. He's a slippery fish. He got the name by being everywhere and nowhere all at once."

"You know about the *Alabama* incident, right?" Alex continued.

"Of course, the first American commercial ship to be hijacked for over two centuries. I know my history."

"Correct. You may not know that the three pirates slotted by the Navy SEALS were part of his clan. He's now out to get revenge and vowed to slaughter any Americans he captures."

"And there's one other thing…" Cameron left it hanging as if to add charge to the room's electricity.

"What now?" Phil said, exasperated.

"Big Mouth and Garaad are the guys that pioneered multi-million dollar ransoms. They now pretty much control the Somali coast. It's got the Chinese and Russian crime syndicates' attention, there's even investment from Dubai. It's attracted a whole new set of interested parties. They run their operation like a business. Garaad is the new role model. When he sets the ransom, it's going to be high, he has stakeholders to impress."

"OK," said Phil, hoping for alternatives; "What happens if we don't pay?"

"Let's make this clear," said Alex, assertiveness now his primary weapon. "Once a ship is hijacked it's game over. It's either pay a ransom or condemn your crew to torture, mental, physical and sexual abuse and death. Secondly, your ship and cargo will be lost. You have to justify that expense to insurers, will they pay out knowing you could have paid a fraction of what a ship is worth? There's also a legal argument to say that by not removing seafarers from harm's way you'd be in breach of Article 2 & 3 of European Human rights,"

"Bottom line? Don't let your ship get hijacked," added Cameron.

Phil slumped in his office chair, took a swig of water to lubricate his parched throat and called the MD of Zodiac. "Brace yourself for more bad news." It's never a good way to start a conversation.

Not only would the ransom be high, with two ships lost, action had to be taken to protect the rest of their fleet. Phil hoped the MD would see the crisis as he did. It was time to take up arms.

Phil scanned the document that he'd requested Jacob compile. It listed the top five maritime security companies.

As a former Royal Marine, Alex was asked for his opinion.

"Dom Mee from Protection Vessels International would be worth a call. He's a larger than life character and gets shit done. Last I heard he ran a couple of gun boats down there, I didn't serve with him but his lads have a fearsome reputation as he only hires former Royal Marines."

"Only bootnecks eh? OK, well I suppose if we are going to get anyone on board it's probably best we get those blokes."

***

Salalah, Oman
16'58N 54'00E

The changing security climate was finally being recognised by some organisations putting common sense before political pandering. Our Omani in-country shipping agent and friend Captain Siad had advised me to get on a plane to Muscat as soon as possible. The Royal Omani Police were about to grant licenses to allow armed guards to land at their ports.

It was rather timely. My Spanish friends, Jesus and Alejandro had recently been stung, their sixteen Mossberg pump action shotguns subsequently impounded in Suez. As a result, they'd asked for my help. I rang my good friend and agent, Mr Nabil.

"Let me talk to someone. I will get the authorities to release them to you."

It was good to have such friends. I'd sent Nige to oversee the transfer and bring the weapons to Oman assisted by Captain Siad.

At the gates of the Salalah Airport, I immediately spotted Captain Siad dressed in his signature pristine white *dishdasha* that mirrored the trimmed beard, striking on his mahogany skin. His perfectly tailored *Kuma* hat that reduced his already small bespectacled face didn't move an inch as he greeted me with a true Bedouin salutation, "Dom! Dom! What is your news?"

Historically, the Bedouin Arabs' greeting to fellow travellers roaming the deserts would be a triple nose kiss and to ask, "What is your news?" The standard reply being, "The news is good," even if they had only been parted for a few hours. I loved the fact that many Bedouins kept these traditions alive.

I never tired of seeing Captain Siad. In his younger days, he'd been quite a celebrity, first as the captain of the Omani National Football Team, then as a TV sports commentator. Now he ran Dhofar Shipping.

"We don't have much time," Captain Siad explained. "We need to meet with the Royal Omani Police and the Coast Guard to discuss the arrangements for armed guards. You will be the first."

We entered the Omani restaurant and walked towards the friendly smiles of two influential officers. Gilded walls bedecked with traditional tapestries offered us a traditional welcome and pungent spices satisfied my nostrils. As soon as we were seated on the floor, I was given *kahwa*, the renowned Omani cardamom coffee that Sir Wilfred Thesiger, the great traveller of the 1920s, called 'the black bitter coffee of the sands'. The coffee is a symbol of the *diyafa*—the hospitality that lies at the heart of the Arab and Bedouin culture. They believe fervently that how well you treat your guests reveals what kind of a person you are. I found it easy to engage with such friendly people. Crossing the cultural divide always seemed more enjoyable when humble and before I'd shaken my cup to signify I wanted no more coffee, the deal was done.

The opening up to armed guards in Salalah was a big breakthrough in the fight against the surge of piracy. Nige had just arrived on a tanker with the Alejandro and Jesus' weapons now released from Suez to test the process. I was confident we could trailblaze the future.

En route to the Salalah Hilton with Captain Siad I finally switched on my phone. Such a simple action was becoming an exercise in dread and the courtesy extended to Captain Siad by not turning it on had been blessed relief. In our game, anything could happen on the savage seas in just a few hours. I didn't even bother to count how many missed calls there were.

I checked in with Killer just to be on the safe side.

"A guy called Phil Shaw from Zodiac Maritime needs to speak with you urgently. He's called about five times," he said.

"Roger the cat. I'll get onto it."

I called Phil. He explained the situation. With two hijackings in one week and so many ships heading to the high-risk area, he wanted armed teams on board as quickly as possible. "Simply put, we can't lose another ship." It was clear he was going through his own personal crucifixion.

"I'll make sure it never happens again," I said bluntly.

We talked money. Naturally, he was reluctant to put all 800 ships under the protection of one untried company, but I knew that if he gave us a chance, my men could deliver the best security in the business. I gave him the best price I could and waited to hear back from him.

I was glad he called. Whether we got the gig or not, Phil was being smart to beef up security. In the last few months, yachts, fishing vessels, cargo ships and tankers had all been hijacked in an ever-expanding area from the Gulf of Aden to the Seychelles to Tanzania. MV *Almezaan* had been hijacked twice. The Maersk *Alabama* had just been attacked for a second time. This time Nic the Greek's Ex SEAL security team returned fire and repelled the pirates with the arms I had leased to them. It was pretty much a no brainer to up-arm vessels.

At the Hilton I met with Nige. It had been nine months since leaving each other after the *Star Clipper* escort. It was great to see him and, as always, our greeting was a man hug— the true greeting of brotherhood.

"How was Iraq?" I asked.

"Complex."

"No shit. You can tell me all about it over a beer."

There were four PVI teams currently in Salalah. It would be a good time to get them all together and chew the fat.

"Get the Brothers together. 7pm in the Whispers Bar. No excuses," I said.

"That sounds dangerous, see you there."

The Whispers Bar was empty. The last time I drank here I'd met a couple of Filipino crewmembers from the MV *Stolt Strength* just released by pirates. They enjoying their first beer after nearly five months held hostage, their suffering exacerbated by the extreme violence meted out by pirates high on khat and class A drugs. They were simple mariners earning a Western pittance sailing eleven months of the year to provide for their families—cheap qualified labour rarely looked after by their paymasters—yet their humility at accepting their hand always made me feel slightly guilty at my own privilege of being born into relative comfort. While a hijacked vessel may mean a delivery being delayed much to the hubristic annoyance of a company, these sailors were the forgotten victims of piracy, reinforced by the fact that some shipping companies would not pay their wages while taken hostage. This stuck in my craw. I paid for their night. It was the least I could do after all they had endured.

Dave Seaton arrived first with his team, shortly followed by Mark Rippin with his. It was a good to see everyone. We moved to the pool bar and restaurant and set about to create one massive table. We looked like the 'Knights of the Square Table' and, in a strange way, that's how I felt. Gallantry doesn't have to be dressed in armour. Here, polo shirts, flip-flops and cussing were equal, albeit not as grand, indicators of men stifling the flourishing of evil.

With such a group it wasn't long before the conversation started to flow.

Mark kicked things off "I think the UKMTO is a fucking waste of space."

"Tell me about it," cut in Les. "Did you know that when Livy phoned UKMTO when attacked, the bloke had the gall to say that Livy was interrupting lunch with his wife?"

It was now a free for all.

"The fucking navies are taking the piss. They catch pirates red handed then just release the fuckers. A week later, they'll be shooting at me on the bridge wing. It's fucking nuts," added Smudge with his usual pleasantries. "It's like some twats breaking into your house, you catching them, taking the crowbar off them then giving

141

the fuckers a lift to the nearest hardware store. It's all bollocks."

"It's all well and good politicians in their ivory towers voicing disgust at violence on the high seas yet it's either naivety or arrogance thinking that pirate masters making millions will listen," added Nige.

"Garaad would slot Mother Teresa if she captained a ship."

"Exactly, these bastards need to be treated *in specie*," I said, just as my phone rang. I may as well have had it surgically attached to my ear. Phil Shaw. I excused myself from the table to answer.

"Dom, I'll be brief. We have two ships just leaving the Suez Canal heading south toward Bab-el-Mandeb where *Asian Glory* was hijacked. If you can send two armed teams to these vessels north of Djibouti right now, you've got a deal."

A last-minute escort of two armed teams was impossible for any company. Normally, it would have been a challenge even for us, but as *AM230* and *DM234* now sailed north after finishing escorting the cable layer *Nexans Skagarak* up from Tanzania, there was a chance we could assist.

"No worries, Phil. Give me the lat and longs of the ships." As he read me the coordinates, I hastily wrote them on a beer mat. "Give me five minutes, I'll call you back." I picked up the sat phone and called Karl Stott on *DM234*. Karl was one of the toughest mariners I knew. Give him enough coffee and cigarettes and he could stay at sea for months.

Karl punched the coordinates into his navigation system and told me he was thirty nautical miles from Phil's first ship and 42 nautical miles from the second. It was close enough to work, but only if Phil made a decision in less than two hours. Any longer and all the vessels would pass each other.

I rang Phil and told him we could cover his ships heading south by transferring my gun crews from the patrol boats to his ships.

He didn't need two hours to decide. "Do it," he said. "I'll get the ships phone numbers for your captains to co-ordinate."

This was a big risk for the patrol boat captains. Cross decking their gun crews would mean he and his first mate would be on their own, defenceless with 300 miles of pirate infested waters to cross before hitting Djibouti. But the upside was huge; my guys understood that.

I immediately received a call from Bruno in Djibouti. I knew the job would have been offered out and he was fishing for information. He had two teams from MAST meant to be boarding two Zodiac vessels. They were too late.

"Dom I have to transport these guys but no one is talking to us, do you have the contract?"

"Tell them to go home, Zodiac is mine," I said with an air of satisfaction.

Around midnight I got up from the raucous table to take another call from Phil. He wanted to know if I could provide an armed escort for MV *Carrera* that would reach Bab-el-Mandeb in five hours.

"If you can't handle it, it's OK, I'll farm it out to another company."

He was testing me. That was fine. "It's no problem Phil, seriously."

My confidence threw him somewhat. What Phil didn't know was that there were no other teams from any company near enough to cover such a transit. I had two patrol boats and four guys who had just arrived in

Djibouti. I knew my guys. They would have all been set to take a long shower, grab a couple of beers, enjoy a hearty meal and hit the sack early after a long, three-week mission at sea. I felt a little bad about interrupting that, but rang Les Page, captain of the *AM230*, and explained the situation, emphasizing that this transit to Salalah short as it was, could make the company the biggest on the seas. "Are you and other lads prepared to crack on?"

"We'll do it." Like Karl, Les replied with typical alacrity.

I called Phil back and told him we could do the job.

"Do this right," Phil replied; "And we'll talk some more. I'm sure you know how big the Zodiac fleet is."

Every company wanted this contract; it was huge. PVI was now number one in the market. We made the deal without signing a single of paper. Just like in the old days, when a man was as good as his word, a verbal agreement over the phone was enough for both of us. I knew Phil was a good guy and he knew I would deliver.

As the call ended I knew things would never be the same. It was known as the 'Zodiac moment'. The guys always came through. That's why it was so special to return to a table of men who had helped make it happen.

I paused. "Gentlemen, our lives have changed forever."

***

PVI Headquarters, Tiverton, UK
50'54N 03'21W

It wasn't going to be a simple task of putting armed guys on Phil's ships. I needed to review their entire security procedures to make this work.

Killer and Titch hit the phones to call every Royal Marine cohort we'd ever served with. Zodiac had 30 ships passing through the high-risk area at any one time. Meeting the needs of Zodiac alone meant having hundreds of former commandos ready to board in teams at any port from Alexandria to Durban.

Most of us had taken a hard landing in civilian life. A superhero in combats able to pick off targets with a sniper rifle at 2km, reconnoitre hostile forces in enemy territory, survive for weeks in the most extreme conditions as well as motivate, plan and operate to the highest corporate standards were ignored by HR departments too lazy to fit transferable skills into their narrow tick boxes. If the guy had children at home and a mortgage to pay, he took any job and sucked it up, his talents wasted to a society too cossetted to understand.

A lot of former bootnecks found work in Iraq and Afghanistan as private security contractors. In the formative years it was a well-paid job, but as in many security environments, wages were lowered as the risks heightened, shareholder dividends far more important than the livelihoods of those who provided them.

The Jo Tankers contract made me see that PVI might be the turning point, not just for me, but for others who struggled to find employment post-service. The Zodiac contract would reunite many more and give lads the chance to use the skills we had worked so hard to attain. For many, it would be a homecoming.

***

Zodiac HQ, London
51'30N 00'06W

"Fifteen million dollars," repeated Phil. It was a crazy number and no such ransom had ever been paid before, but this was Carlos demanding it.

"That's maybe because of the weapons on board." Cameron's words were pointed, accusatory.

"What?" answered Phil, his mind thrashing with indignant confusion.

"According to Persian news sources, *Asian Glory* is carrying weapons for Saudi Arabia to launch additional attacks on Yemen's Houthi fighters. We need to know these things, it changes the playing field."

"Fuck Persian news. *Asian Glory* is carrying cars."

Alex recognised Phil's anger as the conduit to truth. "OK, well, there's no problem then."

"Other than a fifteen million dollar ransom," shot Phil.

"Well, I said they would bid high. Don't worry, they know they may only get a fraction."

Nothing Phil had read about Mohamed Garaad gave him any hope of a favourable outcome.

Alex instructed Phil to hold his ground with Garaad, no matter what. "He's all about strategic manipulation. If he threatens to shoot the crew, feign indifference. He's more likely to leave them alone if they can't be used as bargaining chips. It's all a game. Respond to a threat as if you don't care."

"Captain Velikov is one of my most respected men and takes shit from no-one," Phil said. "He's a gnarly old Bulgarian skipper, ex Navy, with a tough Eastern bloc crew. No matter what you throw at Velikov he always takes charge."

Alex sighed. "If he enters into a power struggle with Garaad, it won't end well."

***

I liked Phil; he was stand up guy. He'd served in the Royal Fleet Auxiliary in the Falklands War on board an unarmed ammunition ship. I couldn't possibly think of anywhere worse to be in an air raid. He'd spent five days in what was known as 'Bomb Alley' of San Carlos Sound, but today another Carlos rented a space in his mind. We worked around the clock reviewing security procedures and setting up clear lines of communication between our companies.

"Do you fancy pint after work?" It was clear he needed to get something privately off his chest, so accepting was easy. As well as a business client, I just wanted to help a bloke in need.

We met at a nondescript pub on Northumberland Ave near Trafalgar Square, a place I last frequented when working in Special Forces Intelligence. The last time I'd downed a pint here was in the company of MI5, MI6 and a whole host of mysterious characters whose job descriptions weren't posted on recruitment websites. We grabbed a couple of pints of London Pride and found a discreet place to sit.

"How are the negotiations going?" I asked.

"Not good, to be honest. That's why I wanted a chat. Do you know the pirate 'Carlos the Jackal'?"

"Garaad? Yeah, of course. It's ironic, he started pirating about the same time as I started in the anti-piracy game."

"He's a total nightmare to deal with. The other hijacker, Loyaan is more about the money and slightly less volatile, so I can work him. Have you had direct dealing with either at all?"

"My dealings with pirates are generally down the barrel of gun," I joked. "I ran into these guys once on the water when I delivered a super yacht. They were out in a group of around twenty skiffs hunting for ships. They'd attacked a cargo ship off Al Mukalla and the next morning we literally ran into them. When I say we, I was with an ex Mossad guy, totally ruthless, but a really nice bloke—your

147

boss would love him. We were very lucky, or they were depending on how you look at it. It was 05.30am, very foggy and they were all asleep. By the time a few boats had started their engines we'd disappeared into the fog. They searched for us for about twenty minutes. Good job they gave up or this would be an altogether different conversation."

"Oh right. I was thinking if you knew someone that could speak to them?"

"Sorry Phil, that's not my part of ship. The only message I post to a pirate is strictly via 7.62mm. Negotiation is admittedly an important job, but I don't care much for the practice. I prefer to deal with dangerous criminals with an axe or a gun. But that's just me."

* * *

Phil left the pub to return to the normality of everyone else's life. He wandered aimlessly around the hardware store in a vain attempt to find paint to re-coat the front door—an overdue job he hoped would take his mind from reality. His hands searched for brushes, his mind searched for answers. His phone rang making him jump, as it now always did. The dreaded 'blocked' number. "Hello?"

"Phil Shaw, today you are going to choose. Do you understand?"

"Yes," he replied, deadpan as NYA had briefed.

"I have your captain at the back of the ship. Do you want me to throw him over the side or shoot him? This is your choice and you must decide now."

It's all a game. Respond to threats as if you don't care. Phil paused, he could hear Captain Velikov pleading in the background. "Do want you like, I don't care."

He heard a single shot. The line went dead.

CHAPTER 12
Colombo, Sri Lanka
06'55N 79'51E

I sat patiently on the veranda watching the palms sway in time with the cool sea breeze that flowed pleasantly through the old white colonial building of the Sri Lanka Navy Headquarters. Harsh echoes of footsteps followed the elaborately outfitted Naval officers in pristine whites adorned with an array of shiny medals. I closed my eyes and drifted momentarily to a bygone age when Britannia ruled the waves and Sri Lanka was Ceylon. With history so palpable, it was easy to have such romantic connotations in a setting so preserved.

According to the chronicles of Mahavamsa, Sri Lankan history spanned over 30,000 years with the arrival of the great Indian Prince Viyaya. In more recent times, the Portuguese had been the first Europeans to arrive, followed by the Dutch. The British Empire were the last colonialists to grace this land of Horace Walpole's Serendipity. Usually, when a country was conquered the victors would often destroy all memory of the vanquished. Sri Lankans embraced each era, preserving the past and intertwining it with their own identity.

My visit to this teardrop shaped island could not have been in starker contrast to my first visit to board *Jo Oak*. The country had since defeated the LTTE but at great cost, with thousands killed. Peace had arrived after 26 years of internal hell, and now I too shared the optimism evident on the street. I had risen from the rubble of a bombed out bank account, a small fry in a sea of corporate sharks to be the dominant force in maritime security.

In the immediate aftermath of winning the Zodiac contract, I kept on winning more and more. PVI was an

149

unstoppable bellwether in the industry. The competition that previously mocked and attacked my character became nothing more than remora feeding off my scraps. I always took the moral high ground in the vicious world of security; my energy was better focused on my team and customers. I never denigrated the competition; indeed I was immensely proud that fellow Britons were flying the flag,

We'd been waiting for over an hour. Anil leaned over and whispered, "All the Admirals are coming. This will be make or break."

I put my hand on his arm reassuringly. "Don't worry, I'm prepared."

The pirates were now operating over the entire Indian Ocean. No route was safe. We'd secured the Gulf of Aden between Djibouti and Salalah, but I needed to board my guards entering the ocean from the east.

We'd looked at India as an option due to their long and proud maritime history but after brief exploration we found their over-engineered processes weren't conducive to the fluidity we needed. Sri Lanka, we hoped, would be more accommodating.

A commander arrived, smart and authoritarian, to lead us to the conference room where the entire command of the country's navy waited curiously to meet this *Britisher* who also commanded a sizable private navy. Trepidation tinged my confidence, as my proposal included landing up to 500 armed former commandos per month at the small port of Galle in the south only a few weeks after the end of their civil war. I stood at a large round table, plugged in my laptop and started my presentation.

I fielded a number of questions from the senior officers around the table who felt at ease in my presence. The Royal Navy and the Sri Lankan Navy retained strong ties and the officers paid special respect for the Royal Marines who I indirectly supported, whether the Royal Navy appreciated it or not. The meeting ended positively and they would accept my guards on the proviso that the Djibouti government would send a letter confirming that all my men boarded legally from their territory.

Anil looked worried, he'd spent months setting up this meeting. "Will you be able to get such a letter?"

"It won't be a problem," I smiled.

The solution to the problem was simple. I'd hand over a highly inflated fee to Bruno who would theatrically procrastinate, like the 'official' Suez Canal measurer, and say it was 'very difficult'. Unlike Egypt, I'd get a result and Bruno would hope for a sizeable tip in lieu of flowers thrown on stage for his melodramatic performance.

That evening I met with Anil and his boss, Reza, to discuss the implementation of our guards boarding in the languid southern port of Galle. We were taking dinner at the Cinnamon Lakeside hotel when my phone rang. Phil Shaw. "MV *Triumph* is under attack."

As Dave Seaton was the leader of the onboard PVI team, I wasn't overly concerned. "Phil, relax. Dave's a great guy, let him take care of business. All will be well," I said confidently. It was our first test on a Zodiac ship and with Phil having two ships currently hijacked his concern was understandable.

That fact we were getting attacked more regularly was simply a numbers game. We were looking after more ships and in most cases, we stopped the attack before the pirates had a chance to fire a shot. My teams would, if weapons were sighted, fire a volley of warning shots around skiffs sending out a clear signal that the vessel was armed. The pirates immediately backed off. There were many unarmed ships to prey upon.

Kenyan waters had seen a recent spike in attacks. Dave spotted the mother ship five miles after clearing Mombasa. He'd observed a skiff launching from the Dhow that, after 40 minutes, managed to catch up with MV *Triumph*.

The pirates stood up and raised their weapons. Dave issued the order for his team to open fire. The water erupted around the skiff as his team fired well-aimed shots from their 7.62mm T3 Tikka sniper rifles. The pirates took cover and wisely aborted their attack. Simple drills, simple execution, simple result. Everyone who mattered stayed safe.

Dave checked in by sat phone. I thanked him for his professionalism and yes, I would cover their bar bill when they hit dry land. I loved my guys, they were the best and I was humbled to be their leader, even though it was costing me a fortune in bar tabs.

As we finished our meals, a troop of Kandyan dancers started their *Ves* dance performance. The male dancers wore traditional sarongs and spectacular headgear, their bare chests decorated exquisitely in silver. With the backdrop of hectic *gata beraya* drums rhythms mesmerising the crowd, I felt totally relaxed, and more importantly, so too did Anil and Reza. I liked this new Sri Lanka.

***

Marina Bander Al Rowdha, Muscat, Oman
23'34N 58'36E

I flew from securing Sri Lanka to see the new addition to the PVI fleet. The first time I saw her after refit, I'd sparked with excitement. Powered by two 4000HP MTU engines that could rapidly accelerate her to 30 knots, *AL345* was a beast. At 25 metres long with a large stern deck space for a tender, a bridge at deck level and a fly bridge on top giving a commanding vista, she was the PVI flagship and demonstrated how far we'd come as a team.

Taff stood proudly on her deck to welcome me on board. The voyage was to fulfil a personal ambition: to escort a large cruise liner through the high-risk area—a prestigious task for my fleet. As with all jobs undertaken by the company, if it was a first I would personally lead it. This also reinforced my commitment to my teams and kept me in touch with the realities at the sharp end. The plan was to head south to Salalah, bunker and procure provisions, then escort the cruise liner to Djibouti.

I entered the bridge. It had a steering wheel akin to a Greyhound coach rather than a fast intercept vessel. I smiled at the fifty or so warning lights of the panel. Compared to the agricultural S200, this was the *Starship Enterprise* but instead of Scotty dressed in his smart federation uniform, I employed a rather scruffy Taff in his signature off-white underpants. Despite our advancement, we were still pretty rock 'n' roll. We never catered to conventional wisdom creating, instead, a rock solid business hewn from our own spirit. I liked it that way.

Taff dashed down to the engine room for final checks before I fired up the engines ready to leave the Marina. I hit the button and the MTU's leapt into life with a roar of 4000 wild, unbridled horses, causing the rickety pontoon to shake. The engines' out pipe shot water 20 feet horizontally across the marina. There was nothing gentile about *AL345,* she was all raw power. For me, this was way better than all the Ferraris in the world. I didn't do cars. I was all about boats. It can't have been particularly pleasant for the other members of the marina pottering around on their serene yachts. To the relief of the crowd, we slowly manoeuvred from the marina finger pontoons and onward to the wide ocean. After clearing rocks and obstructions, I opened her up. She was a powerful, scary beast with a life of her own. The noise deafened me as we powered out along the Omani coastline. My cheeks ached and my jaw locked. Roy took a photo of my inane grin to send to the guys back in the office. As we passed Al Hadd heading south, I backed off the throttles to conserve fuel. Like Randell Memphis Raines's 1967 Shelby GT500, *AL345* was my Eleanor. I was living the dream.

I reflected on how I'd managed to own such a vessel. Captain Siad in Salalah had tipped me off the Omani Coastguard were selling some of their fleet for an upgrade. The Harras Class were designed to operate as a fast intercept vessel or perform offshore rescue operations. The boats were Japanese built and confusingly, still promulgated their instructions in Japanese, a language where my vocabulary extended to '*konichiwa*' and '*saki*'. It was hardly helpful.

We'd bought the boat under the terms as in most military sales—'sold as seen'. If it didn't work, tough shit, it was our problem. Luckily Captain Siad had utilised the services of Major Hashil, a commander of the Harras Class in Salalah, who knew which boat to pick. I received little notice on the auction and by the time I'd arrived at Muscat airport's baggage reclaim, Capt. Siad called.

"I have bought your ship. Meet us, please."

AL345 had been named in honour of our Financial Director Andy Lynes and suffixed 345 as we'd bought it on the 28th October, the Royal Marines birthday who, that year, were celebrating 345 years of service. A few teams were located in Muscat so I invited everyone to join me in the Safari Bar to celebrate the Corps birthday at my expense. As per usual, it had ended up rather messy, I'd have been disappointed if it hadn't. Surprisingly, no one was arrested.

Taff's shouts from the stern deck brought me back from my reminiscing. "Dom, I need to shut down the starboard engine to do a filter change."

"Roger that," I replied easing the starboard throttle into neutral.

We continued down the coast running parallel to the Rub al Khali. Known as the 'Empty Quarter', it's the largest continuous sand desert in the world spanning Saudi Arabia, UAE, Yemen and Oman. Wilfred Thesiger mapped the desert in the 1940s and wrote a number of books on his travels with the Bedouin. He served with the Special Air Service and fought in Sudan during World War II. The grateful Bedouin bestowed him the name *Mubarak Bin London*—'The Blessed One From London'. Like Thesiger I served in the desert during my time in the military but our experiences were vastly different. While he occupied the romantic sublime, I was stationed in the Saharan desert with 40 Commando in 'Camp Cholera' an outpost that swayed between ludicrous and mutinous. After weeks of being chased by T62 tanks in 51°C heat, the unit had lost 10% of its strength to dysentery and without mail for four months, morale plummeted. It was a miserable time in which our Commanding Officer cared little for the men under his charge, a fundamental mistake of leadership he would later regret. Royal Marines are free thinkers, we question things and often when we saw weak leadership there were consequences.

During the six-month deployment, we'd only been given six hours R'n'R. This was not an operational tour so time off could have been allocated, yet the CO chose not allow any due to his intrinsic need to control and his failure in trusting the very men that were professional enough to support his rise to the highest ranks. By the end of our desert time the unit hated him, an anomaly within the Corps, as Commanding Officers are usually held in the highest regard, yet this man stood against everything we fought for as Royal Marines and, quite frankly, a disgrace to the appointment.

At the end of any tour, the Royal Marines always hold a 'Sod's Opera'—an improvised performance by the men recalling funny events during the deployment. The desert Sod's Opera had few funny moments to use as material, so it became the 'How Shit Is Our CO' show. As the beer flowed, the personal insults became nastier. As an audience member it must have rather uncomfortable being the butt of everyone's ire, and rather than weather the storm, he stood on the stage to close proceedings—yet another poor decision to add to his ever-expanding catalogue. A couple of empty beers were thrown, followed by full ones. It became open season. The night sky rained bottles, like a Saturday night on patrol on the Falls Road in Belfast. It was a mutiny. The Regimental Sergeant Major restored order by sending each company back to their lines with extra beer to calm the rabble.

As we stumbled back to our tents, our Company Sergeant Major announced, "Drink as much beer as you like, but don't go near the CO's tent or you'll be shot by the sentry."

We'd regressed back to the days of Lord Nelson where Marines stood sentry against mutinous sailors. The craziness of the night worked—the following day we were given five days R'n'R and the mail miraculously arrived.

When Thesiger described his desert as 'found freedom unattainable in civilisation, a life unhampered by possessions, since everything that was not a necessity was an encumbrance' he was describing the ocean I now sailed. We lived by the same ethos but in realms far removed.

Back in Salalah, we had four days to ready *AL345* for the voyage, the only burning issue being how much extra fuel we'd need to carry. We estimated that she could cover 250 miles at 25 knots, but our journey to Djibouti was over 700 miles. I sat down with Roy and Taff to crunch the numbers on how much fuel we would need travelling a 12 knots—the intended speed of the cruise liner. Roy, a newly promoted captain, was Karl Stott's brother, not as gruff but a mariner from toe to crown and especially knowledgeable in boat systems and navigational equipment. The fuel calculations brought worrying results. The nine tons of fuel we needed to carry on deck would make *AL345* dangerously unstable, but in this game it was truly 'no guts, no glory'. As the boat drank more fuel than a squadron of Spitfires, we gambled that if we constantly refuelled the main tank from the tow tanks we could quickly reduce weight off the deck.

The following day, we loaded all fuel on board. *AL345's* stern sat ten inches *below* the waterline. I can't recall ever having set off in such a dangerous state. Roy and Taff shared my dread. As lives of all my crew were on the line I gave everyone the opportunity to have their say before casting off, adding I'd understand should anyone want to stand down.

The weather needed to be checked before we made our final call. The forecast from Mike was good, yet we all knew we would encounter a dangerous beam on sea when turning right out of Salalah. The added weight on deck could, in principal, capsize the boat if the sea state deteriorated.

Ryan returned from the supermarket with the provisions he'd been tasked to procure. As we unloaded, it became clear that only obese kids shared Ryan's idea of nutrition. For every ten packs of chips, there were nine

157

packets of Skittles. The only inclination of anything fruit-like was a crate of cherry cola.

Since our first voyage on *DM234*, I'd retained a soft spot for Ryan and hoped he would go on to be one of my captains, certainly not one of my chefs. This relationship wasn't missed by the men, who named him 'SOD'—Son of Dom.

With pamphlet 101 'How To Shop' glued to Ryan's head, Dolph disembarked to re-provision with a request to lower the e-numbers and raise the content of meat and cigarettes. I guessed I'd smoke more on this voyage.

Dolph's real name was Darren, but was so named as he was a blonde, chiselled Adonis reminiscent of Dolph Lundgren in his prime. I imagine he'd have been rather attractive to ladies until he opened his mouth to reveal a terribly harsh Birmingham accent.

Azamara Quest entered the port. At two football pitches long and eleven decks high, she dominated the port basin, slowly moving into position along the dirty dock that didn't deserve such a beautiful cruise ship—her royal blue hull dotted with glass glistening below a white balustraded superstructure, the grandiose front to luxurious cabins.

All passengers stood on deck eager to see their new Arabian destination. With 400 ship's company to look after 710 passengers, the enormity of my responsibility started to sink in. We did our final checks in silence. We all knew we were pushing the boundaries of safety.

The ship left port as the evening sun dipped its toes in the darkening ocean. Roy and I stood on the upper fly bridge, agonising over mutual tension. A capsize would be disastrous to the reputation of the company we'd worked tirelessly to build; moreover my crew would be in grave danger.

We turned the corner into the open sea. The swell hit us. We rolled slightly and *AL345* was worryingly slow to return upright. My heart leapt from my chest, by the paled expression on Roy's face, so had his. We pressed on. Taff watched the tank level like a hawk to immediately transfer fuel. I hoped the swell would remain this manageable for the four hours we had to endure it. Once between the land masses of Yemen to north and Somalia to the south, we would be sheltered and the passage, in theory, would be easier. Throughout the night, warning lights signalled the exhausts were overheating slightly but thought it due to the extra 9 tons on the stern.

After a hearty breakfast, morale onboard was good, as the threat of being capsized had reduced with three tons less on deck. I sat on the fly bridge scanning the horizon for the new threat—pirates.

We'd employ a shoot first policy on this escort. The cruise liner's accommodation all faced out to sea, if a pirate managed to fire on the ship there was every chance of a casualty. A few years before, the *Seabourn Spirit* was fired upon with AK47 rounds and two RPG's hitting the ship injuring ex Gurkha, Som Bahadur pointing the useless LRAD at the pirates.

I wouldn't take such chances. *Azamara Quest* wouldn't have to defend itself with the LRAD, which I officially claimed stood for 'Literally Rubbish Acoustic Device', I brought along my own insurance policy to add to our arsenal—a 50 calibre sniper rifle. This would enable us to engage identified targets over a mile away shutting potential threats down immediately.

I noticed that we were dropping behind *Azamara*. I asked Ryan to take the helm while I investigated. Roy stood in the lower bridge staring in disbelief at the Enterprise panel lit up like a Christmas tree.

"They've all just come on. We're overheating on all systems," he stated without breaking his stare.

Both engines were losing power and the temperature gauges were about to break the glass. Taff ran into the bridge.

"Shut the fucking engines down, the exhausts are white hot. We're going to start a fire down there."

Roy killed the engines immediately.

I ran down to the engine room with Taff and saw the smouldering manifolds. He was right to call a shut down. A fire would sweep through the entire boat in minutes. Other than a fibreglass hull everything was made from marine plywood. We were a Guy Fawkes' floating wet dream.

"Get some water on the exhausts. Let's try to cool them down."

Roy managed to shut down around 40% of the alarms while we wrestled with what the problem could be. *Azamara* was now over a mile ahead.

Dolph called up on the security radio from the ship. "We have a dhow and three skiffs ahead. The captain is asking were you are."

"We've a slight technical problem we're working on. Stall the captain we'll get back to you ASAP," I replied. "Fucking great, the fucking pirates turn up now we're dead in the water."

I told Roy to try and restart the engines. Nothing. *Shit. Shit.*

"Three skiffs closing Dom. Update," said Dolph urgently over the radio.

"Roger, wait out." I turned to Roy. "Try again."

The starboard engine responded. Heat warnings immediately lit up. Roy edged the throttles forward. No power. The Port engine started. More warning lights. It was imperative we reach the ship before it was attacked.

Taff ran back up to the bridge. "It's getting hot down there again."

I ignored him, transfixed to the starboard engine gauges. "Give the port engine more power."

As *AL345* started to pick up speed the temperature gauge started to drop.

At 10 knots the warning lights were shutting down one by one as we increased speed, the seawater cooling the engines as we used more power.

20 knots. We headed towards the skiffs locked on like a US Tomahawk.

25 knots. I leapt up the fly bridge ladder in two strides with my AR10 closely followed by Wil and Ryan also tooled up. Adrenaline refocuses the senses amidst impending danger. Through the binoculars I couldn't see any weapons on the skiffs that would surely see us thundering over the horizon. I positioned us to do a fly by at 50 metres. I could see fear in their eyes as we bore down, weapons ready. They froze. I bulldozed a huge stern wave at them as a salt water 'fuck off'. They did. I then returned towards the ship. At full power, we leapt the waves like a Martini offshore race boat blasting across the ocean at 30 knots.

"Great stuff guys," Dolph hailed from the ship.

"Get the cameras rolling, I'm coming in hard and fast to your location." Now high on adrenalin, I aimed for the stern before hauling the wheel over, the stepped hull dug into the water as we leaned into the corner like a Japanese bullet train. The waving passengers appreciated our victory loop of the ship, totally oblivious to the near disaster we'd averted. Like Taff all those years before, we'd quickly gone from zero to hero.

161

We still had 500 miles to go and our seaborne animation show had burned plenty of fuel. While continuing on our voyage in escort, I asked Roy to crunch the fuel numbers. We'd most likely be running on fumes by the time we hit Djibouti. Roy suggested we tuck into the ship's stern to get sucked along in the vortex, similar to a cyclist slip-streaming. The ship would do all the work and save us vital fuel.

Azamara Quest's two massive Wartsila Vasa engines created two huge stern waves. I manoeuvred *AL345* inside the second wave and became immediately locked in. At night, with a hypnotic phosphorescent sea bubbling to our front, we felt were sat on the top of a huge reverse waterfall.

We approached point A and thankfully the end of our escort as *AL345* started overheating again. Losing power, we fell off the stern wave and managed to pull 10 knots out of the engine just as the cruise liner crossed the line.

A mile behind we were radioed by the captain. "Thank you *AL345* for your escort we are now Suez bound. Safe onward journey."

"*Azamara Quest* it was our pleasure. Fair winds, out."

We had done it—the first privately owned patrol boat to escort a cruise liner. My immense pride in the moment was short lived.

"I don't think we've enough fuel to get back to Djibouti," Roy said grimly.

I shut down the port engine and limped in gear on the starboard, making three knots. With everything crossed, we would make our home port. Just. That was if another problem didn't rear its head.

"Three skiffs and a dhow up ahead," said Ryan staring at the radar.

Wil tossed up an AR10 as I scanned the water looking for boats ahead. Three skiffs spread about 50 metres apart approached. I called the order for the crew to arm and make ready.

We steered a course to put some distance between us, but with low fuel they were on our route. I didn't want a firefight; I wanted a big night on the rum. All good voyages have to end with rum—it's the law of the sea.

Our two vessels neared. It was countdown to Armageddon. This could go turbo nasty. With my guys peering down the barrels of our armaments I knew our balls were bigger. We were now within a stone's throw of each other. They stared intensely. I could see them weighing up their chances against our weapons that cast menacing shadows across the boat. This could only mean one thing—they too were armed.

The sea slept calmly as the sun hovered over the horizon, a beauty that would be scarred should they pick up anything resembling a weapon. We drifted slowly past each other, with only the soft growl of a slow engine to disturb the tranquillity of stonewalled violence. Like thieves in the night, we passed without a word being uttered. Our body language said it all.

As we drifted into the night we discussed the skiffs. Our gut instinct that they were pirates was confirmed two days later when an unarmed bulk carrier was attacked in the area. As always, evil feeds on the weak.

CHAPTER 13
Hamburg, Germany
53'33N 09'59E

I was enjoying a fine beer after some highly detailed negotiations with a German ship owner. I'd closed the deal straight after completing the *Azamara Quest* job but stayed to comb through the incredibly long contract driven by the German government as we'd be the first company allowed to put armed guards on German flagged vessels. Bureaucracy is a modern day hindrance to any vanguard business eager to pioneer routes so I had to play the game to succeed. I brought Barry Roche along to pore over the finer details of the more mundane parts of the contract. Due to PVI's expedited growth, Andy needed some help, so I'd given Barry a job as he'd shown strong business acumen after successfully running his own business. Behind the Donald Trump ego, he was a nice guy; a little insecure but would be an ideal administrator for the office. He knew little about security but since I had that covered he didn't need to.

As we celebrated the contract's signing, my phone rang. Phil Shaw. "Hi Dom, we're getting near with the negotiation of *St. James Park*."

"I'll see you tomorrow." It was all that needed saying.

I called Killer for a current location of all my patrol boats. *DM234* was heading south on an escort. *AM230* was in Salalah and *AL345* was in Djibouti.

"I need *AL345* armed to the teeth and sent to Salalah and *AM230* to bunker and get ready for tasking."

Killer instinctively knew my priorities. He made it happen quickly.

Phil and I already had a plan in place in the event that the pirates released either or both of his hijacked ships:

164

I would lead the operation on the ground, delivering the ransom by one of my patrol boats to the ship sat at pirate anchorage. My patrol boat would drop me to the hijacked vessel. I would board, meet the pirates and get proof of life (POL). This would involve me checking the crew against photos supplied by the company to make sure everyone was alive as per the deal. Upon me confirming POL to the company, my patrol boat would come alongside and deliver the money. The heavily armed guys on the patrol boat would be supplemented with smoke grenades ready to cover our extraction if the drop took a turn for the worse. If all went to plan, we'd leave the area to wait for the ship's release, then escort her back to Salalah. This would also give me a chance to meet Garaad face to face. I really wanted to look my nemesis in the eye.

As always happened in this game, the plan needed revisiting. Hizbul Islam, commanded by a former Somalia National Army general turned jihadist, were keen to cash in on the little Las Vegas port of Haradhere, so had taken it back from Garaad's ally Big Mouth whose subordinates were only interested in money—fighting hard core jihadists was not part of their individual business plans. Fear and panic spread through the enclave like another pirate strain of tuberculosis. They crammed all their worldly possessions into their luxury 4x4's and fled at high speed to the northern pirate base of Hoybo. It seemed they didn't have the stomach for a real fight, preferring the easier option of shooting at unarmed sailors for high profits. The Hizbul Islam jihadists were more volatile than 'normal' where 'normal' was pretty explosive during the ransom phase.

I rang Roman. We'd been fortunate enough to work together in Special Forces before he was promoted to run

3 Commando Brigade's intelligence branch. We discussed the mood of the pirates generally and we both concurred that turning up in a military style patrol boat like an S200 to pay the *St. James Park* ransom could result in the pirates getting spooked enough to engage us in a fire-fight or worse. All the work that everybody had done to get this far would be pointless if any of the crew died. I simply couldn't let that happen on my watch.

I met with Phil at Zodiac head office and told him the best option was to do a ransom drop by air. Doing anything else would jeopardise the lives of the crew. Phil fully understood, but the guys from corporate didn't due to it being a more expensive option. I joined these armchair warriors in the boardroom offering my explanation face to face to give them the reality far removed from their comfy leather armchairs where they could each masturbate about being the tough guy. I have no time for arrogant pricks, especially ones who try to swing their dicks in front of colleagues.

"What are you scared of?" he asked with a smirk that needed wiping off.

In an imaginary second I leapt over the desk to head butt him, then throw his limp body through the reinforced glass window to watch him fall fifteen stories onto the wet London pavement.

I snapped back. Pointing my finger was a less satisfactory, but more corporate solution. I wasn't taking any shit from some Yale upstart talking tough in a suit. In my world he'd be eaten up alive and spat out on the sidewalk.

"I'm afraid of no man," I spat, staring into his blinking eyes. "If you want to get your crew killed, do it alone. I'll have no part in it." I stormed out. It was Marlboro time.

Phil followed. He didn't smoke but joined me anyway. He could see my anger. "Don't worry, Dom. They're just hotshot lawyers trying to justify their fees. Let's sit down and make a new plan based on an air drop."

The new worry was that after the crew and the ship were released, it could be immediately hijacked again. My new plan would see two of my vessels escort *St. James Park* back to Salalah. *AL345* would go first as the fastest and biggest patrol boat, followed by *AM230* as a backup and to carry spare fuel to resupply *AL345*. The emergency plan was that if *AL345* ran low on fuel she could take a tow from *St. James Park*.

AL345 was already on standby floating off Salalah. Due to her carrying a ferocious arsenal she wasn't permitted to enter Omani territorial waters so would wait in international waters to transfer weapons to *AM230* before entering port to refuel and then accompany *AM230* to the pirate anchorage.

There were two weaknesses in my plan: Phil wanted me to stay at head office so I couldn't lead the operation myself, and *AL345* had a trainee captain—'Leghorn'—nicknamed after 'Foghorn Leghorn' the overbearing cartoon chicken full of bluff and bluster. Taff had already shown resistance to my plan, but I could work on him. *AM230* was less troublesome. Roy was the skipper, and the gun commander was Wil, an indomitable ex SBS operator whose scars showed him as always one step ahead of the grim reaper. Nige was deployed for two purposes: to ensure the job was done and to assess the crew of *St. James Park*. They'd been held captive for 138 days, so we didn't know their physical or mental conditions. Nige was the perfect guy. He'd once been kidnapped when Nigerian militants from the Delta Region attacked the oil platform he was working on. Forty heavily armed boats fired thousands of rounds at the platform and an unarmed Nige, as the security advisor, relied on the onboard Nigerian Naval detachment to protect the platform who soon withdrew under the hail of bullets.

The militants had boarded the platform, stealing away the Westerners to their jungle lair. Nige had suffered pretty rough treatment as a hostage and on many occasions thought he was to be executed. After finally being released, he walked malnourished out of the jungle, riddled with malaria.

He'd lead the first boarding party onto *St. James Park*. After clearing the ship to ensure no pirates remained on board, his second remit was to support and offer a kind ear to any distressed crewmember who wanted to talk.

***

Zurich, Switzerland.
47'27N 08'32E

The transference of ransom money to pirates was becoming far too complicated. The US State Department, after intervening in the Maersk *Alabama*, stated that no money should be paid to pirates. That was all well and good but the US only had a few merchant ships in the region amongst the 22,000 ships that annually transited the Indian Ocean.

At the time of the State Department's announcement, there were around 700 sailors held hostage, mainly from India, Philippines, Bangladesh and Estonia. There would be no US warship coming to their rescue.

In the beginning, ransoms were paid simply and quickly in London using *Hawala*—an informal value transfer system based on the performance and honour of a huge network of money brokers throughout the Middle East, India and the Horn of Africa. It worked based on trust of the honour banking system that traced its origin back to the Romans. The insurance company would draw $2 million from a bank and visit the *Hawala* broker to pay in cash or transfer it to an account. The pirate's broker in Somalia would immediately honour the money once the broker in London rang to say he had the cash.

Various governments, including the UK and US, ironically closed down this honourable system and as *St James Park* was British flagged, they couldn't use *Hawala*. I found it ludicrous that these governments, who offered no solution to free the hostages or fight piracy, would place so many obstacles in the way of well-established shipping companies trying to get their crews home safely.

At Zurich airport a charter aircraft would start the ransom money's journey to the pirate anchorage of Garacad, just south of Eyl. The flight would land in Dubai airport where in the secrecy of a hanger, like bank robbers after a heist, the money would be stuffed into a fluorescent orange search and rescue tube then transferred into a Cessna 172. Depending on the size of the ransom it may require two planes. The tube would then be fitted to the undercarriage of the plane then parachuted onto its target.

Previously, the ransom planes landed in Djibouti from Dubai for a refuel to offer a relatively short flight to the drop zone before returning safely to Djibouti to accomplish the mission. However, the US Air Force jointly controlled Djibouti airport and the US State Department had therefore banned the use of its air space for aircraft carrying ransom payments. The drop for *St. James Park* would now require a refuel at an isolated airstrip inside unstable Yemen.

Al Qaeda on the Arabian Peninsula (AQAP) operated throughout Yemen from remote outposts all over the country. Flying a plane carrying millions of US dollars into a highly hostile environment required a slightly deranged pilot. The Russians are renowned for their crazy flyers, many ex Soviet veterans ply their trade flying into hotspots no one else fancied; however, we knew a man even crazier—'Fang'. A Stetson wearing, cigar chewing, former Apache helicopter pilot with the US Air Cavalry, Fang already had a few drops under his belt. He'd be paired with a fearless Zimbabwean called Finlay who'd operate the communication equipment and get POL. On approach to the hijacked ship, the aircraft would call the pirates on sat phone to ready the crew. The pirates would parade the crew on the open deck so that a photo could be taken to show the crew alive and well. This would be transmitted to the company to verify. Only then would the drop be approved and the tube dropped into the sea to be recovered by a pirates skiff before returning it to the ship for the official count.

As Fang pushed the throttle knob to taxi onto the runway, he donned his Cavalry Stetson, took a gulp of good luck scotch and chewed on his Opus X cigar.

"This is my last drop. After this one I'm out of this bullshit," said Finlay.

Fang laughed as he pressed David Bowie on his MP3 player. "Let's Dance."

The front wheel left the tarmac and powered into the unknown

**

Salalah, Oman
16'55N 54'00E

On *AM230*, Roy was busy at the dock taking on extra fuel and loading freezers with food for *St. James Park*. Zodiac had sent one of their superintendents for oversight and give a damage report to the company on the state of their ship after boarding with Nige and the PVI team.

Once cleared by Port Control, Roy pushed to full speed to RV with *AL345*.

"What the fuck was that?" shouted Roy, handing Joe the wheel.

He followed Leon down to the engine room. It was clear where the deafening bang originated—the bushes on the clutch had failed. It was a two-day repair. This wasn't an option. They had to continue to the RV.

"OK guys, bottom line is we've only one engine," Roy reported to the crew mustered on the bridge.

A debate ensued. Due to safety considerations, Roy didn't feel that *AM230* should go down to *St James Park*. If they lost the remaining engine in bad weather it could be a disaster. Roy was right. All the crew agreed apart from one man—Wil.

At the RV, *AM230* and *AL345* came alongside secured by lines. All crews came on deck for a final brief. Taff brought up all the excuses why *AL345* could not go down to the *St James Park* either despite it being the plan. He and Leghorn had convinced themselves that *AL345* could not make the voyage because of fuel, and that a tow from *St. James Park* would not work. With both crews unwilling to move to *St. James Park*, it was looking like our mission was over before it began.

Wil had heard enough. "This is bullshit fellas, I'm going in *AM230* to get the ship. Anyone who wants to come, raise your hand,"

All the doubters put up their hand and fell in line.

"Taff, you and Leghorn can stay on your boat with two engines and explain to Dom why you're fucking him off," he boomed across the deck.

Wil briefed me on the change of plan. The alterations would cause a delay in getting to *St. James Park* and make PVI look like amateurish in front of Zodiac. I felt helpless shackled in a boardroom; I would have much preferred to be directing operations from the sharp end.

I told Taff to get his arse down to Socotra and be on standby to go and assist if *AM230* ran into trouble. Although the sea to Socotra was a millpond, I was concerned that as she was running on one engine any emergency would leave a run to Somalia as their only survival option. I didn't sleep that night.

The weather forecast was good but a small depression had been forming off the Seychelles heading north. The crew gave their position every hour so I could update the Zodiac crisis management team. Fang had dropped the ransom without a hitch and returned to Dubai where there was a high chance he'd now be throwing back rum at the Rattlesnake Club surrounded by Russian hookers.

The *St. James Park* crew was now in the most dangerous phase of the ordeal. When super tanker *Sirius Star's* ransom payment was dropped, pirates, after counting the money, fought each other on the way back to shore. Five drowned with millions of dollars floating around their bloodied bodies.

At payment time, pirates are at their most agitated. Armed with AK47's, paranoia fuelled by khat and nervous at the drop unfolding, the situation becomes a witch's cauldron of violence and greed-driven brutality. Even from a plush London office I could feel the tension. At Zodiac, the negotiators had informed Roy and the *AM230* team that if things went wrong, some of the *St. James Park* crew could die. Warnings were one thing, but for *AM230* reality was to become far worse.

Roy turned to the sky. The foreboding dark clouds pulsated with charged particles, producing blinding flashes into the black sky. They were heading towards a biblical storm.

Nige and Joe joined him on deck. As the thunder sounded across the ocean, they felt the beast's first cold breath. Roy immediately instructed the crew to lash everything down and re-check the emergency equipment.

I studied the satellite weather image. The weak depression had now strengthened into an intense storm cyclone. I rang Mike for an update. The spectre of being shipwrecked on the Grand Banks haunted me. It was expected that winds would reach 45 knots with a six-metre swell. I sat silently and questioned myself. *Is it right for me to expect the crew to go on in such conditions?*

I knew only too well what could befall the crew and that scared me more. The storm would push the boat far beyond what it was designed for even running two engines, with only one had I sent my men to their deaths?

I rang the boat to pass on the bad news. Wil picked up the bridge phone. I briefed him on the weather and told him if they felt it all too dangerous, they should return to port.

"Don't you worry, pal, if we sink we'll swim ashore and hijack a pirate skiff. We're going to be on *St James Park*, be sure of that, big man," Wil said calmly in his thick Fife accent.

I'd check hourly just to make sure they were still alive. If the phone was dead so were they.

Phil poked his head around the door, "The pirates have left the ship, what's the latest RV time for *AM230*?"

"The boys are pinned down in this storm, they're only making 1.5 knots over the ground. It's looking like it will be another 24 hours," I replied.

Phil looked worried.

"Get *St. James Park* to make best possible speed towards *AM230*. It's the best we can do." There was no point in making excuses or pussy footing around. "On the upside, it's unlikely skiffs will be hunting in that weather."

Roy struggled with the wheel while Ryan operated the power throttles to try and keep the bows pointing straight into the snarling ocean. Each wave bit *AM230* like a rabid dog. Full power was required to climb the 40-foot waves then backed off to avoid the flat-bottomed vessel being catapulted from the foaming crest into the next wave that could rip her open and send her to Defoe's locker.

The angry sea relentlessly pounded *AM230*, each bottle green wave probing for weakness. Down below it was miserable. Supplies for *St. James Park* took up most of the space of the already confined sleeping area. Condensation ran in torrents down the hot bulkheads, the steamy air the only thing not being thrown about. Nige marvelled at Joe who slept hovering mid-air before crashing hard into the bunk as the boat smashed down on the back of a wave. Nige mused that in Joe's former life as paratrooper he was used to floating before a hard landing. Most crewmembers were seasick, projectile vomiting onto the deck from the rear bridge hatch. They hadn't seen the Zodiac superintendent since entering the storm. He'd withdrawn ashen faced to the rear cabin and locked himself away from the violent ocean. They would check if he was still alive when the weather settled, it was too dangerous to go on deck in the gale.

I stared at the live weather map on my laptop. The cyclone had stopped moving and now sat on top of *AM230* as if angry that this intrepid small patrol boat dare enter its domain. *AM230* would have to go toe to toe with the beast until they reached the other side. I prayed the engine would hold out.

Phil entered my office. "The Royal Navy is sending a frigate down."

"Great, hopefully they'll put a detachment of Marines on board and we can relieve them in place when *AM230* arrives."

I informed *AM230* of the new development and for them to keep radar watch for the warship. As *St. James Park* was the first British flagged ship to be hijacked, it seemed the Royal Navy were finally stepping up to the plate well after the buffet had finished.

St. James Park was underway, the captain keen to put miles between the ship and the pirate anchorage. After months of neglect and pirate vandalism it was not an easy task to get the ship moving. After sitting at anchor for so long the hull was crusted in barnacles and sessile kelp, reducing her speed.

After twelve hours, *AM230* picked up *St. James Park* on radar. My crew were keen to meet the ship as they could then turn around and run for Salalah in a following sea. There was no sign of the British Frigate on anyone's radar.

St. James Park limped along like a resurrected ghost ship. Roy approached her from downwind to give the boarding team the best possible chance of cross decking. Nige, stolid in his eagerness to get on board with the PK machine gun strapped across his chest, even if only to escape the hellish experience on *AM230*. He leapt across the divide onto the small pilot ladder and climbed aboard. Just this small leap lifted the mood of Zodiac. They were getting the boys back home.

Taff and Leghorn, after swanning around Socotra, RV'd with *AM230* for the final leg. The Royal Navy frigate never arrived. Instead, they hosted a cocktail party in Salalah. Sunset canapés took priority over the safety of merchant sailors.

Phil and I had flown to Salalah to greet everyone and as I stood on Salalah dock my heart burst with pride as the PVI flag fluttered from the bow of *AL345*, *AM230* on her one engine still diligently escorting *St. James Park* into port.

Three security teams from other companies waited for their transfer vessel as my boys sailed past. Their look of envy was priceless. Nige gave me a wave from the bridge wings of *St. James Park*. Mission accomplished.

The *St. James Park* crew was debriefed and mental health assessed. I put all the PVI lads in the Hilton, with the exception of Leghorn and Taff who would sleep in the boats berthed in port. The Zodiac and PVI teams would meet in Whispers Bar for a debrief over rum. My lads had gone the extra mile on this one and we had pushed safety to the limit. I was just happy they were alive.

I handed my card across the bar and challenged the lads to break it. Ryan created mayhem trying to drink a flaming Sambuca, but had accidentally set fire to Wil. Everyone was in hysterics, apart from Phil who nodded tersely into his mobile before signalling for me to join him outside. I recognised that look.

"*Battery Park* is under attack."

CHAPTER 14
MV *ASIAN GLORY*
13'38N 56'12E

To the left, Garaad could see the warship approaching. It was sleek, menacing, almost like a space ship he had once seen on a TV. To the right, Scarface's small cargo ship— limp, destitute, pointless.

"I am closing in," he said to Scarface down the phone. "Tell the warship you will kill the hostages if they come closer." He turned to the captain and dug the muzzle deep into the back of the captain's matted skull. "More speed."

Scarface and his band of pirates had captured the small Pakistani cargo ship *Faize Osamani* a month before off Kismayo claiming it was dumping toxic waste—an oft-used excuse for the attackers to beat the crew to feeble puppetry. They were now using her as a mother ship to hunt other commercial vessels. Breaking down mid-ocean had not been part of the plan. Garaad now closed in, intent on rescuing Scarface and his team before the warship intervened.

The VHF maritime radio burst to life. "MV *Asian Glory*, this is Warship HDMS *Absalon*, please state your intentions, over."

Garaad was surprised it had taken them so long, but their inefficiency helped now that he was close enough to make his intentions perfectly clear. He instructed two of his pirates to drag the first officer onto deck. All the warship would see was a man knelt with two AK47s pointed at his head.

He grabbed the VHF. "Come closer, I shoot him."

The silence told him all he needed to know. Western impotence would give him the time he needed. He picked up the phone and called Scarface. "Collect the men, get everything valuable, and get here as fast as you can."

Pilot ladders were slung over the side to assist Scarface and his men scale the massive superstructure of the *Asian Glory* and the skiffs brought on board.

Scarface came aboard and hugged Garaad. "Thank you, brother. I thought I was done for. What about my ship?"

"Why do we need it when we have this? I need men. With this ship, we have the biggest weapon on the seas."

***

Pirate anchorage
08'03N 49'57E

The bridge was now a sauna, but this was not one you could escape from. And normal saunas weren't awash with khat phlegm, piss and shit that coated the floor as *Asian Glory* rocked gently on the lazy swell. The large windows gave good visibility for navigation at sea but acted like a greenhouse in the face of the Somali sun. The generators had been switched off once the ship had anchored and left an eerie silence only broken by a pirate moving his weapon to a more comfortable position and his spitting of yet another globule of thick, rancid phlegm onto the floor; the acrid odour of a forgotten armpit lost amongst the filth and squalor of the surroundings.

The intense heat siphoned off any energy remaining in the crew. The disgust of sitting in bodily fluids had long passed, and only the threat of death kept them alive. Every one of the crew stared blankly at the floor, longing for the love of a distant family etched inside their deteriorating minds—home but a mere slip of a dream. They may see neither again.

Every ship needs a captain. His steady hand navigates a ship across the treacherous seas, guiding the ship and crew to the safety of the shore. He is the glue that cements all hands onboard, and when the tempest rages, all eyes look to the captain for hope and salvation. When a ship loses its Master, terrible things can happen.

In 1816, French Frigate *Méduse,* commanded by Viscount Hugues Duroy de Chaumareys, headed to Saint Louis, Senegal to deliver Colonel Schmaltz as the new French governor. Chaumareys scored high on aristocracy but low on seamanship. He was an arrogant fool without the knowledge to navigate but with too much vanity to ask his deck officers for help. He found solace in a passenger called Richefort whom he made unofficial navigator. Richefort was a philosopher and member of the philanthropic society of Cape Verde—hardly qualifications to safely navigate the ragged coast of wrecks and reefs. The hapless pair soon floundered, grounding *Méduse* on a reef off Mauritania. With the ship still intact but with the weather mocking their plight, the viscount wasted precious time by constructing an overcomplicated raft to transport the 400 passengers and 160 crew to the shore 30 miles away. The ship's boats towed the raft for a few miles before the winds turned foul. As the storm increased, the viscount cut the lines of the overloaded raft and rowed to the safety of the shore, abandoning the passengers and crew to their fate. The raft quickly descended into the anarchy of insanity. Sailors fought soldiers, and officers fought the passengers. The first night saw twenty killed. The raft's faulty construction meant that only the centre was secure, so many more died over the course of three days, fighting to get to the safety of the middle. After the fourth day, only 67 remained alive, but the primeval darkness of frightened beasts would see brutality descend

179

further. African slaves were shot then eaten as the mariners turned jackals, greedily tearing at the gruesome flesh, fighting with blood-smeared mouths over the human carcasses strewn across this radeau of death. Humanity was replaced by primordial degeneracy, purveying the evil of the Gorgon after whom the abandoned ship was named. After 13 days, the *Argus* rescued the raft. Only 15 of the most savage remained alive.

Captain Velikov had been a good Master. His time at sea started in the Bulgarian navy before moving to a career in the merchant service, and the high esteem afforded by Zodiac was only surpassed by his loyalty to the company. Even when the pirates had burst onto the bridge, filling the bulkheads with bullets, he'd stood his ground. His order for the pirates to leave the bridge had earned him a sickening rifle butt to the face, yet still he stood resolute. Velikov was not a man to break easily.

Garaad had forcefully taken him from the bridge in a demonic rage after yet another refusal to dance to his tune. The crew had heard the shot. None believed Velikov could be dead, even after a bloodstained Garaad stood before them to announce the murder and to warn a similar fate would befall anyone who didn't follow orders.

Yet, the fact that it had been so long since Velikov had been seen or heard now started to sink in, and that his secret diary was now waved in the hands of the pirates made the likelihood of his demise all the more real. What information would be in there? Would it compromise the crew and the company? Without their captain, without a plan, some of the crew started to fall apart. As unbelievable as their dead captain, there was treachery emerging within the crew. Confinement brings on mental stress not helped by the regular beatings they endured from the pirates. Tangible fear was one thing, but the paranoia of suspecting everyone around you was becoming unmanageable.

Rajith sat like the rest, forehead down, praying to wake up from this four-dimensional nightmare. The heat and the smell made it impossible for him to escape the reality of being taken hostage, cramped like a caged market chicken back home in Mumbai, with the same uncertainty of fate. The guiding light of his father slowly dimmed, and the ensuing hopelessness and fear made him want to cry; yet, he knew the pirates would prey upon weakness as they'd done the night before. The savages had beaten him for looking at a pirate in the wrong way. He didn't even know the right way. He'd been dragged to the deck below, where a pirate had smashed his head into the bulkhead and stolen his beloved Sacramento Kings baseball cap. As he lay on the floor waiting for further blows, he'd seen the Ukrainian, Chief Officer Petro, talking to Garaad in the pilot's cabin. Maybe it had been the blow to the head, but it looked a cosy chat.

With the captain gone, Rajith fully understood. Like Jim Hawkins, he'd witnessed treachery, but what could he do? Were others involved with the chief officer? Crewmembers were regularly taken from the bridge, often returning bloodied and bruised from another beating, yet some returned without a mark. Were they collaborating with Petro and Garaad, or were they just needed for a task? Why did some smile? Had they been given food, water, a toilet? Why would they be treated so well? Rajith wondered if anyone else thought the same. If he was sent on a task and returned unharmed, would they think him a traitor too? His head swam, searching for reason in the situation; yet his mind drowned. He just wanted to see his family.

He was woken by a sharp dig from a roughly wielded AKM slant compensator and forced up onto the stern deck to parade. Garaad stood menacingly before them, his weapon slung low. The third officer knelt limply at his side, his shirt crusted with blood from yet another beating.

"We need to move the ship. If you don't help," Garaad shouted as he rifle-butted the kneeling man between the shoulder blades, "He dies."

The threat was used every time, but the crew never wanted to tempt fate to see if Garaad cried wolf, so co-operation made life easier. Forcibly preparing the ship for sea, each crewmember was accompanied by a sadistic pirate. Rajith's mind raced. *What does this mean? Are we to be released? Has the ransom been paid?* He kept his thoughts to himself; paranoia over the chief officer and his secret mutiny still blighted him; beside, he was just happy to be off the rancid confines of the bridge. He deeply inhaled the delicious sea air as he walked forward to help raise the anchor, his knees joyous in their release. Having not eaten for the past three days, he felt slightly dizzy after his first burst of activity. He squinted at the clarity of his surroundings and noted another ship at anchor close by, then another and another. He counted eleven ships. Were they also hijacked? Were their crews going through the same hell? Was it wrong to find comfort in finding he wasn't alone?

Task finished, Rajith returned to the bridge herded along by Scarface, his tormentor-in-chief, who took great pleasure in indiscriminate beatings. Scarface received his grotesque facial wounds from an explosion in a Mogadishu marketplace while accompanying his father to buy gifts for a family wedding. An Al Qaeda suicide bomber had detonated in the crowd, killing ten, including Scarface's father, whose body was never found. Being a pirate was far better than eating from bins back on land. The bonus of taking out his frustrations by beating others made it worthwhile.

As Rajith walked past what was once the captain's pristine sanctum, now awash with bin liners full of khat leaves as the pirates drifted from their self-made squalor into a khat-induced trance, he noted Petro in deep conversation with Garaad staring at navigation charts. The first officer was also present, and smiled as the second engineer brought a plate of food and bottles of 7Up. Rajith's hunger heightened both his sense of smell and anger in witnessing what was unfolding. Scarface, sensing Rajith had seen something he shouldn't, hurried him along in his usual way—a dizzying rifle butt to the back of the head.

There were seven other Ukrainian crewmembers on the sweaty bridge; would they join their countrymen, siding with the Somali devils forever high from sucking on their khat gobstoppers? Especially now that he, the cook, and the motorman had been described as the captain's most trusted men from the translated diary entries. Rajith could see the glint in Scarface's eyes; it could only mean more beatings. Scarface didn't disappoint, his boredom often eased by pulling Rajith's hair sharply, kicking him as he passed, or just using Rajith's face as a good old punching bag.

Rajith was thrown back into the swamp of the bridge and into the effluent of others. The pirate guards stood on the starboard side with the crew sat on port. But as Rajith's mind swirled, he wondered, whose side were they really on?

∗∗∗

Garaad stood proudly on the bridge wing of the *Asian Glory*. Such a huge ship gave him ultimate sea power in the area and he couldn't afford to lose it to Hizbul Islam who Big Mouth had warned were planning on attacking ships at anchorage. With no port at which to land them, the 2,405 cars on board were of little worth. However, they held a highly important commodity—fuel. After analysing the logistics, he decided to first resupply his dhows and skiffs with diesel and petrol at sea. He'd posted his heavily armed men at likely boarding points, taking proper security measures against hostile pirates in the area.

This was the first car carrier ever to be hijacked and at five stories high, Garaad had turned it into a floating fortress, possibly the biggest ever pirate ship in history. Not only did her high sides give perfect cover and protection, she was armed to the teeth with one extra special weapon in her armoury—the Red Ensign. There was no fictional romance in flying the *Jolly Roger*. In modern piracy, Garaad could sail under the esteemed British flag, virtually camouflaged to attack vessels. He wasn't in a hurry to hand it back to Zodiac.

"The Londoner is coming. Inform the crew," Garaad said to Chief Officer Petro now stood at his side.

Petro, was a short, stout man resembling Danny DeVito, and his helium-pitched voice only added to his comedic appearance, yet never once did he make the crew smile. He was a survivor, hustling his way through life. For him, he didn't see himself as someone working for the pirates; chicanery offered the best chance of surviving the ordeal. If the captain wanted to be a hero, fine, but he wasn't getting paid enough to be killed in the crossfire. He'd approached Garaad and offered his help immediately upon the ship being hijacked. Garaad, in turn, needed help from the crew to operate the ship. Petro had offered a hand, Garaad had returned with a detachment bordering on disdain. He finally shook it with a limp and lifeless motion, devoid of decency, barely sharing a glance. The treacherous pact was made.

Petro had approached "Arty," the second officer and one-time mafia errand boy, who agreed immediately. Petro just needed the engineering team to join him. It wouldn't be too much of a problem—they both hated the Bulgarian captain, and Ukrainian blood ran thicker than seamen's honour. The dirty deal was finalised on the car deck under the supervision of Garaad while pirates siphoned car fuel tanks to replenish the many dhows hunting for prey. When you sell your soul to the devil, rarely do these complex affairs end well.

The skiff, transported from another hijacked ship, pulled alongside. It was the second time the Londoner had visited *Asian Glory*; the previous occasion had been when escorted from the *St. James Park* anchored a mile away prior to its release. Despite his name, the Londoner had never even visited Europe, but had a better upbringing than most of his countrymen. Abdi Saed Bafe Looyan, known as "Loyaan" to hostage negotiators, was born in the Puntland administrative capital Garowe. After finishing primary school, he was educated in Dubai then India, where his university studies furthered his competence in English, Arabic, and Urdu to complement his native tongues. He'd returned to Puntland to work as a manager for Jubba Airways in Bassaso before working for a women's NGO charity. After the desperation of subsequent unemployment, he'd linked up with a childhood friend, who happened to be the son of pirate kingpin Big Mouth. He soon used his language skills as a pirate negotiator for Big Mouth and Garaad.

The game had changed. With ransoms getting higher, pirate negotiators became a useful asset and highly sought after and, as such, targeted by rival pirate gangs. One of the pioneering negotiators, a UK national called Khalid, was killed before he made a penny. With Garaad's strength, Loyaan soon rose to the top of the food chain. He possessed a friendly demeanour and always remained pleasant to the hostages, even handing out fines if pirates broke any posted rules. Loyaan's presence was a good sign for the crew; it meant he would be speaking to the company to hopefully release the ship.

Loyaan stepped onto the bridge to address the crew. "I am really sorry, your company doesn't care about you. We have been very reasonable with them; we are only interested in the money. We don't like to keep you here, but your company is not interested in your release. They blame you for getting hijacked. I can help. You all have the chance to call home. You must tell your families to pressure the company to pay and get them to pressure your governments. Maybe then the company will take your situation seriously."

Calling home was too attractive an offer for the crew to resist, yet their calls would be interrupted by an AK47 being shoved to their head with the threat of death should the money not be paid. Loyaan's duplicitous offer was a savage psychological trick designed to heap even more emotional burden on families already worried sick.

Loyaan and Garaad were at the top of their criminal game—a classic good cop, bad cop combination. Garaad was unpredictably violent, with Loyaan steadfastly calm. He would often tell the hostages he was on their side and only working for the pirates as they had kidnapped his family. He believed he was a businessman and that holding people against their will was normal. In his confusion, he disclosed to the chief officer about how he wished he wasn't a player in piracy and asked whether it would it be possible if they could sail to Australia. The chief, although up to his own neck in deceit, wasn't buying any sob story so told him they didn't have enough fuel.

"That's OK. We could hijack ships on the way and take their fuel and food."

The chief ignored the statement; Loyaan, whether he liked or not, was complicit in his own misery.

Garaad, on the other hand, knew exactly what he was and took great pleasure in purging the high seas of millions of dollars. He didn't possess the adventurous spirit of Blackbeard, he was just a predator on the herd, a money hungry cutthroat, with honourable endeavours his transparent shopfront who used the brass of a bullet in his hunger to storm towards currency of a country he despised.

He stood on the stern deck out of earshot of the crew and pirates, the nacreous sunset a contrasting calm to his palpable ire. "I want more money for this ship; it's bigger than *St. James Park*."

"I am trying," Loyaan replied; "but they want to settle for the same figure. Let's see what problems the family give the company after the crew call home."

"What about the other ships?" Garaad asked.

"We are on course to receive payment in the next two weeks: $3.8 million for the chemical tanker and $4 million for the other, Insha'Allah."

"OK, delay the company further. I need more time to transfer all the fuel from the cars. I have a plan for this ship."

CHAPTER 15
Raffles Hotel, Singapore
01'17N 103'51E

It was important I kept all my shipping companies briefed on pirate developments and made sure we were meeting their expectations. After flying for ten days straight between a blur of European cities, Durban and Madagascar, I hauled myself wearily across the peanut shell–strewn floor of the Long Bar on the second floor of the iconic hotel.

Captain Tong Boon created the Singapore Sling here in 1915 within the pulley fans and teak plantation shutters, but this captain was strictly Havana Club. The bar provided an escape. With no clients to meet until the following afternoon, I didn't want to speak to anyone. Everyone needs rum in their fragile life and it would be my companion to help stabilise my mind that rolled like a bottle in a car. Mort Künstler could have painted a fine picture of me at the Long Bar enduring the solitude of command.

Loneliness never bothered me, despite being a fairly social creature on the outside. I was a loner, more at home on the wild ocean or in the wilderness of the Arctic using my skills against the elements to survive. My life had become all consumed with the fight against piracy, but it had to be that way as the stakes were so high. In these rare, uninterrupted moments of dislocation, I'd try to unravel the mess that masqueraded as my personal life. My marriage was pretty much over, and I couldn't remember when I last crossed any threshold I could call home. With so many families relying on me for income, I blocked out domestic dystopia to keep focused on the job. The bartender poured me another drink without a word. A malcontent soul makes people nosey. When you're down, many want to dig, under the veneer of assistance, just to polish their own existence. I couldn't handle self-congratulatory concern, so was thankful that years serving in such a high-class establishment had taught him to allow space for self-reflection.

Again, Phil Shaw broke the serenity. "Hi, Dom, I want your advice. The British Embassy in Nairobi has just contacted us. They've had a man walk in saying he can get a deal with the pirates on *Asian Glory*."

I wrote down all the details of the individual and told Phil I'd get back to him. Phil would have been a great poker player in another life; he remained unemotional, but from my days as an interrogator, I sensed the stress in his voice. I knew he was grasping at this hope of a breakthrough as negotiations hadn't moved forward sufficiently. He also lived with the guilt of Captain Velikov, agonizing over whether he could have done more to save him.

I stepped outside and took shelter from the afternoon showers common here in May during the inter-monsoon season. I leaned against a white colonnade to fire up a Marlboro. I had a friend in Kenya, an ex-SBS commander who'd spent his last service years hunting down Bin Laden in the notorious caves of Tora Bora. He'd carved a niche in piracy delivering ransoms by ship. Like me, he led from the front. I hugely respected his approach; plus he was a really nice guy.

I dialled his number. "Hey brother, I've a strange one for you. Not really my line but any advice is really appreciated." I carried on to explain this mysterious man dropping into the embassy, including his name.

"Dom, lose him. He's just trying it on. This happens all the time. They just want to make a fast buck before disappearing into thin air."

I hung up and fired up another Marlboro for good measure; Phil wasn't going to be happy.

The millions of dollars in ransom payments had attracted all manner of crackpots trying to cash in on the Somalia gold rush. Opportunists and scammers claimed early successes duping desperate ship owners. NGOs in Somalia and Kenya were also a good source of income to those who wished to exploit the benevolence of the international community.

A colourful German called Julian Bauer claimed to be a professor and had set up an NGO to protect the Somali marine environment. His PhD seemed to be in meddling in the misery of others. In a strange set of events, he'd positioned himself as a middleman to many pirate groups, including ones Loyaan worked for, on the pretence of helping the hostages. In fact, he worked with the pirates. He was delusional to the point of being sectioned. When the Korean-flagged MV *Rim* was hijacked, he convinced the pirates the ship carried missiles, pushing the ransom up to $3 million. The vessel carried nothing of the sort and was due to be scrapped. Fuelled by greed, he interfered with many hijack negotiations. He reached the ethical gutter when he advised pirates holding a fishing vessel *Prantalay 14* that they should keep the four Thai nationals so he could hammer out a better ransom from the Thai Embassy. Luckily, the Indian navy successfully launched a rescue mission. In many of the bungled Bauer cases, his interference unnecessarily extended negotiations, meaning more time for pirate beatings, hostage despair and separation from families.

He was not alone in his pirate-obsessed madness. The Virginian socialite Michelle Ballarin joined the ranks of the loony bin, calling herself Amira, the Princess of Somalia. She toured the country, conjuring up claims of how she would save the country from poverty and free all the hijacked ships by "unwinding the situation," whatever that meant. Of course, nothing happened other than interfering with the negotiations of the British couple held in Somalia, demanding that she should handle the ransom payment for the exclusive PR rights to their story. She wanted to deliver the payment to the pirates personally before being dropped by the negotiators for being a crank and a liability.

Such clowns would be deemed a joke if it wasn't for them adding to the hostages' misery. I would have been happy to line them up against a wall to be shot for their ego-driven fantasies.

I finished my Marlboro and returned to my leather stool at the bar.

"Tough day?" the bartender enquired, instinctively pushing another rum and coke in front of me.

"Every day, my friend, every day. Keep those Havana Clubs coming."

I scrolled through the ten messages missed while on the phone. One was from Ang: *When are you coming home? I can't take this anymore. We need to talk.*

She wanted a divorce. She talked about it more than ever. I agreed, but simply had no time to attend to it. Divorce means admin and lawyers. I have little time for either. Finding somewhere to live and, above all, the heartache of parting with someone with whom I had shared most of my life, I couldn't deal with; far more reason, then, to bury my head in the sweet Cuban nectar. I needed to be back on the ocean, some sea time would soothe the soul.

***

Southeast Al Mukalla, Yemen
13'58N 49'31E

"Dom, I need some guys! The engine room's flooded!" Taff yelled from stern deck.

I sounded the general alarm to muster the off-watch crew and directed all hands to help Taff.

The voyage had been an ordeal from the get go. I'd felt a strange disquietude over the cruise ship we escorted as if it were a Jonah. After a recent refit that had cost the lives of four workers, en route to our RV a passenger died. We escorted her back to Salalah while she transferred the body ashore for repatriation. On the way, *AL345* had lived up to the name of Eleanor, yet on this escort she behaved much worse. We'd spluttered into port, the result of water in the fuel. New fuel had been pumped feverishly on board while the cruise ship had steamed ahead keen to make up time after the delay of the death.

I'd contacted the company security officer to explain our issues and to confirm that we'd continue the escort; yet, my concern had lingered, as the ship's bridge had not responded to any VHF calls since transferring Nige and Dolph on board. I'd managed to phone Nige, who informed me that the Italian captain viewed our presence as an irritation rather than a necessity.

Yet, as professionals, we were committed to doing the best job possible; our focus was protection rather than a clash of egos. In Nige, I had the best man on the bridge, so knew he could work magic on this most ignorant of captains.

"Dom, what's happening?" called Nige over our private security radio.

"We've just had to shut down the engines. We're working on it."

We were now three miles behind the ship. Even without a damage report from Taff, I guessed they had things under control as we were still afloat.

Nora rushed onto the bridge. "It's a bit of a mess down there. We've blown the starboard engine water intake, but Taff has managed to do a temporary repair. Can you restart the engines?"

The light panel's blinking illumination showed Eleanor far from happy.

"Tell Taff I want to take her up to 25 knots to try and cool the engine systems down." I wasn't sure how long the repairs would hold, but I increased power slowly, and the guttural growl of the two MTU power plants churned the ocean behind as we hit 20 knots to finally gain on the cruise ship.

Even with this relief, the bridge mood remained fraught. The captain's sole aim was to reach Safaga in Egypt on time, no matter the consequences, and became increasingly agitated with delays. Nige was more concerned about the 700 passengers getting there without being hit by a pirate's RPG.

I manoeuvred *AL345* to within half mile of the ship. My pulse slowed as I felt we were regaining control of the escort. Mischievous Eleanor sensed it. We started losing power. My heart sank.

"Dom, I need to shut down the port engine to change the fuel filter. We've still got water in the fuel," said Taff from the engine room.

I cursed. With only one filtered fuel line, we needed to close down the engine to change it. Pushing the remaining engine harder to keep up with the cruise ship caused another problem—overheating of the exhausts.

With warning lights and alarms reflecting my despair, we started to drop back again. Taff entered the bridge to restart the engine. His concession to the interminable heat was to be constantly dressed in only saggy stained y-fronts and steel-capped boots. With a submariner's etiolated pallor and spindly legs best suited to a chimp, a catwalk model he wasn't; yet, despite his outward gruffness, when his grubby hands tinkled the metal, he could make engines smile. Until now. He was covered in grease and diesel and totally exhausted after wrestling Eleanor's recalcitrance for five straight hours. I threw him a bottle of cold water.

"It's not good down there," he said after swigging eagerly. "I'm not sure how much we can keep pushing the engines."

For a moment, he again reminded me of a scruffy Welsh version of Scotty from *Star Trek*. It was the levity I needed in an otherwise dangerous situation.

"We've only got ten filters left," he said with a foreboding air.

The reality then hit me. "We'll push them until we've completed the mission. Get back down there." I needed respite. Sometimes, we never get what we wish for.

Nige radioed in. "We've spotted a capsized boat a mile from our position."

"Roger that. We'll take a look," I replied.

"The captain is ordering you to ignore it."

"Kindly inform the captain that as AL345's skipper we *will* investigate."

How could any mariner ignore a stricken craft? There could be someone alive clinging to hope while tied to the wreckage. I'd been there myself, hanging on for dear life when my boat had capsized in the north Atlantic.

194

Assisting a mariner in distress was every seaman's duty, whatever the circumstances.

We approached the upturned vessel, its dark blue hull bobbing like a giant fishing float. Italian Rob leaned over and tapped the hull with a boat hook to alert any survivors underneath. Nothing. He tapped again. Still no reply. Whatever had happened, sharks had probably put these guys out of their misery. The sea gave no quarter to the stricken.

We headed back toward the cruise liner. I felt a pang of sadness for those lost. Having personally been sledgehammered by the terror of being shipwrecked, I felt more empathy. I doubted the Italian egotist on the cruise liner would have had much experience of the gritty edge of sailing small craft.

My repeated request for the captain to slow down to 10 knots had been repeatedly refused. At 10 knots, we had a fighting chance of providing the escort. At 13 knots, we were pushing *AL345* to breaking point. The captain was hell bent on his timetable. I'd met his sort before: those dangerous in their arrogance who'd be prepared to sail into a hurricane rather than change course.

Frustrated by us slowing him down, he sent his chief engineer across to *AL345*. The German chief stepped on board, his smartly clipped hair framing a look of disdain. After 30 seconds in the engine room, he reappeared on deck. "It is clear that you are likely to break down and be a further problem to us."

He glanced around, unimpressed. Maybe it was our engine, or that his virgin white overalls had been defiled by an oily pipe somewhere down below. His world was far removed from ours. He would pride himself on being able to eat from the floor of his huge engine room immaculate in high gloss.

Taff and I explained that we only needed to reduce speed by 3 knots to protect them, leaving us with enough power to accelerate to intercept any vessels that posed a threat. Taff asked him again to come down below to detail the issues we had.

"No, I'm sorry, I've seen enough. I'll report to my captain; he'll decide."

He stepped off *AL345* onto his spotless launch. I expected he'd immediately shower after being exposed to such a filthy boat.

On the route ahead there'd been three attacks in the last 24 hours. The fact that none had resulted in a hijacking meant the pirates would still be hunting ships. They were my tormentors—not dirty engine rooms.

Nige radioed in to tell me that the captain believed that we were a liability and wished to proceed without our escort.

"Have you briefed him on what's happened up ahead?"

"Yes, mate, but he's adamant. There's nothing I can do."

"Can I speak to him directly?"

There was a pause. "Sorry, mate, he sees no point in it."

Although livid, I had to wear my professional head, a part of the body I'd like to have ripped from the captain. I sent Italian Rob and Nora over to bolster the cruise ship security for the rest of their voyage. Nora was a good hand, and we'd served together for years. He'd a face that would frighten a police horse, yet had turned his unappealing visage into an advantage by becoming his village's gurning champion, unseating the long time winner—his father.

Although Nora's head could be used as a battering ram, the flag state did not allow weapons, so the team would be unarmed for the next 1,000 miles through pirate alley. Such stupidity was risking passenger safety.

I shared my crew's despondency. They'd worked so hard to keep us in the game. Like me, they hated failing.

The shipping company would rightly want an explanation, but there was no way I'd take any shit. The cruise captain was a modern day Viscount Hugues de Chaumareys, and his inability to compromise was complicit in the escort failing. What the arrogant captain didn't know was that I knew the owner of the company exceedingly well . . .

We tied up in Salalah and after post-escort admin, I took the crew out for a slap-up meal at the Oasis Seamen's Club. Despite the escort being our first misfire, my crew had given everything, so I made sure they understood how much I appreciated their commitment. I'd also ensure the problems we'd encountered would be fixed ready for the next escort. Every day is a learning day at sea; the key is to remember to stay ahead of the game.

"Dom, what happened with the hijacking attempt on the *Battery Park*?" Wayne enquired as I ordered another round of beers.

"*Battery Park* came really close to being boarded." I then recounted the report stating that the ship had been sailing in poor visibility due to fog. Matt Horncastle had been on watch trying to focus through the pea soup that surrounded the ship. He'd heard a voice on the water but thought it impossible in the conditions. He'd then seen a white skiff right next to the ship with pirates about to hook on their ladder onto the portside deck. Matt had quickly grabbed his SIG 542 rifle and fired five rounds down onto the pirates. They'd panicked and fled without firing a shot back. "That's why I changed our SOPs for all weapons to be made ready, safety on," I added as a footnote.

The following morning, Captain Siad escorted me to the military side of the port to board Major Hashil's Harass-class vessel. Although the same class, it looked as if it had been spared the hard yards given to *AL345*.

I outlined our problems, and he agreed with my request for Taff to link up with his engineer. It transpired that the vessel had a manufacturing fault that meant the engines would overheat between 12 and 13 knots. The news was as bitter as the pitch coffee we drank. If we'd known this before the last two escorts, life would have been much easier.

With the guys working on the boat, I took the opportunity to walk the dock—something I always enjoyed as it offered the chance to see all manner of craft from around this seafaring region. The playful water raked the rusting stanchions and Great Cormorants, drying their wings by crucifixion, blissfully ignored my stroll. The port was a hive of fishing dhows, and I stood fascinated by their manoeuvrability as they came to rest alongside many others rafted together, bobbing 20 deep. A favourite vessel for pirates on long-range attacks, a dhow's elegant crescent lines resembles a piece of ornate furniture with high bows and a high stern, the steering positioned at the rear under the shade of a simple wooden roof. The design hasn't changed for centuries, but nowadays many had a small inboard diesel engine rather than the more elegant sail.

The dhow is believed to originate from India, and Omanis in the sixth century used to buy their dhows in Beypore as the timber from the Kerala forests was believed to be the best for dhow construction, along with highly skilled Indian carpenters. Later in the 18th century,

Al Hudaydah in Yemen became the epicentre of Arabic dhow construction for the Red Sea and the Gulf of Aden.

I met an old fisherman sitting on the dockside, his face worn from a struggle his eyes seemed to have escaped. His son welcomed me in perfect English. We talked about their dhow moored close by, the son entertaining me on how they fished and enthralling me when describing his father's skill using only sails.

"Would you be kind enough to take me out for a few hours?" I asked.

The father's puzzlement accentuated the wrinkles on his weathered face; each, no doubt, told a sea tale. The son explained that they were not due to fish for the next few days. The old man's youthful eyes glinted once more when he agreed to take me on a sightseeing trip for $300.

We cleared the port, slowly traveling at 5 knots before turning east toward Mirbat, a place heralded in British military folklore. We kept within five miles offshore to avoid running into pirates. The father switched off the engine, and we drifted downwind at around 1.5 knots. As it often does, the contentment of breathing briny air overwhelmed me. I felt at home here amongst new brothers of the ocean.

The son cast out some hand lines off the stern so as not to waste any fishing time. He explained that dhows could cover great distances with little support as they used sails to collect condensation in the cold nights for drinking water. They were supremely efficient on the sea but needed to drift with the winds and currents, the dhow's high sides designed to catch the wind perfectly.

This small voyage gave me great insight into how the pirate dhows operated. They'd drift in the shipping lanes, using only their engines to run after a failed attack. This enabled them to fish and carry more water than fuel to sustain months at sea trying to hijack ships. I'd also wondered why pirate dhows towed skiffs behind, as their drag caused more fuel use and, therefore, seemed rather inefficient.

"No dhow captain wants combustible petrol on a wooden dhow, so it's all kept on the skiffs. As the dhows drift most of the voyage, they hardly use any fuel anyway."

It was simple yet brilliant. With this information, I could return to the UK to develop a matrix for tracking pirate movements adopting newly found mariner knowledge to complement our security experience. It may prove invaluable, giving my team's vital intelligence on how and where pirate groups operated and future areas of commercial shipping vulnerability.

***

PVI Headquarters, Tiverton, UK
50'54N 03'21W

I'd just arrived from Muscat. Titch, as per usual, gave me a hug as I entered the office. Killer, as per usual, was busy on the phone. In the five months since delivering on Zodiac, we won two further blue-chip shipping contracts. Sam Osborne, my new sales guy, was signing up new companies daily and the bank of computers expanded every time I returned.

Killer finished his call. I gave him a big bear hug as he had been holding everything together. He was my pillar of strength; we could never have grown the company in such an expedited fashion without him. Beyond his permanent smile, I could see he was exhausted. He'd literally moved into the office and had slept under his desk for the last six months. Pushing my concerns aside, he was steadfast in his actions, understanding how high the stakes were when the lads' lives were on the line. We didn't look on the guys as "contractors" or "employees"; they were truly our brothers, and we'd inadvertently created a big family for ex Royal Marines.

Titch brought in a mug of tea for Killer's briefing on the operational picture. I stared at the map on the wall; I had to pinch myself sometimes on how fast we'd grown. Over 200 of our guys were on the water protecting 50 ships. Other companies must have thought we'd concocted some dark alchemy to achieve success, but our business model was simple: we were totally honest and cared for our people, paying them well and looking after their welfare. In turn, they delivered the most professional service in the business.

"It's been busy out there while you were in the air. Paul Storey's team on MV *White Sea* was attacked. Pirates managed to fire off an RPG but missed the ship. Paul's team returned a volley of shots so the pirates immediately aborted the attack. Nige's team has safely disembarked from the cruise ship in Safaga with no reported incidents. I'm guessing you want to speak to the team leaders? Their numbers are on your desk."

There had also been a firefight between pirates and an armed security team off Aden; the security team had killed one pirate before a warship arrived. All pirates were arrested and later freed with enough fuel to get back to Somalia. In response to the incident, the International Maritime Organization issued a warning that escalating violence between security teams and pirates could put sailors in danger. The fact that the ship was not hijacked and no crewmembers injured seemed to have been lost in bureaucratic translation.

I gave Phil Shaw a quick call to see how negotiations were progressing with *Asian Glory* now entering its fifth month under hijack. It wasn't positive. In London, the

Zodiac and NYA negotiation team had presented a generous dollar figure to Garaad, who threatened to kill more crew if they again submitted such a derisory offer.

"One thing that strikes us as strange," Phil continued, "is that the *Asian Glory* has left anchorage and is moving north."

CHAPTER 16
Dar es Salaam, Tanzania
06'49S 39'16E

Captain Borkovsky confirmed the correct loading of his final consignment of containers. Efficient as always, he ensured his ship was on schedule. The weather forecast for his voyage to Mumbai was favourable, and he'd received security updates from his CSO before briefing the crew.

The new third officer finally arrived. After solving the problem of clearing customs by giving two packs of cigarettes to a corrupt official, he reported immediately to the bridge, keen to make a good first impression on Borkovsky, the legendary Ukrainian, who, at 6'3" with thick grey hair finished off with a matching beard, portrayed a true mariner. With over 30 years at sea, he had five years left before retirement.

"Good morning, Sir. Third Officer Linnik reporting for duty."

The captain gave Linnik his orders before they exchanged pleasantries while waiting for the steward to take Linnik to his cabin.

Linnik had spent most of his career in the Atlantic. This would be his first post operating in the Indian Ocean, so one burning question stung his lips. "Sir, what's the situation regarding pirates on our voyage?"

"Pirates are out there, that's for sure. Not that I've seen any in the ten years passing through these waters."

"Do we have armed guards?"

"We don't need them. Company procedure dictates that if we see anything suspicious we mount fire hoses along the deck and switch them on if necessary."

As Linnik was escorted to his cabin, he felt a little unnerved by the captain's solution, but as the new man on board, his will to voice such a concern was hidden under a blanket of subservience.

Back in Odessa, the ship's management company, like many, thought piracy always happened to someone else.

The ship pulled away from the dock typically jostled by three tugs all with different ideas of how to move the ship. The first officer stood on the portside bridge wing using angry hand gestures to guide one especially imbecilic tug.

"Dar es Salaam Port Control, this is MSC *Anafi* requesting port clearance," the captained called over VHF.

"Captain MSC *Anafi*, Port Control you are clear to proceed."

The Anafi was built at the great Polish shipyard of Gdansk. At 206 metres long she was well suited to African trade, equipped with three large cranes on deck, allowing her to load or unload her cargo into small ports with limited infrastructure available alongside. The ship, like the captain, would be retired within five years and run up Alang Beach to become another metal corpse in the world's largest ship graveyard.

The ship steamed ahead through the narrow entrance before heading NNE to avoid Outer Makatumbe Reef, keeping the two cardinal buoys to port as they entered the vast ocean. The captain adjusted the ship to best economical speed of 14 knots. The crew slipped effortlessly into their sea routine of watches and meals. Linnik stood on the bridge wings and tingled with excitement. It was all new, and the thought of visiting India fired his imagination as the molten sun dripped over the yard arm into the iridescent ocean.

***

MV *ASIAN GLORY*
04'00N 55'48E

Rajith busied himself on the car decks. The ship had been at sea three days, and with a possible storm coming, Petro had ordered him to check that all vehicles were properly secured. The inside of the ship resembled a huge multistorey car park, so any multiple car movement could be catastrophic to ship stability.

Rajith worked slowly; the task offered relief from boredom on the bridge. He felt normality in the strangeness of working on deck with the ship underway, apart from the red-eyed Somali with an AK47 on his heels. Scarface's departure to a pirate dhow the previous week had lifted him from his hopelessness and depression; even the captain's secret diary revelations seemed to have been forgotten by the pirates in the mist of khat.

The pirates' moods had also shifted. They seemed more purposeful, and Garaad spent forever poring over charts with Petro. Supplies had been brought on board including two goats that were treated better than the crew until they were individually slaughtered on deck. Rajith had winced. Although no stranger to killing animals, this was not a butcher's clean slaughter, more of a crude attempt at throat slitting, prayers to Allah an afterthought when watching the goat's feeble struggle while it bled out. Fresh meat wouldn't pass Rajith's lips; he would have to survive on the last few tins of chicken the chef had said was pork.

He'd also noticed many rocket launchers, machine guns, and belts of ammunition being moved from the car decks to the accommodation block. It looked like they were preparing for war. He hoped it was in preparation for the ransom payment delivery.

After completing two decks, he returned to the bridge. A shot rang out. He froze. *Who was attacking them? Other pirates? Commandos?* He could hear Garaad shouting as he climbed the ladders to the bridge. He entered as silently as possible, quickly sitting on the floor.

Garaad, wild with anger, stood behind Petro with an AK pointing to the back of his head as he stood at the controls. "Get the ship closer!"

"I'm trying, believe me." Petro now understood the cost of his pact with an unstable killer. Petro reduced to 11 knots, with another ship approaching astern at 14 knots. He was allowing the ship to overtake, at which point he would increase speed and adjust course to bring both ships together.

Twenty armed pirates were directed onto the stern deck primed with darkness as their camouflage. Garaad forced another pirate to keep a gun on Petro as he leaped out onto the starboard-side bridge wing with binoculars. The bridge was tense; every crewmember tried to look for comfort from another, but all they saw was fear and confusion. *What was going on?*

"Dabka, dabka, dabka!" Garaad yelled from the bridge wing down to his men on the stern deck.

***

On MSC *Anafi's* bridge, Captain Borovsky paid particular attention to the erratic course of the huge ship he was passing to port. Under the rules of navigation, he was obliged to keep clear of the vessel he was overtaking. The ship was not transmitting on AIS, which was unusual for such a large vessel, especially one flying the Red Ensign. British-registered ships usually had fine captains, so he was curious as to what punishment the officer of the watch would receive once the captain realized the mistake.

The deck lit up in a blinding explosion. Borovsky sounded the general alarm, thinking it was an explosion from the cargo. He needed to check for a fire, but before he could issue the order, the bridge erupted into a hail of bullets. Everyone hit the floor as hundreds of rounds spat around the metal bulkheads. The port watchmen crawled into the bridge on their bellies.

"Captain, that ship is shooting at us," reported the shocked watchmen.

The captain froze for a moment. *A British ship firing at us?* It didn't make sense. He tried to make sense of the situation. "Everyone keep low. Ivan, steer five degrees to starboard." He turned to the new third officer, bleeding from the splashing of glass, "Linnik, call UKMTO to report our position, and tell them we are under attack then gather the crew and move everyone to the engine room." He crawled through broken glass as bullets continued to search for a human target. "Chief, I need full power from the engines. Keep your people in the engine room. We are under attack; it's too dangerous on deck."

The ship's engines started to build speed. "Another five degrees to starboard." He checked the speed—18 knots.

"Sir, it's the car carrier firing at us," shouted the watchman.

The captain's heart sank. Any such vessel could match her on speed. Gunfire now strafed the containers on deck, his course change putting the bridge out of the firing line. Another explosion lit up the sky as an RPG round hit the middle crane on deck. He scanned the deck for a fire, but it looked clear. He checked the speed again—18.5 knots. That was all she could give.

***

Garaad entered the bridge of *Asian Glory*, pointing his weapon into Petro's face. "We need more speed."

"It's all we have." For once, Petro was relieved, despite the madness of the situation. He knew he'd be complicit if they managed to board the target. They'd been chasing the container ship for far too long and unless the target had an engine issue the distance would extend between them. The engines were at full power but only giving 16.5 knots. She could normally reach a top speed of 18 knots, but months at the anchorage had taken their toll. Not running an electrical pulse through the hull had allowed it to become the home for hundreds of thousands of tiny barnacles; harmless on their own, in their masses, they were powerful enough to slow down even something as huge as *Asian Glory*.

After several hours of receiving hostile gunfire, the escaping MSC *Anafi* had become the first ever vessel to be attacked by a British-registered pirate ship. Not a word of it was reported in the open press.

Garaad tried using *Asian Glory* as an attack vessel twice more. Neither attempt was successful. It was time to demand cash. He realised his previous tactics were far more profitable.

Innovation in a booming market would always see Garaad one step ahead of his competitors. Mergers and hostile takeovers had made him the most dominant force in the market, but with power comes envy and Garaad knew there were many factions keen for their slice of pie. He understood he had to be shrewd on land to ensure his war was at sea. There would be many more ships to take. With over 200 teams to call upon, no navy could stop him.

***

Dubai, UAE
25'13N 55'20E

A loud knock on the door slowly stirred Fang. He slowly opened his bleary eyes to focus as two startled girls ran naked for the cover of the bathroom. He fell out of bed, cursing last night's excess as he stumbled over the floor littered with beer bottles. He peeked through the door's peephole to see a stressed looking bellboy. He opened the door slightly, allowing the bellboy to thrust a message through.

"Your company has been trying to reach you all night."

Fang searched for his phone, lost in the sexual turmoil of the night's entertainment, finally finding it in the inside of a thigh-high black latex boot. He smiled. *What a night*.

The phone showed 20 missed calls from his boss. He checked in.

"Where the fuck have you been? I've been calling all fucking night!"

"Good morning to you too, Sir." Fang returned in his usual 'I don't give a shit' tone.

"I've a drop for you, but it's a fast ball. The money arrives tonight. Is the plane ready?"

"Yeah, we're always good to go," he lied. "Don't tell me, the refuel strip is in Yemen again."

"Yeah, it's Yemen, and the drop has to happen tomorrow. Details are at the hangar." The dial tone left Fang with little choice.

Enough time had passed since his last drop to build up a tab at the Rattlesnake that would bankrupt most men, and girls here weren't as cheap as in the Far East. He'd promised himself too many times that he'd done his last drop, but he was hooked on Dubai's high life. He glanced at his watch. He could squeeze in a little more fun before he started work.

Arriving at the hangar, the ground crew had worked through the night to get the plane ready. He'd a new British guy riding shotgun with him on this drop—Connor from Yorkshire, wherever that was. He hated new guys on a job, especially ones who didn't like Bowie; he didn't know how they'd cope if shit went down, and in Yemen, the shit was deeper than in most places. He slept that night in the hangar, with a half pint whiskey nightcap to ease him into slumber.

At 0530, he donned his lucky Stetson hat, cracked the top from his cigar tube, and took a slug of whiskey. It was a perfect breakfast for the day ahead.

The plane flew low to get a better visual on *Asian Glory* somewhere in the vicinity. Connor scrutinized the area ahead through a set of high-powered binoculars to look for the blue and white behemoth.

"I have visual," Connor reported.

The plane passed low to alert the ship to their presence. The pirates immediately lined up the crew on deck to be counted by the plane.

Connor called Zodiac. "25 crew members on deck. I've just sent a photo. Please confirm when you want us to drop."

Phil was taken aback. *25? There should be 24.* "Reconfirm crew number."

After a brief pause, Connor's voice came through the Zodiac office speaker "Confirmed 25."

Alex smiled at Phil. "I told you Garaad was bluffing."

The picture transmitted from the aircraft arrived into Phil's inbox. He counted them again just to process it in his own mind. He then scanned it carefully. 161 days as a hostage could not alter his unmistakable figure. A huge weight lifted from Phil's shoulders. Captain Veliko Velikov was alive.

CHAPTER 17
Hurghada, Egypt
27'10N 33'48E

The second Marlboro still hadn't satiated my post-flight nicotine thirst, yet I decided three would be greedy, besides, I was burning to death under an unrelenting August sun. I moved under the shade of a palm tree and smiled as a noisy flock of jetlagged Russian tourists, clumsily herding belligerent children and badly packed bags, converged on the infinite line of orange and white taxis. This was an unfamiliar realm, and one I was unsure of being part of. The airports I usually frequented were far from the beaten track or ones where aircraft carcasses paraded along the runway told their own story. Here it was a cheap concrete hive, where swarms of transiting passengers, pale or blistered depending on their holiday phase, were congealed into a gelatinous mass by holiday reps who barracked them to make sure their holiday was orderly. Tourist packages were the antithesis of freedom and far removed from the only holiday I'd ever taken backpacking across Mexico.

I fended off waves of Egyptian touts with my well-practised serial killer stare that I knew had a physical effect on people. "Where the fuck is Leghorn," I muttered angrily.

Induced into my third Marlboro, I checked my phone to confirm the hotel address. I wandered aimlessly around the scorching car park while I searched for the hotel's details in a sea of emails. I flicked my cigarette in the drain before bumping into a young Egyptian man.

"Do you need taxi?" the gangly teen asked.

"I need to go to the Seagull Hotel. Do you know it?"

"Yes Sir, I know the place."

"OK, don't mess me around and don't talk, I'm not a tourist. Follow these simple instructions and you'll get a better tip than any holidaymaker will offer." I threw my bags at the grateful youth.

We drove through the confusion of Hurgharda, a jumble of tacky hotels and disparate enterprises, interspersed with incomplete buildings—it was Dolly World meets Gaza. The contrast appealed to my mild anarchical streak. After years prescribed with military order, I found a shot of chaos refreshing.

Hurghada was a simple fishing village until the 1980s when the government and private investors started to develop the place for tourism. It was one of the most popular destinations for Russian tourists and many had settled down in the town now boasting 20,000 Russian expats. The majority of British and West European tourists headed to the more upmarket resort town of Sharm el Sheikh on the Sinai Peninsula, the most fought over piece of land in human history where modern day warriors planted their towel on a pool lounger to signify territorial rights.

Mustafa, the taxi driver, had followed my brief and drove responsibly, both rarities in an Egyptian taxi. I took his number before heading up the steps to the Seagull Hotel that welcomed me with a security portal where my bags and I were x-rayed. The government had issued a directive to bolster security at all tourist destinations after 62 tourists had been massacred in Luxor by a Jihadi splinter group sponsored by Bin Laden.

Ryan met me in the lobby. His long unkempt hair made him look like a cross between an arts student and Man Friday. After our customary hug, he explained the rest of the men were refitting the boat. I sensed a problem. He was evasive when pressed but I thought better of pushing it until I'd freshened up.

The room was basic, softened with bland sheets and tired fittings along with an austere bathroom adorned with cheap tiles. It was all-inclusive hell. How could vacationers see this as relaxation? On the plus side it had a balcony. On the downside it overlooked a dusty building site. I fired up a Marlboro. No frills covert operations. It'd been a while.

Taff looked timid as we met in the hotel beach bar.

I pounced on his furtiveness. "OK, what's happened?"

"The Egyptian crew put the boat on the reef."

"Has it sunk?"

"No, we managed to get her back to the dry dock in Safaga."

This wasn't a great start to the mission, but thankfully I hadn't paid the full amount for the boat so any repair costs would be borne by the current owner who also happened to own the Seagull Hotel.

Leghorn emerged smiling from the sea of dance floor foam where scantily clad young Russian girls energetically danced, their provocative moves memorised and replayed later through the minds of the salacious middle aged voyeurs stood timidly on the periphery—a far cry from my lads causing self-inflicted injury by badly break dancing in the middle of the suds. Ryan and Scotty arrived, thankfully bereft of bubbles so could at least retain some level of professionalism in this highly distractive environment.

They all shared one thing in common, and it was Leghorn who broached the subject. "Dom, why the fuck have you bought a dive safari boat?"

"Have a guess," I smiled.

"Dive safaris?" answered Scotty, never one to shy from stupid answers.

Allowing the mystery to continue, I turned the conversation to what damage had befallen the boat. They'd hit the reef doing 7 knots, ripping a massive hole through the underbelly and smashing one propeller and rudder.

We should have been setting sail in less than two weeks. It was clear that was never going to happen. I rang Andy back in the UK and told him to withhold payment until I gave the nod.

I turned to the bar tender and ordered four bottles of rum. I fired up a Marlboro and downed three rum and cokes in quick succession as if the day was my last. Those sweet molasses were always the activator to my thoughts.

***

Safaga, Egypt
26'46N 33'55E

The desert road stretched endlessly, pockmarked with military outposts all poised ready for the imminent Israeli attack they'd waited nearly forty years for. My mind drifted into the beautiful dune waves that took my thoughts away from home where the situation had become unbearable.

I'd arrived back early from an overseas trip so rang Ang to inform her I was on my way home.

"Don't bother, find a hotel." Five words to confirm our marriage was just names on paper.

I'd slept in my car at a motorway service station. Enough was enough. When I left for Egypt I promised myself I was not going to return. I didn't tell Ang. I couldn't deal with the conflict; I felt so much responsibility to the business and the lives of my men. That they always came first, I guess, was the problem, so I understood Ang's frustrations. I wasn't an easy guy to be married to.

Taff snatched me back from my marriage woes. "We're ten minutes out."

I acknowledged him as we entered the ancient town of Safaga. Founded in 282BC, it was originally named Philotera by the Greek Egyptian Pharaoh Ptolemy II Phiadelphus in honour of his deceased sister. When the Pharoah left he clearly took all the builders with him— Safaga was as unimpressive as most towns in modern day Egypt. Town planners clutched to some ridiculous notion that creating an unfinished clutter of structures was the way to go, but in reality, it was a melancholy symbol of a bright past decaying into an uncertain future. The great Pharaohs of antiquity would be sorely disappointed with the lack of progress since their golden age.

Safaga possessed a bigger port than Hurghada, and cruise liners transiting the Red Sea would regularly stop here before entering the Suez Canal. We passed through the town before arriving at the boat yard south of the old port. The road paralleled a disused and forgotten railway track hardly raised an eyebrow to the locals but stood as a personal reminder of the erosion of Victorian Britain. Its construction was an incredible feat of engineering, connecting Alexandria in Egypt to Khartoum in Sudan. At the planning stage many hailed it as impossible, the concept of building a railway through the desert sands was radical in engineering terms. The purpose of the Sudan Military Railroad was to transport thousands of troops, under the command of General Kitchener, to retake Sudan from the Mahdi khalifa. It worked.

The boatyard was popular for dive boat refits after the holiday season and unusual in that railway tracks ran through it to the sea. Each boat was loaded onto a modified train bogie then hauled up onto the dock where wooden supports would keep the boats upright. *Sirdar* Kitchener would at least be happy that the railway still retained some relevance.

A short Egyptian guide darted ahead of us, bobbing and weaving through shipyard entanglements and the jungle of boats stood up on hard standing to arrive at *Sea Scorpion*. I inspected the damage to the hull. It was substantial but fixable; however, the propeller shaft and propeller looked more complicated. I stared up at the most rickety ladder in Egypt that led 30 feet up to the deck. I climbed with the torment of Casablanca flashing before me. *Sea Scorpion* was just over 30 metres long and 8 metres wide. Her teak stern open deck was in contrast to the pure brilliant white hull, and designed to allow divers easy access into the crystal clear waters of the Red Sea. I walked into the large saloon where in the middle of the lounge area steps led me to ten guest cabins on the lower deck. The forward end of the saloon led to the ship's galley that was small but functional. I continued my inspection, ascending the outside stairway to the first deck that opened out to a sun lounging area and six crew cabins with the captain's cabin next to the bridge. The bridge was my sanctum where I would plot courses and plan all aspects of the operation. She was a good size but needed a great deal of work to meet my requirements. Leghorn's assumption of voyage readiness in two weeks was delusional even before the ship hit the reef. The final stairwell led to the highest point—the fly bridge. It was open apart from a small bimini giving welcome shade to the steering position. It provided a commanding 360° vista and most suitable as the primary steering location.

"This is pretty awesome, eh Dom?" Ryan offered.

"It has potential but it's way off being operational. I'd suggest not thinking about leave for the next six weeks."

I left the crew in silence and called Killer. "Hi shipmate, do you know where Harry is at the moment?"

"You know Harry, he could be anywhere from Tehran to Lagos."

"Try and find him. If he's available get him on a flight to Hurghada and also put Lasse on standby to come out as well."

I booked Leghorn onto the next available flight back to the UK. He'd been out for six weeks but achieved little—his parting words being the vessel's engines and machinery were sweet. I certainly hoped so.

I gathered the team for a briefing in my hotel room away from prying eyes. I issued each a crew uniform. The shirts and shorts displayed a logo of a shark surrounded by the wording 'Shark Watch Expedition' and was our cover story whilst in Egypt. The secrecy of the operation was paramount both commercially and for our own security.

***

I walked from the street past two armed officers with AKM assault rifles and into the depressing concrete office. At the far end of the room two more sombre looking policemen guarded another steel door that led to the mysteries beyond. Many who'd passed through were never seen again. Three women accompanied by a guardian all wore the same look of foreboding as they sat stewing from fear and the uncompromising heat. I mulled over the cover story again and again in my head until I believed it as the complete truth. I pictured my opponent on the other side of the steel door. He too would have been trained as an interrogator but our methods were poles apart. I'd use sleep deprivation as the star of my toolbox.

He'd use iron bars and electric testicle clamps in his search for answers.

I'd only been out of Egypt for 24 hours due to an urgent meeting in Athens. Ryan and Scotty had unloaded the support rigid inflatable boats (RIBs) from sea containers sent from Alexandria, but the police had intervened and sent the boats back. On arrival back to Hurghada I'd been summoned to report at the office of the State Security Investigations Service—the feared SSI.

As Egypt's main security apparatus, SSI reported directly to the Ministry of Interior—the powerful organisation that spread terror amongst citizens. Any Egyptian arrested by SSI would endure harsh interrogation and torture in the underground cells found in every city, and in many cases executed if found guilty. SSI members lived secretly within the community, even close family would never know of their dark side. Like the Iraqi Mukhabarat, SSI watched everyone.

The police officer standing guard at the door motioned with his rifle for me to enter. I walked through the heavy door into a dark courtyard. On the right stood a decaying building with broken masonry, windows secured by rusty iron bars. I walked towards the torture chambers but was called by a voice from the left. My eyes focused into the darkness to see another armed guard in full dress uniform. The building he guarded was, by contract, much smarter, even palatial. I entered through the oak door and instructed to sit in a small waiting room decorated to fine taste. A large door with a brass plate opened. Invited in by an orderly, I was escorted past oak panelling and beautiful artwork. I took a seat in a subtly lighted leather chair that complemented the expensive brass fittings. I could have been in a swanky Upper East apartment. Whomever I was to meet was high ranking. My stomach shrank as if starved and seeds of doubt stumbled in to my consciousness. *Had we been compromised?* It was impossible; I'd kept a sealed box on operational security. Before I could fully recap, my host arrived and walked directly to his desk leaving an overpowering trail of expensive cologne rich in agarwood hanging in the air. He sat down, closely sizing me up. His mouth turned up intricately at the corners as if in a permanent half smile to accentuate his middle aged charm. He spoke with an air of sophistication backed up by an expensive education, yet his coal black eyes betrayed him. He was totally ruthless. I dived into full cover mode. In the world of deceit I was a good actor and would have to give an Oscar winning performance against such a shrewd critic. A falter on stage would not end with a bow but the flickering of lights as electricity passed through my scrotum.

For around fifteen minutes we chatted like long lost friends—he asked me where I lived in England, where I'd travelled, if I had kids.

"So tell me about your RIB boats. What is their purpose here in Egypt?" The niceties abruptly finished leaving no conduit to business.

I explained we were embarking on an expedition to tag and record Tiger Sharks off the coast of Sudan and to film a documentary for National Geographic. I didn't want to bring up how ludicrous the Egyptians had been by claiming a shark had been remotely controlled by the Israelis to attack people and so disrupt tourism. I supported my story with print outs of my previous expeditions across the Pacific, Atlantic and the Arctic. He carefully studied the paperwork analysing every detail. My expeditions were real. They would check out to the most rigorous inquisition. The key was not to trigger too much digging. It was better to project oneself as naïve bordering on stupid. He bought the ruse and issued a no objection letter to allow my RIBs to be launched in Hurghada.

I walked back out through the steel door and onto the street, immediately firing up a Marlboro. I jumped in Mustafa's waiting taxi, and hastily drove off heading back to the hotel without saying a word.

After twenty minutes he could not hold his silence any longer. "Are you OK? Did they hurt you?"

"No, the guy was a perfect gentleman, he was very helpful."

"Don't trust them. They killed two of my friends for protesting against the electric company. I hate them."

I didn't respond. In a police state it's always better to stay neutral on anything, anywhere.

Ryan and Scotty returned to Alexandria to check the condition of the RIBs. The customs officials had ripped the boats apart damaging most of the equipment, even puncturing the tubes.

After extensive repairs in Safaga, *Sea Scorpion* was moored at the Seagull Hotel jetty allowing us easy access to make preparations for our voyage. The project was two months in but we were no closer to leaving. The vessel was Egyptian flagged and could not be transferred to sail under a Red Ensign due to her design and Egyptian government restrictions. We'd walked into another ambuscade of Egyptian bureaucracy or stupidity depending on which department you visited. I spent most of my days visiting different ministries trying to obtain mythical stamps from idiotic officials who made me wait for hours before realising I was too complex so referred me to another ministry of equal incompetence. I'd often visit the local coffee shop, clouded in apple-tinted smoke, to meet a middleman who knew someone who could help. The 'someone' turned out to be as mythical as the quest for the holy stamp. It was hopeless. With the onset of Ramadan, we also had the added bonus of the whole country shutting down.

Scotty and Ryan had managed to get the RIBs unloaded from the containers and were on the way back to Hurghada on flatbed lorries. The best place to launch was from the marina but when the boats turned up, the lorry couldn't get through the gates and caused a huge traffic jam. Right on cue, the cops arrived who I stalled until I'd thought of a Plan B.

Mustafa called his friends, one who owned a crane and another who knew a safe place to park the boats until the dust settled. We arrived at the friend's place that resembled the Golan Heights after a serious pounding. The crane, precariously balanced on loose rubble, lifted the boats to rest comically on a squalid rubbish pile. At least it was soft and a step forward in the war of officialdom in the kingdom of the elusive stamp. Mustafa's friend watched over the boats totally out of place in their new urban setting. It had been a long day.

"Lads, it's Saturday night, I fancy dinner at the Hard Rock Café. My shout."

After the last two weeks of unrewarded hard work, the team needed a blowout.

We'd become regular visitors to the Hard Rock, and as a group who always gave decent tips, we were hastily waved to the front of the long queue and given a prominent table where the boys immediately ordered stupid looking cocktails, drinks best suited to people-watching in Hurghada's most popular nocturnal hang out. The place was in full swing, the dance floor full of writhing women, ranging from gorgeous to stunning. When surrounded by ugly males for 99% of my time, it was easy to look at the opposite sex with reductive instinct.

Scotty and Ryan dragged me up to the dance floor and Havana Club always made me enjoy a good boogie. As we thrashed around like idiots, my eye was turned by a figure across the dance floor. She was beautiful, but danced similar to a wounded ostrich. My eyes melted into hers, and we exchanged ticklish smiles. She awkwardly moved towards me, mesmerising me with her moves. I mentally crowned her the worst dancer in Egypt.

She now danced right in front of me, and looked directly into my eyes. "Hi, how are you?" she asked in a strong Russian accent.

"Would you care to sit down?" I offered; mainly to protect her from further dance floor embarrassment.

We talked for a while. Her name was Anna. She'd only been in Hurghada for two months, working as a Hotel guest relations manager after graduating from university in Russia. An early start the following morning stymied any lengthy carousing so she departed far sooner than I'd hoped. There was something about this girl I really liked. She purveyed that hint of confident aloofness I found both challenging and hugely attractive. With alcohol my armour, I exited the club, catching her just as she slipped into a cab. "Would you like to have dinner sometime?" I asked with a tinge of desperation.

"Sure, that would be nice," she smiled.

I gave her my number and before I could ask anything else, the taxi curtailed romance in a valedictory cloud of blue diesel smoke.

CHAPTER 18
Hurghada, Egypt
27'12N 33'49E

Through long nights, hard graft, much rum and infinite laughter, we'd managed to keep within our six-week schedule to ready *Sea Scorpion* for sea and pass the required inspection to leave Egypt.

I stood in a long queue of fishermen, safari boat owners, glass bottom boat drivers and all manner of seafarers. They were all trying to get a stamp so they could feed their families, nothing more. The man they waited to see was Abdu who headed the Marine Department responsible for issuing the legion of different licences for vessels in the Hurghada region. He was also one of the area's most hated men, demanding high bribes that drove many Egyptians out of business. Although he'd ruined countless lives, working for the Marine Department meant equally corrupt police and the slightly less corrupt navy protected him. Anyone who dare confront him would end up at SSI and I doubt they'd end up sitting in a swanky leather chair.

I was finally sucked into the admin vortex of Abdu's office. He was a small man with a contorted face and a slight limp. He looked how he acted in life—bitter and twisted. After two minutes, he asked me to wait outside while he spoke to my interpreter who usually worked in the accounts department of our hotel. After ten minutes he came out to say he'd scheduled an inspection for the following Tuesday. I was surprised it had been so simple.

I wasn't surprised when no one arrived on Tuesday. On Wednesday, a man arrived to say he was a friend of the inspection team and would arrange a meeting with the head of the department. *Here we go again, yet more financial friendships.* After a further two weeks of false meetings and general deceit, the inspection team arrived. Fifteen minutes later they left informing us we'd failed. I made them write down every point they needed us to rectify and sign it so I'd be ready for any tricks at the next inspection.

My phone rang. Killer. It was time for our regular Friday phone meeting to update me on pirate activity and how the business was running, most of the latter being in relation to the unwelcome rise in administration since Barry's arrival. Earlier in the week, an intelligence contact had sent me a strange selection of photos of a ship damaged in the Strait of Hormuz off the coast of UAE. It seemed like the vessel had been in a collision with an unknown object. Two explanations were offered: a possible freak wave caused by a recent earthquake, or a collision with a nuclear submarine. Killer reported that it was, in fact, a suicide bomber in a speedboat. The Abdullah Azzam Brigade, more associated with firing rockets into Gaza, claimed responsibility for the attack. This was yet another danger in our already complex threat environment. I assured Killer I'd write a directive to my men on the ground. It was key not to overreact. This was a fairly isolated incident happening years after the USS *Cole* and the *Limburg* were attacked in the Gulf of Aden. My biggest concern was if the shipping companies panicked and wanted to extend armed protection into the Persian Gulf. No Arab countries would allow us to disembark with armed teams so logistically this would be a huge problem. The other concern was that armed guards moving through the Straits of Hormuz could cause tensions with the extremely professional Iranian naval units forever on high alert. I knew only too well the risks—I was the leading expert for the BBC when an Iranian Revolutionary Guard unit intercepted a Royal

Navy boarding team from HMS *Cornwall*. The boarding team had strayed into Iranian waters. Within minutes, the Iranians surrounded them. The sailors and marines were detained and transported to Tehran for questioning. After negotiations, the group were released and for some reason the Ministry of Defence permitted the sailors to sell their stories. It was a media disaster giving the Iranian's a PR coup and making Royal Navy look even more incompetent. If my men were in a similar situation while transiting on a ship, they'd be afforded no such luxury. It was a situation I was keen to avoid.

I received yet another text. Finally, it was welcome. Anna: *Do you want to meet tonight?*

Things were moving rapidly with Anna. After meeting for our first dinner weeks before, our relationship had blossomed to full bloomed love. The relationship was far from transparent, however. She believed I was a dive boat owner conducting a shark watching expedition and knew nothing of my real life; it was too complex. I wanted to be with her but it seemed everything was against us. Living on the fringe of society for so long, my personal life could be viewed unconventional at best, dysfunctional at worst.

Anna was kind hearted, intelligent, funny and I felt at peace in her presence as she made the purgatory of Egypt bearable. I didn't deserve her. I knew I should end it but I couldn't. I tried to fight it but it was impossible. The irrational feelings of love scared the hell out me.

***

I waited with the guys for the Marine Department inspectors to arrive. We'd rectified every fault to the letter, but this was Egypt. The biggest problem was no one wanted us to leave; the hotel, the marina, the shops, the Marine Department, all saw us as a big cash cow and the whole community seemed hell bent on milking us dry. At every corner we encountered a problem that led to several more. Enough was enough. If we didn't pass this inspection I was going to make a run for it and put to sea.

The inspection team buffoons finally arrived. I forced a smile but, in reality, I wanted to strangle them all. I was too ill tempered for these corrupt bastards, and if provoked I would throw them all over the side which would certainly not help the situation. It would be more advisable to keep a low profile and let the crew be the interface. They procrastinated at all the work completed.

Eventually the head of the inspection team approached carrying a brand new lifejacket he'd helped himself to. He was a walking advertisement for gout having pigged out on luxuries at the expense of the common man, "Mr Dom," his Janusian face smiled; "the boat is nearly ready but..."

"…We are ready to go." I stopped him mid-sentence raising a peremptory hand. It was the only way I could prevent using it as a club hammer on his face.

He recognised the malevolence in my eyes. "OK Mr Dom, we issue the license," he responded.

"I'll be at your office first thing to collect it." It was my 40th birthday. I was glad I hadn't killed him to make it memorable.

The following morning I searched for my interpreter at the hotel. He was nowhere to be found with no explanation from the manager. They were stalling, trying to get us to stay longer. I ran around until I found the owner and cornered him. I took his photo on my phone. "Get me the interpreter now."

He tried to make a lame excuse but by now I was wise to his deceit. He'd previously told me he regularly travelled to Europe as his wife originated from the Czech Republic. It was the angle I could work him.

"Get him now or I'll have men waiting for you next time you're in Prague."

The interpreter miraculously arrived five minutes later. We headed to the Marine Department. I sat in the car with Mustafa for five hours. He explained this situation was the norm for everyday Egyptian people. The government took everything; it was impossible to make a living. Daily he would give money to the police. If he didn't, he would be detained then forced to pay even more for release. The society's whole moral fabric had been corrupted to such an extent that the people could never succeed—and that's exactly what the regime wanted. They kept the people down to line their own pockets. If the country's leaders did it, why shouldn't they? There was a palpable mood on the street that life was changing. Like me, they were fed up of continually being abused. The seeds of discontent were spreading.

The interpreter arrived with a big smile. "I have your licence, Mr Dom."

I immediately rang Taff. "Get the boat ready for sea, we leave tonight."

It was a flurry of activity on board. The team came alive with the prospect of finally returning to sea. I ran around Hurghada settling all the bills and making final preparations. The word soon spread the cash cow was leaving. All pigs arrived on the dock sniffing for their final truffle.

We downed a beer at sunset and took our last look at Hurghada. As much I was looking forward to leaving, I felt a pang of sadness leaving Anna, but the mission came first.

I contacted Omar our agent, as jaundiced as Abdu, to arrange our port clearance and exit stamps for the crew. I put Ryan and Scotty into each RIB to drive independently.

I didn't trust the Egyptians and was certain they would attempt some sham tactic to delay the vessel at the last minute. I stood on the lower bridge as the lines were cast off, slowly putting *Sea Scorpion* into gear. As we left the dock, I felt a great wave of relief.

Three small boats headed towards us. I was in no mood to be messed around any longer by these parasites. Omar, plus some other non-entities who I didn't recognise, arrived on the stern.

"Hi Mr Dom, these are my friends, they helped you get clearance," Omar said as he boarded.

"If they attempt to board my vessel I'll throw them in the sea. They're not welcome." I stared down at the takers bobbing around looking to take their last score. *Not tonight.*

With passports finally returned, I radioed Ryan and Scotty to go ahead in the RIBs. I'd already given them an RV to meet at on the eastern side of Giftun el Kebir Island. Port Control tried to call on VHF. I turned off the radio. *Bye Egypt.*

***

The full moon illuminated a silver staircase on the rippling ocean waves. The navigation screen picked up a ship on its AIS displaying the name.

"That's her," I pointed to the steaming lights. "One mile out."

Ryan pushed the throttles. The RIB's 150HP inboard engine accelerated to 35 knots in pursuit of the tanker. We both wore helmets fitted with VHF radio and an internal boat radio. I called the captain who instructed us to approach on the portside. I moved forward as Ryan manoeuvred the RIB to an open hatch about 10 feet above the waterline from where a small pilot ladder dropped.

"What the fuck's going on?" The team leader shouted from the hatch.

"You'll soon find out," I said, nonchalantly. "Just get in." I helped them pass down the Peli cases and the security team followed.

With the transfer complete, Ryan pushed from the hull and sped away, the security team all looking at each other in communal bemusement.

Sea Scorpion finally came into view. I could tell the guys were impressed.

"This is all a bit James Bond," exclaimed one.

They weren't the only ones surprised. Our three Egyptian crew, Sammi the chef, Mohamed the steward and young Chesni the deckhand started to understand the reality of their life on board, when the Peli cases were opened to reveal weapons.

"Fellas, welcome to the world's first floating armoury."

We were finally executing a plan that I'd secretly plotted over six months. I'd come up with a plan to have our own floating armoury over rum with Killer in his local Cornish pub. Lying in international waters a floating armoury would negate the bureaucracy in the many countries we operated from. By also having a ship big enough to accommodate teams we could operate autonomously if Egypt went offline for any reason. I'd monitored the situation closely in the Red Sea, an area where our only other option was Port Suez, if that went off line it could bring down the business. Garaad and his men were regularly operating in the southern Red Sea and had successfully hijacked a number of ships there.

It was almost revolutionary, but the problem of being a pioneer is that you make all the mistakes. We'd been further burdened by the Egyptian authorities not allowing us to go offshore to check the engines and onboard systems, meaning our maiden voyage was on live operations, which is never a good place to start. On the plus side I worked with a 'can do' crew and together we'd pick up and embark crews onto ships as we steamed towards our permanent operating location.

***

International Waters, Southern Red Sea
16'26N 39'34E

Dragging anchors woke me from my already fitful night, a full night's sleep was a cruelly ironic dream. I stepped onto the bridge to check the radar and the AIS plotter for any ships in the immediate vicinity before heading down to the bow to help Taff, Italian Rob and Sharky struggling to haul in the anchor line. The wind had picked up and a choppy sea sent spray over the anchor handlers.

"It's a poor holding here, Dom," said Taff, half in greeting half in despair.

"It's the only anchor holding in the area, it's over a thousand feet deep anywhere else," I replied, grabbing the anchor line.

The southern Red Sea off the Sudan coast was way too deep to anchor. I'd managed to locate a small sea mound 20 metres below the surface that gave us the best chance of hooking on to the seabed using simple coral anchors that resembled a large Gamakatsu treble fishing hook—the main type of anchor found in the Red Sea. We also needed to be within striking distance of the north and southbound shipping lanes. If the weather stayed calm the boat sat happily attached to the mound but the minute the wind got up we would lose our holding and have to constantly re-anchor. Such is life at sea.

We'd been on the water for two weeks, encountering many initial problems with *Sea Scorpion* necessitating an unscheduled repair stop in Port Sudan. Now the port generator had broken down again. Titch had organised a specialist engineer to fly out from Scotland to Egypt then board a tanker to meet *Sea Scorpion* and fix the ongoing problems. The engineer's main request had been a flat calm sea so he could use his gauges. In our permanent location we'd been bouncing in steep sharp swell in 24-knot winds. I pored over the chart looking for a solution. I noticed a tiny speck of land 50 miles to our south.

The Imray Red Sea Pilot guide stated: *Romiya Islet yachts have found respite from northerly winds hanging off the shelves on the SW corner of the island.* The main advantage of Romiya was its isolation, handy when sailing with a boat full of guns. I rang Chris Collison, our Djibouti in-country manager and tasked him to obtain a cruising permit for Eritrean waters. According to the yachting community such a permit did exist but we found no tangible evidence.

Isolationist Eritrea had always fascinated me. Three years before, Killer and I had planned to visit Lebanon, Tripoli in Libya and Massawa on the Eritrean coast for sightseeing on the road less travelled, but after two Israeli soldiers were taken hostage by Hezbollah, Lebanon reignited once more so we cancelled the trip. Eritrea had become a misinterpreted country, seen to many as the North Korea of the Red Sea, yet I saw it as fiercely independent. The Eritreans were great warriors led by Isaisias Afwerki, pitted against a superior force of Soviet-backed Ethiopia. During the bitter thirty-year war, the longest in African history, the Eritrean's not only held off mass attacks, but also defeated the mighty Ethiopian army. The siege of Barentu and the battle for Massawa were at the cutting edge of guerrilla warfare. Despite close air support from Soviet ground attack aircraft, the Eritrean's drove the invaders back to Ethiopia forcing the Soviet Union to withdraw its support. Eritrea, through self-determination, won independence for its people. I really admired their resilience.

Tensions still remained along the border. Eritrea has an asset that land locked Ethiopia needs—a port. Due to their failure to conquer Eritrea, Ethiopia's sea trade has to pass through Djibouti who takes 16% of Ethiopia's GDP for the privilege. It's clear why Massawa was of such strategic importance. Eritrea still remains on high alert, just in case Ethiopia makes another move. The need to defend its borders is a great burden, especially for the country's youth and young men unwilling to defend their country flee to Europe to seek asylum and the easy life away from the trenches of Badme. I'd call them deserters but I'm sure a human rights lawyer would disagree, the irony being a weakened Eritrean army would mean more human rights atrocities in the long term.

***

Romiya Islet, Eritrea
16'18N 39'45E

Only a pauper's oasis of hardy acacia scrub broke the barren landscape. I scanned for any signs of life, only a solitary Grey Heron seemed interested in this rocky outcrop. The islet stood motionless, almost frozen in time. My marrowbone tingled with mariner's zeal. This was a true desert island.

I'd stopped *Sea Scorpion* half a mile offshore. Sharky, Italian Rob and I motored ahead in the RIBs to look for a suitable anchorage and check the uncharted depth around this low lying forgotten outcrop. The island, located fifty miles off the Eritrean coast is one of the northern most islands of the Dahlak Archipelago, the most pristine marine park on planet earth. We approached the crystal clear waters surrounding the island, and found a favourable place to anchor. We soon set up two anchors on the island as we didn't want to hurt the coral below and one stern anchor in deep water. With *Sea Scorpion* rested in still water, the crew started getting the boat ready to receive teams. Despite our mechanical problems we still needed to protect ships.

I took the opportunity to pilot the Gemini to the island alone; the place attracted my pioneering spirit. I stepped on the island's powder sand and a lightening bolt of positive energy shot through me. Like John Locke's Hydra Island, the place triggered profound reverence. I wandered for a time, allowing my bare feet to befriend the bleached earth below before resting on the eastern side where I felt an unaccountable feeling of belonging.

I returned to *Sea Scorpion* slightly forlorn to have left the place. The boys organised a BBQ ashore while I stayed on the bridge with my thoughts, at peace hearing their laughter around the glow of fire. I checked the instruments and saw us drifting in the slow easterly current. All was well.

Romiya offered little protection in a gale so it was imperative we find alternative anchorage. It was wholly plausible that pirates, smugglers or worse could use these remote islands as a base. I erred on the side of caution, so, while Taff and the Scottish engineer were busy stripping down the generator, I loaded two SIG 542 assault rifles into a RIB and set off with Matt into the unknown.

***

I put the throttles into neutral and stood off about 500 metres from the small island of Entaasnu ahead. Matt and I scanned every inch of the coral outcrop lying just off the larger Harmil Island to the east. We slowly motored closer with Matt off the bow calling the depth of these uncharted waters. While nerve wracking, it was exhilarating to live the life of a New World discoverer. The coral surrounded the island like an outer undersea wall, so far too dangerous to get in close. This place offered nothing for shelter. We motored off to Harmil, its southern part hosting a small bay marked on the chart as an anchorage. We proceeded with caution, even with a beautifully calm turquoise sea.

We found a suitable spot should we have to endure a strong northerly wind, but the low laying land provided little shelter for anything else, yet it was better than nothing in an emergency. The charts indicated some gun emplacements, probably Italian from the Second World War, but not much remained of them other than a few square steel boxes. The Italians colonised Eritrea and it played a key industrial role for the fascists until the British invaded in 1941. After pockets of fascist diehards conducted a short guerrilla insurgency, the British secured the country in 1943.

The seabed had less coral so I hopped ashore. Scanning the island further north, I noticed a radar antenna about half a mile away. We jumped back into the RIB and hugged the coast. A small rusty post flying the Eritrean flag hung limp in the still air, behind it stood a small building with a small curtained door suggesting it contained occupants. We didn't have to wait long for confirmation. Two men burst through the door brandishing AK47's.

"Shall we get the weapons out?" Matt whispered.

"No, they're military. We've no right to be here." I didn't want a bloodbath.

I pushed the throttles to full speed. In the flat conditions we effortlessly planed to 35 knots. I steered a course dead east leaving the island behind us as we blazed through the azure ocean. Three miles out, the island was no longer visible to the naked eye so I pressed on a further two miles before turning north. It was important not to give away *Sea Scorpion's* position so I boxed an area to avoid detection, pushing further north before heading west then south back to Romiya. My hope was that the outpost may think we were from a large yacht offshore, but knowing these guys probably had no visitors for months they would have little else to think about and cocking their weapons was too good a chance to miss. Time would tell but by then we'd be back in international waters.

Returning to *Sea Scorpion,* Sharky welcomed me with a message. "Headquarters wants you back, Killer has a tanker arriving to take you to Suez."

As I stood on the tanker's salt-flecked bridge wings and watched the RIB disappear over the horizon to join the fire streaks of a dipping sun, I felt a tinge of sadness leaving the islands and *Sea Scorpion.* After such a Herculean effort I had achieved the objective—to create the first offshore armoury and mobile base for operations. It'd been such a rollercoaster journey with so many twists and turns, it challenged even my eternal optimism, but this only enhanced the liberation from the experience. I enjoyed being around my crew and looking after my teams when they came aboard. The adventurer in me preferred being a ship's captain rather than a president of a large company yet I needed to reengage with the business. Barry and Andy had been unsupervised for too long and I sensed Machiavellianism afoot. First, a more pressing personal matter required resolution, and it involved Anna.

***

Mustafa, my now regular taxi driver, drove me to Hurghada. As endless dunes passed my dusty window on the windswept road, I pondered on England. It no longer felt like home. No one loves the green and pleasant land more than me, yet I felt detached through constant travelling. I reflected upon my epiphany on Romiya Islet. No matter how difficult it was to do, things had to change.

I waited outside Golden Five Resort until I saw her walking in her own unique way that was thankfully far more elegant than her dancing.

We spent the evening together but I sensed her sadness. Anna wasn't stupid and realised I wasn't a safari boat owner. She confessed to worrying whether there hid a darker side to this elusive man she'd fallen in love with. It was confession time, the main problem being my life was pretty unbelievable—'*I have a private navy fighting pirates.*' Imagine trying to chat up a girl in a bar with that line? It wouldn't be the first time someone had poured a drink over me.

I carefully laid out the truth, trying to portray my chaotic life as somewhat normal. It was a big revelation. Unsurprisingly, she became upset.

I needed to lay all my cards on the table. "Technically I'm still married."

She walked out.

I jumped into a bottle of rum as is customary on such occasions.

***

Touching down at Heathrow, Verity, my long-suffering PA, was first to call. "Hi Dom, your suite at the Ritz is booked. I've your pin stripe suit, cuff links, RNSA tie, handkerchief and new shoes. You're meeting with a few people at Lloyds then Phil Shaw for Christmas drinks with Barry."

"Thanks V." I was eternally grateful for Verity's efficiency. I could have done with her earlier that morning to help find my trousers that had somehow disappeared down the toilet. Finding solace in rum often has dire consequences.

"How long are you in the UK for? We've a number of issues to address."

"That's a very complex question, I wish I knew. Can I just ask you remain flexible?" The truth was I didn't know. In my line of work, storm clouds hid behind every ray of sunshine.

I walked into the Rum Bar at the Artesian and immediately spotted Barry and Phil who by their inane grins had already been there for a couple of hours. It was good to see them. Phil appeared more content than I'd seen him in a long while. It was almost the first anniversary of the *St. James Park* hijacking. The Zodiac fleet had been hit ten times since. My guys had repelled them all. He was happy with PVI's service and I relayed how my lads had gone beyond the call of duty to get there. PVI was on the up.

But in spinning the wheel of life, my worst nightmare was about to unfold, scuttling me to the darkest depths of the vast profound.

CHAPTER 19
Taunton, UK
51'01N 03'06W

Winter had started early with snow laden Siberian winds assaulting Northern Europe. Temperatures in the UK had dropped to -20°C and Scotland had suffered its heaviest snowfall for 40 years. Dutch canals started to freeze and even Scandinavia reeled in the surprise winter assault recording its coldest and snowiest start to winter in 100 years. The forecasters believed that more extreme weather was on the way in the run up to Christmas.

I peered out of the scratched window as snow morphed into apparitions before disappearing into the blank white air. It was quite surreal; I'd been working away in the Gulf of Aden for so long a British winter had become a figment of my imagination.

"Ladies and gentleman, we will shortly be leaving Taunton for our service to London Paddington. We apologise for the delays due to the weather."

The 'High Speed' service to London was suspended. I was amazed this archaic commuter train ran at all, normally the smallest metrological glitch was enough to bring the British rail network to its creaking knees. This slow service would squeeze past sleepy stations in the south of England: Castle Carey, Frome, Somerton and all manner of quintessential villages on the way to the capital. Taunton station held particular significance—After winning my green beret at the tender age of 17, I'd been posted to 40 Commando located a few miles outside Taunton. I was now leaving for good.

Heavy chains clanked as we slowly lurched forward into the white abyss. I sank into my seat recoiling from the cold compartment. After arriving all those years ago with a sense of foreboding intertwined with excitement of the adventures ahead as a fully-fledged commando, I now departed emotionally drained; my future uncertain and self-doubt weighed heavy as the snow that danced in the tumultuous blizzard outside.

I'd returned to Taunton to finally cut the rope on our marriage. While confirming the inevitable, the reality of parting after over 20 years together was harder to endure. I wanted Ang to keep everything; it was the right thing to do. I left carrying a bag packed with what I thought I needed for the road ahead. No fixed abode. No plan.

In normal circumstances, I'd stay with a friend who'd listen and advise. My circumstances weren't normal. I had no time to search for inner peace, Garaad and his men were never far away, probing our defences looking for weakness. To top it all, PVI had serious issues in the Red Sea.

While families would be cossetted within the bosom of Christmas, I was heading to Eritrea.

***

The run up to Christmas was always a busy time for the shipping industry, and the spike in business meant *Sea Scorpion* was flat out with work. The downside being that she'd used more fuel than anticipated, and by the time Taff had informed me of the situation, *Sea Scorpion* didn't have enough fuel to make it to Sudan. The only reachable port was Massawa. This was far from ideal, Bruno had always warned me never to go there, describing it as an endless horizon of problems with a reputation for detaining vessels on obscure charges. I called my shipping clients to see if they could resupply her at sea. None could assist. She was on her own. It seemed my fascination for Eritrea was about to be satiated.

Her role as a floating armoury was indeed the biggest complication. Neither the Eritrean port authority nor the UN Eritrea and Somali Monitoring Group permitted weapons due to UN-imposed sanctions for Eritrea's support to Al Shabaab and other opposition groups operating in Somalia. The Eritreans denied all accusations, blaming it on an Ethiopian government conspiracy; nevertheless, sanctions heaped more misery on an already impoverished nation.

We'd tried relentlessly to make contact with the port authority in Massawa to no avail so I'd dispatched Chris Collison as an advance party to find a shipping agent who could receive the boat and organise fuel, repairs and provisions. Upon entering the country, Eritrean Customs had confiscated Chris's cell phone, citing they were forbidden. Limited communications were exacerbated when it emerged the highly censored internet service was only granted to authorised people. After two days, he'd used someone's phone to inform us that he'd appointed an agent ready to receive *Sea Scorpion*.

I'd arranged a meeting with Killer at PVI HQ to devise a plan. I felt uneasy about the whole situation but it seemed we were short on alternatives.

I grimaced at Killer with my finger hovering over the send key.

"We'll make this work, don't worry," he said.

I hoped so. I pressed send.

Gents,

Call sign KN252 (Sea Scorpion) is to head to the port of Massawa for resupply of fuel and food.

Romiya Islet - Small arid outcrop with an area of shrubs for potential caching. Islet's waters have coral approaches and short-term harbours. No signs of habitation when surveyed by RIB although this does not guarantee it is always so.

Harmil Island - Two man military outpost sighted by a clearance patrol using the RIB. It is located in the area of a world war two bunker complex on the southern part of the island. The soldiers had clear visual on us. A radar mast was co-located but not switched on. Various antennae were also seen. The status of their communications is unknown but it is assessed they will have comms with units further south. Last month, AL345 was approached by a skiff with two men in what appeared to be in similar clothing and armed near the Harmil military outpost. AL345 increased speed and left the skiff. On my trip around the island a skiff was not sighted in the area of the outpost but we must assume they have access to one.

Your mission is to establish a covert temporary camp at Romiya Islet for the rear party.

KN252 will be boarded at the Massawa anchorage before obtaining permission to enter the port with no exit stamps for the Egyptians - this will complicate matters so they must be left behind with the rear party.

A working party of six men should assist offloading all the weapons and body armour from KN252 for safe storage on Romiya islet. I would advise burying them in a covert location away from the camp. In the event of being detected the cache will not be discovered. One PVI rep will act as the custodian of the equipment and I/C of the rear party. The PVI rep is to check in with operations 1700hrs UTC daily to inform on their status.

The PAC 22 RIB and Red RIB must both be recovered from the beach prior to the move to Massawa. If necessary KN252, with a long tow line, may have to be employed if the RIBs cannot be freed. Leaving RIBs on Romiya is NOT an option.

The Move To Massawa.

Drop off the rear party at Romiya.

The passage plan should avoid the Island of Harmil even if this detour uses more fuel. The PAC 22 RIB has been seen by the military outpost on my clearance patrol we do not want KN252 to be linked to the RIB.

A sailing permit should have been obtained by Chris Collison by the time you start the passage. It will be scanned and sent to you in case outposts board you further south. Manning for the passage should be: 1 x captain 4 x crew split into two watches with two men on watch at all times. Chris will arrange all paperwork and port clearance prior to arrival at the port anchorage.

For the entire passage no PVI clothing is to be worn, nor any military style equipment to be carried on board. Team Quest Shark Watch Expedition to be the cover for this port call and the rear party.

Chris and Dom to act as shore support for KN252 when alongside in Massawa. There is a crane for lifting the two RIBs onto the dock. The PAC 22 RIB will remain in Massawa for repairs. A mechanic will be needed to look at the PAC 22 RIB stern drive. Repair the red RIB damage starboard side and power wash the bottom and load back into the water when repair work has dried.

Shore support party to deliver food to KN252 by hire vehicle.

Full bunking conducted for KN252.

We aim to conclude this operation in 12 hours and proceed back to the island to collect rear party, equipment and weapons before continuing operations.

Sammi to email Tiverton with a 30-day food supply list in the **next 48 hours.** This will enable the shore support team to have all ready when you arrive.

Crew change: Adrian Troy will captain KN252 while Taff goes on leave. Taff will move to Djibouti from Massawa with Chris.

KN252 to make best possible speed back to Romiya to pick up rear party.

Routing should again avoid Harmil where possible.

Recover rear party and all equipment back to KN252. Return to the mound in international waters to resume operations.

The plan was far from ideal but our best option in the circumstances. Heeding Bruno's warning, I'd decided to split the regular embarked teams and weapons to Romiya in case *Sea Scorpion* was detained. The port call was immensely risky but running out of fuel and encountering bad weather would put lives at risk. With no southern Red Sea coastguard, my men would perish if shipwrecked.

We were the good guys protecting ships from pirates but our resources were limited and the difficulty of operating in the southern Red Sea wasn't lost on Garaad. He understood the challenges we faced and started attacking ships in the area, successfully hijacking a number of ships. He was becoming an unstoppable force and had just been nominated No.4 on the Lloyds list for the world's most influential figures in shipping. People had finally smelled the coffee that I'd brewed over three years ago. It was incredible that a pirate had made such an impact and yet still he sailed with impunity. I had political and logistical problems to contend with on a daily basis, my nemesis operated everywhere unhindered by the regulations I was bound by. Like our service personnel who battle those who murder free from scavenging lawyers it seemed darkly ironic.

***

Romiya Islet, Eritrea
16'18N 39'45E

Sea Scorpion had left Romiya en route to Massawa. After finishing their working party on the islet, Steve Regis joined John Miles for a run around the outcrop, enjoying their first time on dry land in over a month, no doubt wobbling initially trying to run off their sea legs. Along the beach of driftwood and cuttlefish, they came across two bloody carcasses—a small Tiger Shark and a

Hammerhead, both gutted with fins removed. They continued their jog and found a pile of about eight shark fins. Their uncertainty at these morbid discoveries was countered by the clarity that other people used the island. Everyone seemed too preoccupied in personal administration to take notice of their findings.

***

Heathrow Airport, UK
51'28N 00'29W

I arrived at Terminal 3 via the chaotic labyrinth of tunnels and escalators made claustrophobic by impatient passengers with wayward luggage. On reaching the surface I headed outside and immediately hit by the freezing air that grated the back of my throat. I fired up a Marlboro to counter the icy conditions.

Smoke lingered as I scanned the departures board for my Air Italia flight to Asmara. Like most it was highlighted in yellow—cancelled. A second cold front had descended on Europe bringing freezing air and snow direct from the Arctic, cancelling even Scandinavian flights and I'd seen aircraft land in horrific weather when working in Northern Norway.

The terminal had been transformed into a seething, swaying mass of overcoats and anger, with elbows used as weapons of rib destruction. I stepped over a carpet of travellers who'd accepted their fate and converted the terminal floor into a temporary home. I finally saw my touchline of Alitalia check-in desk and lunged forward as if scoring a try, but instead of a celebration I joined the queue of frustration. Five Eritrean women unable to speak English nor Italian wept, unable to understand why they couldn't go home. I finally spoke to the robot-like check-in assistant worn down by endless demands.

"All flights are cancelled. We don't know when the next flight will be. Please check the boards for updates," he regurgitated monotonously, probably for the 99th time.

Clearly no one wanted to take charge, and as I was body packing $20,000, sleeping on the terminal floor was hardly an option. Andy had already transferred some money to the Eritrean shipping agent but because of Eritrea's parochial and restrictive banking system the crew were informed it'd not arrived. In desperation we had sent a further payment at the agent's request to a bank account in New York, again it had somehow disappeared into the ether. The only hope to get *Sea Scorpion* out of port on time was for me to pay in person and leave with the boat back to Romiya Islet.

I decided to head for my place of refuge—the Sheraton Skyline hotel where I could keep an eye on the flight statuses from the comfort of a leather chair and a Havana Club. I rang Verity to speak with our travel company for any updates. She sensed the tension in my voice. "Dom, are you OK?"

"I'm fine, but just to let you know Ang and I have split and this next job is a little complicated. Please cancel any appointments for the next couple of weeks. I'm not sure when I'll be back."

The storm outside taunted my urgency to reach Eritrea by raging unabated. With mountains of snow piling up I couldn't foresee me getting away any time soon. Whatever the conditions, I had to get to Eritrea.

***

Romiya Islet, Eritrea
16'18N 39'45E

The beach camp dawdled in slumber as the sun rose to smouldering embers. The team had left the Gemini on the

246

beach and built a massive campfire. While not tactical it offered respite from the determined sand flies. Steve and John were first to wake and decided to go for another run. On the far side of the featureless outcrop during a bout of push ups and sit ups, Steve spotted a dhow 150 metres off the island heading south. It stopped before hauling in two towed skiffs.

Steve turned to John. "What do you think?"

"Looks like pirates. We should return to camp, we're really exposed here."

The camp, by now, had started the day routine with every man undertaking his respective task.

"Lads, there's a dhow off the island. I think they're launching a skiff," John shouted as he grabbed his day sack before running straight to the weapons cache hidden in the nearby scrub.

Men from the dhow had boarded the skiff and now seemed to be heading for the beach. John and Steve uncovered the cache and located the two Peli cases containing SIG pistols. They set about feverishly charging seven magazines with loose ammunition, each loaded into a pistol and placed in John's daysack before he casually walked back to camp, covertly handing one to every man. Steve crawled on his belly with an AR10 from the cache to a covert firing position amongst the sharp spinifix grass to cover the guys on the beach.

The skiff approached with one man on the bow and two on the stern, their long shadows bouncing on the crystal clear water. The bowman, scruffily dressed in faded black shorts and a filthy once-white t-shirt, started ranting aggressively in an Arabic dialect distinct from what our three Egyptians understood. The guys fanned out into a staggered line staring at the approaching hostiles.

The skiff beached and the bowman jumped into the dancing froth leaving receding puddles in the sand. John spotted two AK47's near the two men in the skiff so tapped two fingers on his thigh to signal Steve they were armed. Despite being outnumbered, the leader's self-assured rant continued. John sensed the two men in the boat felt uncomfortable in this Mexican standoff.

The bowman spotted the team camp and shoulder barged through the guys to have a closer look. The camp seemed to enrage him further.

His actions indicated this was his territory for whatever illegal occupation he plied. The three Egyptians stood quietly to the side watching fearfully at the events unfolding. Mohamed, sensing the situation worsening, boldly stepped forward to calm the leader. "*Habibi, Habibi,*" he repeated.

The leader threw Mohamed to the ground then continued his rant at young Chesni who still couldn't understand anything other than fury. He finally turned to the team, his arms flaying widely, his anger piqued.

The guys tensed and slowly reached for their pistols ready to draw if the mad dog became a tangible threat.

Steve pushed the safety catch off his AR10. With a clear shot on the two in the boat he checked the skiff for movement. If either bent down he would take them both out. They wouldn't feel a thing. After killing those two he'd switch fire to the dhow to stop a follow up. He trained his red dot sight on the skiff and began to control his breathing.

***

Heathrow Airport, UK
51'28N 00'29W

I felt totally helpless. With the stakes so high I was stranded in the worst snowstorm in over 100 years. The next flight to Asmara was rescheduled for late afternoon. The BBC weatherman reported more snow on the way and would cause further disruption. I needed to leave Europe immediately on whatever flight I could find before the airport shut down completely.

My phone rang. Al Sims—the number two on the *Sea Scorpion* berthed in Massawa. I hoped there was at least some good news.

"Dom, we're getting nowhere with these jokers in port. We're planning on not taking on fuel. I've checked the tanks and we've enough to return to Romiya."

"OK, cancel all the resupply and get out of there as soon as you can. I'll try and get some fuel and provisions. I'm stranded so unsure when I can get to you."

A Marlboro calmed me before I called Killer to find out if any ships were coming down the Red Sea.

"The first vessel to embark is the cable layer from your Spanish friends and then *Emerald Park*."

As ever, Killer saved the day.

The cable layer had been off my radar when I'd previously researched *Sea Scorpion's* resupply. I contacted Alejandro in Madrid who organised the cable layer to supply *Sea Scorpion* with enough diesel and food to get to Port Sudan. I was so angry with myself for not finding this solution earlier; my mind distracted by all the emotional turmoil leaving Ang had churned. I wasn't on top of my game. I hadn't taken a day off in years and maybe I'd been running too hard. That could be addressed later; the current situation needed controlling, and fast.

I rang Al on *Sea Scorpion* to inform him of the new plan and for him to get port clearance and leave in haste. If we took on supplies it would complicate matters in the same way as driving from a petrol station without paying. If we left port not owing any money it wouldn't be such a big deal. My phone rang. *Sea Scorpion.* "Hello Dom, Taff here, we've fully provisioned and taken on fuel."

I struggled to contain my ire. "Have you spoken to Al about the new plan?"

"Yes Dom, but we need to get food for the guys."

I hung up in despair. I had no time for self-pity, my phone rang again, I thought it was Al to apologise. It was Matt on Romiya.

"Dom we've been visited by hostiles and are now stood to with weapons."

"I thought I said be covert. How the fuck did they see you?"

"There were loads of sand flies, it was mega uncomfortable so we moved to the beach. I think they spotted the Gemini."

I couldn't believe how stupid they'd been to leave the Gemini on the beach and totally compromise their location. I took a deep breath. Despite everyone and everything seeming to conspire against me, my ranting at Matt wasn't going to help. He was in a shit fight on a desert island with no backup. I needed to offer support and get them extracted as quickly as possible.

"Who do you think it was?" I asked calmly. The thought of a fire-fight with the Eritrean Navy filled with dread, this would cause an international incident and have dire implications for all involved.

"The general consensus is they were pirates or gun runners."

I picked through every detail to understand the intruders. I agreed with his assessment, which brought some relief that they weren't military. I made it abundantly clear that if they had any visit from the Eritrean Navy to stand down and fully co-operate. We would figure our way through as events unfolded.

"What do you want us to do if the same guys return?" asked Matt.

"You know what to do but keep the noise down, I don't want the whole world alerted. And for fuck's sake, clean it up."

"Understood. One more thing, we're nearly out of water."

"Sit tight brother, we're going to get you out of there. You're bootnecks, you'll survive." I hoped I was right.

CHAPTER 20
Massawa, Eritrea
15'36N 39'27E

Arron lowered the red RIB via a squeaking crane—a rusting reminder of Italian occupation during WW2. The dock was an uninspiring long hard strip of concrete to simply park a boat and unload.

Massawa was once the capital of Eritrea known in its heyday as the Pearl of the Red Sea but now the bitter scars of war stood as an indelible adjunct to the blight of subsequent malaise. Once popular for its Italian art deco architecture, locals once enjoyed al fresco dining in one of the many palatial courtyards but after the Fenkill Offensive the city changed forever. The Eritrean Liberation Army launched a surprise attack on Massawa and soon had the occupying Ethiopian troops on the run. The Ethiopians responded in the venom of defeat by carpet-bombing the city with napalm and cluster bombs inflicting huge civilian casualties. Arron noted the sad air, the old men recollecting with affectionate melancholy their once beautiful city that the youth would never see and could never imagine. War—the giant eraser of humanity and hope.

Al's frown indicated a man bearing bad news. He summoned Arron on board for a crew briefing.

"Right lads, things have gone from bad to worse. The lads on Romiya have been spooked by some hostiles and are stood to with weapons. They've also run out of water. Chris is in town still trying to get port clearance from the agent, but we need to go tonight. Is the RIB ready, Arron?"

"We're full of fuel and good to go."

"If this all goes pear shaped forget us on *Sea Scorpion*. You have to reach the island, come what may." Al knew he and the crew would be sacrificed to save the men left on Romiya.

***

Heathrow Airport, UK
51'28N 00'29W

As I barged my way through the security gate for my new flight to Egypt my phone rang. Adrian Troy. As Taff was due leave Adrian would be *Sea Scorpion's* new captain so briefed me on the plan for approval. Adrian had served with Killer at 45 Commando and since leaving the Corps had continued to lead an interesting life working around Asia before skippering a pearl diving boat in Australia. Even though I didn't know him, and the situation hardly ideal for a new captain, the intricate detail of his checklist allayed my fears. My greatest concern was that despite paying twice, we still had no confirmation that the port agent had received any monies. In many African ports, everybody gets a cut, including the navy, who don't take kindly to any boat sailing off owing money.

Undeterred by the challenges, Adrian believed it doable, and because the rear party on the island were on the verge of having a gun fight with pirates or dying of thirst our options were limited. This was shit or burst. Do or die. Big boys rules. Fucking dangerous.

"OK, let's do this. You have the executive order. God Speed," I said.

"One more thing," added Adrian tentatively. "Chris is AWOL, what shall we do?"

"Leave his kit on the dock and proceed without him."

Trapped in the no smoking hell of Heathrow, I needed a big nicotine hit. I'd be boarding my flight as they were leaving. I sat silently in the business lounge envious of other company directors busy on their phones sealing deals with a less complicated product than I provided. I poured an overly large Havana Club with a smidgeon of coke and sat like a man awaiting his walk to the gallows.

**

Massawa, Eritrea
15'36N 39'27E

Chris Collinson clattered onto the dock in a frenzy of sweat and panic, waving manically to Adrian on the *Sea Scorpion's* fly bridge. Chris was evidently shouting something but the RIB engines drowned his words. Chris threw his gear onto *Sea Scorpion* and followed it on board to repeat his message.

Adrian nodded to Billy and Ben on the dock to secretly slip the lines off the cleats. You could only be so covert in such a vessel and sneaking away was difficult as *Sea Scorpion's* throaty Caterpillar engines churned up the foul smelling dock water off the stern as the boat spun around with the assistance of the RIB. He pushed the throttles; speed was key to escape but she was no racehorse and the element of a surprise move was short lived.

"Hurry up, they're here," shouted Chris jumping onto the fly bridge.

"Who?" asked Al, but the answer was already in earshot.

The grinding of gears and the plume of diesel smoke signified the militarised Toyota pickup truck full of soldiers careering around the corner, nearly catapulting one soldier onto the concrete below. It sped towards *Sea Scorpion* now 20 metres from the dock. Ben and Billy were separated on the dock with the shouts of soldiers in their ears.

"Arron, get alongside pick them up!" Al shouted.

Arron nervously manoeuvred the RIB astern and the boys jumped on board, their weight nearly throwing Arron from the wheel. He pushed forward to sit on the blind side of *Sea Scorpion* that now moved slowly towards the heads of the harbour and the open ocean.

"Get a move on Adrian, they're taking up fire positions," Al shouted as the troops on the dock fanned out into an extended line.

While the engine roared he couldn't hear but saw the unmistakable synchronised movement—they were cocking their weapons ready to shoot.

"Stay low," screamed Adrian knowing *Sea Scorpion* was hardly a difficult target. "Come on, come on," he pleaded to the engines.

"Al, we've a gunboat heading our way," Arron said over the radio.

Al peered into the closing light to see the interceptor. He looked down the nose of a light machine gun on the bow with three men crouched in the small high-speed craft.

"We'll never outrun her," said Adrian, realising holding them off as long as possible would allow Arron's RIB to escape.

"Al, the gunboat is nearly on me," Arron shouted over VHF. He could hear voices from the fast approaching vessel. Three men each pointed an AK47 at him.

Arron pointed to the *Sea Scorpion*. "I'm just following him," he shrugged, feigning ignorance of the events unfolding. "Get him to stop."

The leader of the gunboat shouted instructions to his coxswain who swung the craft towards *Sea Scorpion* continuing on its hapless course for freedom. Arron followed before veering to the starboard side of *Sea Scorpion* out of view of the gunboat but back in direct line of fire from the dockside troops. He hoped he was now out of range or that they had terrible aims.

Al watched closely, planning the next chess move. He then spotted an even larger gunboat approaching and, to his horror, saw its bow mounted with modified ZSU23 23mm cannons. *Check*.

Shots rang out across *Sea Scorpion's* bow as the smaller gunboat opened with a warning volley. Their patience had run out. Adrian and Al crouched down to avoid being hit staying on course approaching the harbour entrance.

"Let's keep going," Adrian put his hand on Al's shoulder.

Al assessed the range of the troops on the dock. They held a healthy gap of around 300 metres—a difficult range in darkness for them to hit the RIB. He was about to give Arron the order to run when the both gunboats opened fire. Rounds ricocheted around the fly bridge. Adrian and Al exchanged smiles—another predicament to tell the lads.

They had to hold out until the RIB made a break. To make sure Taff kept the engines going, Adrian dashed below, hitting the ladder, just as two rounds splashed inches in front of his feet. Al remained on the fly bridge as they cleared into open water. The troops had now moved to the end of the breakwater in a desperate attempt to cut off the escape. Rounds splashed water around the RIB.

"Arron go, go, go," Adrian shouted over the radio.

Arron needed no encouragement. He pushed the throttles fully forward, swearing at the small lag from the turbo diesel engine. The RIB's bow lifted skywards as it screamed towards the open ocean. Ben, supine on the bows, looked astern commentating on the muzzle flashes lighting up the breakwater. The recognisable popping of high velocity rounds cutting the cool air above Arron's head meant was stopping for no man; death would be his only brake.

"Looks like the gunboats have forgotten us," added Ben.

As if affronted by Ben's telepathic taunt, the larger gunboat skewed its path towards them. "Get a wriggle on Arron, they're after us again."

More sonic cracks forced Arron to swerve right sending a wall of spray into the darkened sky. The RIB back on line, he willed the bawling engines on.

Seeing the second gunboat firing at the RIB, Adrian flashed the ship's powerful searchlight, momentarily blinding the interceptor's sailors, giving the RIB an advantage. The blinded sailors switched fire to the nearer *Sea Scorpion*, the hull popping as rounds strafed starboard.

Sea Scorpion was now four miles offshore and still holding off the small gunboat. Al started to think they could make it, hoping the chaser did not have enough fuel to continue. His hope was short lived. A navy cutter closed in. They could handle a fair amount of small arms fire, if the cutter opened up it would blow them off the face of the earth. Al's hearts sunk. *Check Mate.*

"Lads, the game's up. Shut down the engine and put the lights on, we have to give up," Al broadcast on the boat's intercom.

He stared at the horizon, the RIB now out of sight. "God speed, fellas."

***

Ben and Billy lay prone on the bow as gunboat rounds whizzed overhead, Arron steering the boat from the deck sitting as low as possible. He was confident he could outrun the gunboat, having noted she was fitted with two Yanmar 60HP outboard engines. With the weight of her four cannons she would not be any faster than 20 knots and he was pushing 38. He focused on adjusting the pitch of the propeller to give him more speed. The gunboat fell behind firing a few angry shot into the night. His pulse slowed. They'd done it.

"Patrol boat half a mile to port," shouted Ben.

The large patrol craft headed at speed towards them. Arron's optimism sank as he made out the silhouette. "Fuck."

"What's wrong?" asked Billy.

"It's a Super Dvora."

"What the fuck is that?"

"It's an evil Israeli made bastard, that's what. Top speed 50 knots with a 20mm cannon up front." Never did Arron believe one would hunt him down.

He decided to stay on course and maintain maximum speed to try and outrun her, taking an educated gamble based on his knowledge that African navies, as a general rule, were poor at maintaining their fleets. The Super Dvora had two 4000HP Detroit diesel engines capable of propelling the 27-metre boat to a comfortable 45 knots, but if poorly maintained she would struggle to make 35. She'd perform especially badly if she'd been collecting barnacles after being static in the water for months. The Eritrean navy was the least funded arm of the military as all resources were spent on the frontline with Ethiopia.

The Super Dvora stayed in the chase as the RIB dashed across the Massawa Inside Passage heading to the Dahlak Archipelago. As the luminance from the instruments and compass offered a target to the gunner manning the powerful 20mm cannon, Arron sped along using the clear night sky as his guide. This would be fine in open water but he intended to run through the garland of islands, reefs and uncharted wrecks caught in the shallows to cover the boat from the hunter's radar. It was an extremely high-risk gamble but in taking the most dangerous route, Arron hoped the Super Dvora might not follow due to her deeper draft. In recovering the lads he could in no way offer the Super Dvora an indication where he was headed.

Ben kept watch astern while they probed through the reef labyrinth. "It's falling back, maybe three cables."

"Roger that." It was enough space for Arron to flash up the navigation console to check their position.

The VHF crackled into life. Four stressed words from Al confirmed the gravity of the situation. "Arron, keep fucking going."

It would be the last contact from *Sea Scorpion*.

The reef could have torn them apart but Arron's risk had paid off. The chasing interceptor was nowhere to be seen. He pulled back on the throttles slowing the RIB between the two tiny islands of Kad Jerom and Enta-idell.

"Fucking hell, Arron good work. That was hairier than Ben's ass," Billy laughed, slapping Arron on the back.

"Don't get too comfortable, we're still in Eritrean territory. Ben, flash up the radar, let's see where that Dvora is." Arron dipped the fuel. His face dropped.

***

Cairo, Egypt
30'07N 31'23E

The Egypt Air flight came in for its final approach. The contrast between England and Egypt from the air was minimal—a white European carpet now replaced by the dirty pink desert rug of North Africa.

The whole flight was one of anxiety verging on hyperventilation, every scenario passed through my jittered mind, from the lads being given permission to leave to the very worst—*Sea Scorpion* and her crew scuttled to the bottom of the ocean. What would I tell their families? Would they blame me? What future could I give the lads if we caused an international incident? Would I be responsible for putting the lads out of work, out of a home and back on skid row?

Touching down was a frustrating evolution. I needed to ring Killer as soon as possible, troubled by my last call to *Sea Scorpion* as it departed Massawa.

Taff had answered with typical understatement. "It's not going very at all Dom, we're being shot at." The line went dead.

Regardless of the illuminated seatbelt sign, everyone leapt to their feet as the aircraft still trundled, keen to free themselves from the claustrophobic cabin.

I descended the steps to the awaiting business class bus on the tarmac. "Killer, what's happening?"

"We've lost comms with *Sea Scorpion*, but Arron managed to escape on the RIB and is heading to Romiya."

"I need to speak to Arron, I'll be wheels down in Hurghada in an hour."

Mustafa waited outside Hurghada airport. I needed to be in a secure location to co-ordinate the rescue and, strange as it seemed, Mustafa's familiarity was a welcome contrast to the situation at hand.

I checked into the Oberoi Sahl Hasheesh due to its excellent security and individual suites away from prying eyes and ears. I immediately set up my laptop with charts for the Red Sea. Killer had started an extraction plan to move the island party offshore to a secret RV with the cable layer currently in international waters. The plan all hinged on Arron.

I called him on the sat phone. "How are you guys holding up?

"We're OK," he answered before summarising events.

"What's your fuel state?" I asked.

"Not good. I reckon we've less than half a tank."

He was two hours away from Romiya Islet. If he slowed to 10 knots he should have enough fuel to collect the men and RV with the cable layer. It was going to be tight.

Killer sent the latest position of the cable layer heading south from Suez. I punched the co-ordinates into my navigation system. "Fuck." My heart sank. "It's 18 hours away."

So much time on the water would give the Super Dvora plenty of time to locate and intercept. We had no other option.

I rang my Mossad contact to send me everything he could find on the capability of the Eritrean Navy to better assess the threat. We'd now spiralled from a simple extraction into a full-blown rescue operation.

Killer rang. "Have you spoken to your Spanish friends about the plan?"

"Not yet, it's going to be tricky. I'm not sure their client is going to be very happy. A resupply is one thing, a rescue of escapees is an altogether different proposition. Don't worry I'll get it squared away."

My Spanish friends were an interesting couple. We'd worked together on a number of operations having first met Jesus, a former member of the Spanish Special Forces *Mando de Operaciones Especiales*, on a surveillance job in

Madrid. He'd bailed me out when nearly compromised by the Spanish Royal Family's protection detail as we'd ended up at the same event on different missions. Nige and Philippe were detained for a short time while Jesus and I had sorted out the problem. We'd looked after each other ever since, including my recent recovery of his confiscated weapons. His partner, Alejandro, a lawyer by profession, rarely did legal work. He was the main trouble-shooter for a powerful multi-national organisation whose identity he never disclosed.

I knew how important this cable contract was to the guys and I didn't want to compromise the relationship but this was an emergency with lives on the line. I knew they'd understand. I harboured less faith in their client.

"Alejandro, it's Dom. My operation in the Red Sea has gone badly wrong. I really need your help," I said as if it was the most natural thing in the world.

"You know we'll do anything to help you, mi hermano. I'll smooth things with corporate. Jesus is on the ship."

Having Jesus on board was a major coup. I felt our luck changing. I called him to explain the situation, hoping he could live up to his name, adding the team's details and RV co-ordinates, and requested the use of their onboard crane to recover and hide the RIB from the Eritrean Navy.

Just to add even more jeopardy, the Iranians rented a nearby island from Eritrea to monitor ship movements in the Red Sea. I didn't want to risk the cable layer being compromised and seized on the homeward straight.

I sat quietly in my room staring at the charts through a fug of smoke, counting down the seconds as the stress built, knowing that the entire Eritrean Navy would be out hunting for the lads in the RIB.

18 hours was a long time to hide on the open ocean.

CHAPTER 21
Isratu Island, Eritrea
16'18N 39'54E

The silence of the night air was in stark contrast to events that had unfolded four hours earlier fleeing under gunfire. Waves gently lapped on the RIB's hull as a light northerly wind disturbed the ocean's surface. Billy gazed upwards; with no light pollution he felt he could reach out and touch the magnificence of the Milky Way as the pinholes of heaven radiated down on the three men.

Arron restarted the engines putting them firmly into gear. He was fortunate to have a quiet inboard engine. "Any sign of the Super Dvora?"

"She seems to have stopped around 20 miles behind us." Ben's eyes stung from gazing at the radar's phosphorescence.

Arron needed to hug as close to any available land to hide from Dvora's radar. He'd also throw in some doglegs to further protect their next destination of Romiya. He skirted Isratu Island as close as he dared; hitting coral would be catastrophic. At least bloodthirsty sharks would quicken their death.

Clear of Isratu, Arron set a direct course to Romiya— 18 miles of open ocean interspersed with deadly shoals and unchartered reefs silently waiting to sink the unwary mariner. The three chatted quietly feeling slightly more at ease now they moved closer to their objective.

Three miles from Romiya they spotted a glow on the horizon. Arron checked the compass. It appeared to originate from the direction of the islet. He pulled the RIB's throttles back to dead slow to cautiously probe ahead.

Ben moved forward to the bow. With binoculars he scanned the red glow ahead. "It's hard to tell from this range but it's a fire of some sort. We'll need to get closer to confirm," he said as he shuffled to the centre of the RIB. "Maybe they've been hit by the outpost on Harmil?"

"Let's check the radar for other craft in the area, I don't want to run into an ambush." Arron scanned every inch of the coastline around the surrounding islands but picked up nothing.

They'd push another mile before stopping to check the area again for any signs of hostile vessels lying in wait, but knowing fibreglass skiffs were hard to spot, the clouds of doubt and foreboding returned.

They edged forward towards the mystery inferno. They weren't armed to defend themselves. What if the pirates had returned and attacked the islet? Every conceivable scenario ran through their minds as they tentatively continued on their uncertain course checking the area with several radar sweeps until they stood one mile off from the islet.

Ben edged forward to check ahead. He saw movement on the beach around a bonfire but nothing suspicious. No other boats were visible. He couldn't believe his eyes. "The lads are having a massive bonfire on the beach."

"If we could see it three miles away you can bet your bottom dollar the outpost in Harmil are probably getting warm from it. We need to move now." Arron pushed the throttles to full power and headed to the fire.

The boat neared the camp but hung 30 metres offshore to avoid coral. John Miles dived from the beach and swam to the RIB with a rope in his teeth. "At last, we thought we'd be stranded. Do you have any food or water?"

"Fuck food, fuck water. We were followed. We need to move fast and put that fire out for fuck's sake, it can be seen for miles," hissed Arron.

A working party quickly assembled to ferry weapons, men and equipment via the Gemini to the RIB.

"We can't take anymore," shouted Arron. "The RIB is becoming unstable with the weight,"

"But we need to recover it all," answered John.

"We wont be recovering it anywhere if we sink. You need to prioritise what stays and what goes."

The remaining guys, enveloped by acrid smoke billowing from the extinguished beach fire, reburied the majority of weapons and equipment before puncturing the Gemini and casting it adrift.

Arron thought he saw a searchlight coming from Harmil Island. It was time to go. He started the engines, putting the RIB into gear. The engine cut out immediately. In the panic and the smoke he tried to restart. Nothing. *Check kill switch.* OK. *Check ignition.* OK. *Check the prop.* Shit. The line they used to ferry the stores had become tightly entangled around the propeller, immobilising the RIB at the worst possible moment. They were highly vulnerable next to the biggest smoke marker for a thousand miles. Ben jumped over the inflatable tubes into the water illuminated by John's head torch.

"Give me a knife, quick" shouted Ben, realising the torchlight turned him into a wonderfully fluorescent shark lure.

Ben hacked through the rope with his Leatherman like a frenzied serial killer and hauled himself on board.

All eyes turned to Arron. He hit the start button. The engines roared into life. Jettisoning off at maximum speed would have been ideal. With all the weight, the RIB meekly limped away at a painfully slow 3 knots. They all knew that they couldn't outrun the navy; their only hope was their size might show as a spurious signal to a lazy navy radar observer.

***

The sun rose, as did the temperature. Clouds didn't have the gall to appear under the punishing sun. The calm sea, so beautiful in its serenity was a mendacious killer—a saltwater desert bereft of anything but allure. The RIB lazed on the swell, its tubing weighted low in the water due to its human cargo. Inside, a dry cough was the only noise offered, dehydration sapping energy to a degree where to swallow was a struggle. In good spirits hours before with humour the balm to their predicament, their laughs had now silenced as sandpaper throats yearned for the lubrication of ice-cold water or the pleasure of refrigerated beer. Sweating had stopped, and uncovered parchment skin slowly sizzled to dark red burns on even the most tanned. Most lads slipped in and out of exhausted sleep, lifeless limbs draped over each other, hands trailing in the water. They were distressed mariners cast onto a beautiful aquamarine sea of hopelessness. Without immediate rescue they would die.

***

Jesus leaned over the guardrails as the cable layer cut through the water heading south. He sipped on his coffee and stared at the horizon searching for answers to his innermost thoughts. The Ukrainian captain had point blank refused to go to the RV as he held no charts for the area and wouldn't risk his ship. Jesus didn't even fit into the ship's chain of command but he knew that men would die if he did nothing. The RIB carried the weapons needed to protect the cable layer when they entered Pirate Alley in another two days. It would be a horrible twist of fate to abandon the RIB and the ship become hijacked later in the voyage.

His sat phone rang. Alejandro. "Buenos Dias, amigo, How are you getting on with the captain?"

"Terrible. How are you getting on with the company?"

"Terrible." They both laughed. In the face of adversity, they knew the importance of cheerfulness.

"I've just spoken to Dom. If we don't pick them up they won't make it. I can't do anything from Madrid. Do what you can."

They were two hours from the RV. Jesus's mind drifted back to Afghanistan. He'd been the Patrol Commander on a reconnaissance mission when they'd unwittingly walked into a Taliban ambush. Completely cut off, having been pinned down for five hours, and with no helicopter extraction available due to heavy enemy fire, the only option was to fight their way out with a counter attack. It had succeeded but two colleagues had been killed before evacuation. It still weighed heavily on his mind. He couldn't let the men on the RIB die. He returned to his cabin to collect his charts for the area before heading to the bridge where stood the haughty captain.

"Captain, can I have a minute please?" The captain approached Jesus at the chart table. "According to the paper charts there's good depth to the RV located just off the Dahlak Bank."

Again, the captain refused to change course.

"We're less than 40 minutes away. If we don't change course immediately we'll miss the RV."

The captain still refused. With the parting words of, 'That is final,' he walked away.

Jesus paused. He knew what he was about to do could be classed a mutiny and would certainly lose him the contract and potentially a stint in jail. He lunged across the bridge and pushed his face into the captain's.

"If we don't get to the RV, the death of these men will be on your hands. You have to pick them up."

"I'm not being made responsible for this." The captain wiped Jesus' spittle from his face and walked back to the chart table.

"Don't worry about your precious job, I'll take full responsibility."

Jesus couldn't care less if the captain registered a complaint, he'd deal with such trivia later. He sent word to the galley to prepare extra food and water on hand for the men's arrival and remained on the bridge in case the captain changed his mind.

***

Arron lay across the console with an oily rag draped over his head in a futile attempt to lessen the sun's ferocity. He glanced at the pitiful snake's wedding of semi-conscious crew.

Killer had called to inform him that the ship was 30 minutes out, but in his delirium he couldn't remember whether it was a dream. As he tried to focus on the empty fuel gauge, the RIB rippled on a series of small waves. No one had the sanity to stir. Arron scanned through the sting of his salt encrusted eyes to see what had caused the disturbance. He saw a large grey ship on the horizon heading towards them. Grey ships were usually military—the Eritreans had found them. He couldn't care less, at least the ordeal was over and he'd finally savour water. He waited for his fate unable to compose an emotion; his only need was escape from the surrounding beauty slowly killing him. As the ship closed, he saw a high white bridge with cranes on the super structure. The hull appeared lighter than battleship grey. He sat up. "Lads wake up, it's the cable layer." A grin split his dried lip.

"Thank fuck for that," croaked a voice from the bottom of the boat.

Ladders were dropped as the ship neared. The team snapped back into action and boarded the vessel with their equipment. Arron and Billy stayed on the RIB to connect the lifting strops from the crane. Just as the RIB was about to be loaded on deck, the crane failed, dropping the RIB 10 metres into the ocean. Both Billy and Arron disappeared under the white water, either to be crushed by the weight of the RIB or sucked under by the cable layer's hull. Jesus stood with his mouth agape. After escaping near death, they'd be killed by their rescuers.

Arron and Billy resurfaced. Jesus cupped his mouth, feeling his sharp stubble on his palm and shook his head in disbelief as he saw them laughing. Re-entering the RIB they hooked up again to the alternate crane and lifted safely aboard. Arron and Billy jumped from the RIB into the waiting arms of Jesus.

"Hi guys, I'm Jesus."

"That you are," laughed Billy. "You're early, Christmas is tomorrow."

"I'm a good friend of Dom. It looks like you guys have had a rough time," Jesus smiled, pushing two bottles of water into their hands. "Come, eat."

"Any news on *Sea Scorpion*?" asked Arron.

"No, nothing."

CHAPTER 22
'Unnamed' tanker
21'27N 39'07E

Caught Red Handed: British Assassins in the Horn of Africa

A six man squad of British mercenaries have been caught red handed in the midst of preparing an attempt to assassinate the top leadership of the Eritrean government in the port city of Massawa on the Red Sea.

Of the six, four were apprehended and two managed to escape, abandoning their mates while blazing out of Massawa Bay into the Red Sea in an inflatable speedboat, never to be seen again by Eritrean eyes.

A search of the vessel they arrived on uncovered a cache of tools of the assassin's trade. Included was a small arsenal of automatic weapons, a sophisticated satellite communications system, state of the art electronic target range finders, and most damning, several sniper rifles.

All of those arrested have since been confirmed as employees of a British "security" firm akin to the notorious US company Blackwater. At least two of the four are former British Special Forces. As in the case of Raymond Davis, the CIA killer caught in the act in Pakistan, the British Foreign Office has been claiming Geneva Convention protections for these gun thugs all but confirming their being on an official mission for the British Government.

Their arrest took place just a few hundred yards from our Red Sea home in Massawa, and happened while we were there. Each time I have driven by that spot, I have felt a sick feeling in my stomach, for the salt embankment they were hiding behind has an unobstructed view of the site where just a few days later all the top leadership of the Eritrean government would be gathering for the annual outdoor celebration of the 1990 capture of the Port of Massawa by Eritrean liberation fighters.

These professional killers were discovered almost by accident by a woman taking a shortcut home through an adjacent out-of-service salt flat. The woman noticed, as all good Eritreans should, that sa'ada, white people, were taking photos (with telephoto lenses) somewhere they were not allowed. These Brit "diplomats" took their sweet time scoping out their firing points and parameters of their potential killing field for their discoverer had to walk almost a mile to the nearest police station to report this and then the police had to drive the roundabout route to the spot in question.

But for the vigilance of one Eritrean woman, Eritrea might have experienced an unthinkable disaster, the loss of Eritrea's President and only god knows how many of Eritrea's top leaders. ~ Tesfa News.

They say never let the truth get in the way of a good story and this wasn't the first politically motivated article charged with emotive language to surface on the crew of *Sea Scorpion*. Of course, it sent the internet into hyperdrive: Eritrean commentators demanded executions, maritime competitors gossiped like playground attention seekers and tabloid newspapers sensationalised events all blanketed the banal truth that the Eritrean government weren't talking to the British government and no one knew what the hell was going on. The Rt Hon William Hague, former leader of the Conservative Party and currently the UK's Foreign Secretary, stepped in to negotiate but had been stalled by President Afewerki's anti-West rhetoric. I would've actually admired his stance to raise Eritrea from the ashes of war and progress free of international patronising but the more I understood, the more fearful I became for the four lads incarcerated especially after seeing an official photograph of them sat in

271

a line, each displaying a pallid dolour suggesting they'd heard their death warrant.

Afewerki's human rights record had been attacked by many quarters and his prison network described as a 'network of repression'. I could take such headlines with the same pinch of salt as the rest but the fact was Eritrea kept their prisoners, many of whom were incarcerated without charge, in atrocious conditions: cells were improvised from shipping containers that baked people alive and stripped them of skin. If they were lucky enough not to be locked in such an asphyxiating furnace they could be shoved into underground cells with no light for the body to digest time nor offer the sanctity of hope— many died of torture, many died of preventable diseases, others died of just giving up hope—suicide their only escape. My mind couldn't process as lies the stories of prisoners being regular beaten on their buttocks so they couldn't sit, or rolled in sand to accentuate the pain of their sweaty welts that would become infected as washing was only allowed on a Sunday. I read a story of an escapee who'd been in an 11-foot by 8-foot cell with 33 other prisoners, where men died on their feet and desperate pleas were met with death threats. If things took a turn for the worse I truly feared for the sanity, and lives, of my lads. I had to get them out.

I walked to the stern of the ship looking down at the troubled waters as the ship churned its way down the Red Sea. I waited with an unease common when the day may be your last. It would be futile vainglory to reflect on a life I'd led so far, the humble concern of future survival was my primary goal. The mission was about as high risk as it could get. Anna passed through my mind. She'd walked back into my life at the worst possible moment, when deep in rum and rumination. Her knock on the door had sent me into paranoia—*SSI? Eritrean Secret Service?* On opening the door she'd fallen into my arms and told me she understood. In that moment I knew I wanted to be with her forever. I held her tightly to my chest and kissed her. After so much emotional strain it felt surreal to feel love again. Despite the overwhelming odds stacked against us I dared to dream of a future together. And in that moment of just wanting her, I had left for a task from which I may not return. As our hearts broke in tandem, I gave her Killer's phone number and told her to call him if she heard nothing from me.

We hadn't heard anything from *Sea Scorpion* since Big Al's final transmission to Arron. The biggest issue was that they'd left weapons behind on Romiya islet. This could be the difference between life and death for the guys detained in Eritrea. It was vital I reach the cache before the Eritrean Navy. Best case, we'd recover the weapons, throw them into the sea and escape. Worst case, we'd walk into an ambush and get shot to shit.

My two patrol boats were heading up the Red Sea to RV with us at which point Arron and I would dive over the side and be picked up. The aim was to be as covert as possible; our names weren't on the ship's crew list so we wouldn't be missed when the ship reached Jeddah, overt stowaways breaking every seamanship rule, but sometimes you just have to do what's necessary. We'd then move to a standoff area to the north of the Dahlak Archipelago.

I flicked my cigarette butt off the stern; it rose and danced above my head like a child's kite before plummeting through the vortex into the sea below, lost forever. I hoped it wasn't a prophetic metaphor for all of us involved.

I walked back towards Arron working on the inflatable—a last minute purchase from Suez for our

273

precarious operation. Egypt never cares for your tears and for $4000 I'd bought the most useless inflatable boat in North Africa—holes outnumbered rubber content. Arron and I would use the boat to drift 20 miles down the Red Sea to the island. Without the ability to call for help it didn't bode well, neither did the clouds on the horizon.

"Not good," Arron said, with an air of understatement, pointing to dark black apocalyptic clouds gathering ahead threatening menace to anything that dare walk their path. We stopped, silently watching as Jupiter's army gathered.

"I'd better call the patrol boats," I muttered with a sense of fear.

Arron returned to his kasbah of rubber and glue to make the boat slightly floatable. As commandos it was fairly standard to work with little or nothing to pull off miracles for the Admiralty who sat on big aircraft carriers painting war in the wardroom. At the other end of the bravery scale was the publicly unheralded Arron. Despite having escaped Eritrea by the skin of his teeth, he didn't flinch in volunteering for an operation that may be his last. There should have been four taking part but two pulled out at the last minute. I didn't hold it against them; people prioritise differently, so it was down to Arron and me to make it work no matter what the cost. I owed it to my guys held in Massawa.

My satellite phone rang. Roy on *DM234*. "Hi Dom, we've fallen behind schedule, the weather's a bit fresh down here."

Roy's description of 'a bit fresh' would have most people heading to the life rafts to abandon ship. Checking Roy's position I saw they sat on the edge of the hellish system we'd just entered. Whips of wind drowned out my voice on the phone as an eerie darkness enveloped the ship; high voltage clouds pulsed, cutting off the call in a maelstrom of static. On the upside, the weather would give us cover to cross deck undetected provided we didn't drown.

A deckhand joined us on deck to inform me of a call. I entered the captain's sanctum where the Russian Master handed me the ship's phone.

"Hi Dom, it's Jim Broomfield on *ChemCon Albatross*. We're heading south to Salalah but the client is taking us off when we've a clear pirate threat en route." He explained that the captain wasn't happy, but nearing retirement, if he signed off in protest he'd lose his company pension.

I stepped out onto the bridge wings and tried to fire up a Marlboro while dialling the large keys on the Iridium phone but the wind had whipped into a gale preventing both. I returned to the bridge to use the ship's phone. I called the shipping company's CSO. It was clear halfway through the conversation that in the space of two years he'd become the world's expert on maritime security. This was a common aliment with certain CSO's.

I warned him of the risk and consequences of his decision. In his goldfish bowl of rumour and google intelligence he believed the route to be safe as the ship was in ballast so her emptiness made her sit too high in the water to be taken. He probably thought I was trying to make a quick buck from his company but this was not the way I rolled. I passionately cared about protecting mariners and this ethos was the cornerstone on which I'd built the company.

The captain patted me on the shoulder as he passed. "Jeddah has been closed due to the weather. The storm is getting worse."

My plan was unravelling before it had even started. Roy had decided to turn back as the seas were unmanageable. Both patrol boats had spent the night punching the waves head on to avoid sinking, each narrowly avoiding capsize. It was clear that neither were going to make the mid sea rendezvous as planned. I'd have to cross deck after our port call at Jeddah.

The storm reached its peak as we approached the outer limits of the Saudi port and gateway to the holy city of Mecca. Purple anvil crawlers flashed across the sky as negatively charged particles of intense white energy, reminiscent of H G Wells' Martian beams, rained down. It was the worst electrical storm I'd ever witnessed and fearful as the mighty thunder seemed to shake every rivet on the ship. Ships are not lightning proof but if hit the steel structure passes the deadly voltage into the sea—In theory. I reminisced a quote from 'War of the Worlds' ~ *suddenly, like a thing falling upon me from without, came fear.* In that moment I understood the trepidation of my primeval ancestors recoiling at the power of Mother Nature, believing it to be a bad omen offering blood to appease the heavens. I decided not to cut my finger as an offering but retreated instead into my cabin where I hoped the Gods of the Internet would be friendlier. I inserted my 3G dongle, less than hopeful of getting a signal, for any news on Eritrea. Despite being five miles offshore and in the middle of electrical Armageddon my emails downloaded. One from my lawyer in Eritrea caught my eye:

Mr Mee,

I am in constant contact both with the courts and the navy. The navy is saying I have not finished my work.

The recent news I've heard is that the vessel at port was tagging the escaped RIB boat, and a certain quantity of ammunitions and weapons was found in, around or about Romiya Islet. This makes the navy cautious of its investigation.

The court is also cautious of the matter and am advised to wait.

This evening, I shall have an update and shall inform you if I find any further news.

Horror enveloped me. The weapons had been officially discovered. This was perilous news for the *Sea Scorpion* guys.

There was no point in continuing the recovery. Fatefully, Zeus' ire had saved us. If the weather had remained clear, I wouldn't have received the email. We'd have sailed straight into an ambush.

I returned on deck. The pelting of heavy January rain turned the ship into a floating waterfall. Visibility was down to zero, so too my hope. I stared out to sea looking for answers. The discovery of the weapons made things far more complicated. Arron joined me on deck.

"I've aborted the op," I said without taking my eyes from the wet static air.

"OK, boss, so what's the new plan?"

"I have no idea."

***

Salalah OPL, Oman
16'54N 54'05E

Captain Chopra stood on *ChemCon Albatross's* bridge. After bidding farewell to Broomfield and his security team in Muscat he'd hugged the Omani coastline hoping it would be safer, but he knew there was no safe passage in these waters. Now nearing the Salalah anchorage, the worst of his tension lifted. He watched the crew coiling hundreds of feet of razor wire, removing reinforced steel doors and taking down other fortifications to ready the ship for its port call. It was a routine undertaken daily by hundreds of ships in the Indian Ocean. He contacted port control requesting an area to drift before being called forward to a berth inside for taking on his chemical cargo.

The crew's mood was upbeat and relaxed. The stress of running south with no protection now forgotten as they beavered away thinking of possible shore leave. The anchorage hummed with all manner of small boats darting between ships at anchor, fishing dhows, having finished a day of longlining, were heading to market sell their catch. Two skiffs skated through, blending perfectly into normal port traffic. They'd launched from a dhow two miles over the horizon. With no security, nobody noticed the first skiff come alongside and its occupants clamber up a hooked ladder onto *ChemCon Albatross*'s deck.

***

At Coastguard HQ, Major Hashil was on duty, sharing a cool *Quwat Jabal* and deep conversation with Captain Siad.

A young sailor burst in. "Sir, forgive me but we have a broken message over VHF that a ship has been boarded by pirates in the anchorage."

"Impossible," Major Hashil exclaimed. "Excuse me, my friend, while I sort this issue." He ran to join his crew on the dock.

The first officer had already started the Harras 7 engines and mustered the crew to emergency stations. He greeted the major and informed him armed men had been seen boarding a tanker off their starboard quarter. "Port Control has tried to raise the ship on VHF with no response. I have the co-ordinates of the suspected ship."

"Uncover the 12.7mm. I want all of the crew armed and made ready," ordered Major Hashil.

Once the vessel's lines were clear, Major Hashil pushed 4000HP to full throttle sending one crewmember stumbling over as the Harras rocketed from the dock.

The first officer plotted the position into the navigation system. They were four miles away but the AIS tracking the ship showed it heading to the ocean. "Sir, they are making a run for it."

"I want four sailors ready as a boarding party and a gunner on the 12.7mm to give covering fire."

The Harras quickly closed in on the tanker, scraping the waves at 3 knots. The light blue hull and white super structure dwarfed the interceptor. With the ship empty of cargo she sat high above the waterline, the gunner on the 12.7mm didn't have the elevation to give covering fire for the boarding party assembled on the stern of the Harras, unsure how they'd be able to get on board the gigantean, this was more a job for Special Forces.

Major Hashil spotted a pirate with an RPG on the bridge wings, so backed off. He decided to hail the ship on VHF. "*ChemCon Albatross* this is Omani Coastguard. Stop your ship we are going to board."

Scarface smiled as he and four other pirates dragged two of the crew on deck and paraded them with AK47's pointed at their heads.

Major Hashil had no back up and a toothless plan. He sat Harass 7 at neutral and watched the ship disappear over the horizon. He'd just witnessed the most daring hijack yet—a ship taken from supposedly safe anchorage waters. Garaad had further upped the ante.

***

Hurghada, Egypt
27'14N 33'50E

After aborting the weapon recovery operation, I returned to an Egypt on a knife-edge. Mustafa didn't pick me up from the airport. He'd been detained along with many other Egyptians in a crackdown for reasons unknown to those affected. Dissent grew on the streets, in particular towards the police. I shared their anger—the whole establishment reeked of corruption.

I'd managed to rent a discreet two-bed apartment—the bolthole I needed to plan and crisis manage. The apartment seemed new but was busily surrounded by demolished structures as if a B52 bomber had emptied its payload levelling everything other than my apartment block. I'd picked it due to the dusty balcony offering a clear view of the port and the surrounding coast.

Having commenced full dialogue with the British Ambassador to Eritrea, Sandra Tyler-Haywood, I disclosed the full story, assuming that upon the Eritrean Navy's discovery of the weapons, the detained *Sea Scorpion* crew would be getting the full treatment, none of which I could see being pleasant. Her attempts to get access to them were continually stonewalled by the fractious Foreign Affairs Ministry in Asmara and we still had no news on their wellbeing.

Barry was placed in charge for the welfare of the detained men's families. While of little emotional comfort, the men would receive full operational pay and I instructed the UK staff to give the next of kin our full support in all matters while I continued to reach out to my network to further help the authorities.

In addition, I also needed to get my three Egyptian crew repatriated. They'd been moving continually around the region in my patrol boats since the incident having left their passports on *Sea Scorpion*.

The gaps in the vertical blinds cast bar-shaped shadows across my body as I lay on the bed, offering a subtle glimpse of my future. I stared at the ceiling fan hoping the mesmerising blur would open up solutions, yet my thoughts and ideas seemed to ricochet from it, crashing to the floor as wasted time.

"I must know someone in Eritrea, for fuck's sake," I muttered to myself hoping someone would answer. I sat on the balcony with a bottle of rum and racked my mental notebook. The TV in the background reported another bombing in Iraq. I reflected on my list of Generals and my previous hopes that the Iraqi people could have overthrown Saddam. It came to me in a flash. *Peter.* Sir Peter Charles. He'd know someone. I still had his Whitehall office number.

"Hello," an unfamiliar voice answered.

I asked for Peter without offering a reason.

"I'm sorry, Sir Peter is no longer with this department." He hung up.

I called back and persisted with the uninspiring individual to give me his contact details. He told me he'd get a message to him before again hanging up. It looked like there'd been a changing of the guard with Sir Peter replaced by a chinless civil servant on a fast track ticket. I racked my brain further. *Trevor.* I scrolled through my phone list thankful that my admin had been on the ball when he'd offered me his number on the Tattershall Castle. He wasn't surprised to hear from me, he'd obviously been making a decent career in intelligence and was surprisingly helpful.

I dialled the number and was met by the baritone whir of a lawnmower. The elocutionary perfect voice told me to hang on as he shut the two-stroke engine down. Ugly growls of the motor were replaced by the melody of chattering black birds. I felt a slight pang of homesickness for a country from where I felt exiled. I pictured him in a quintessential English garden surrounded by gnarled apple trees and tidy rose beds.

"Hello young man, what are up to in Eritrea? Hopefully not trying any regime change, we've had rather enough of that lately."

He'd clearly done his due diligence. I wouldn't have expected anything less from such a seasoned spook. I further explained the situation and asked if he knew anybody on the inside in Asmara.

"I did once, " he said with an air of melancholy. The line went silent, I presumed something had happened to his man on the inside. "Look, Sandra is one of the best and you're already talking to her through the FCO channels if anyone can sort out this mess it's her. Don't do anything stupid you've caused enough trouble. I told you to stay in the service now you're running around like Mad Mike Hoare."

I thought him a bit harsh. I wasn't attempting coups like I suspected he did during his service.

I felt deflated. I hoped Peter could have been my silver bullet but the conversation made me feel even more isolated.

"Dominic," he said, as we were just about to sign off. I expected one final lecture. "Let me make a phone call. All will be well."

As soon as I hung up the phone rang. Leghorn on *AL345*. The Egyptian crew were getting increasingly agitated, wanting to know when they were going home. I said they should be careful what they wished for.

The crackdown intensified with hundreds of young men being rounded up and detained to clear them off the streets. The regime's oppressive strategy of fear and intimidation hadn't worked; indeed it further fuelled the fire of discontent. Tahrir Square became the rallying point for protests but the contagion of injustice spread across the country like a *khamaseen* wind.

Suez was one of our main embarkation points and after losing *Sea Scorpion* it was vital we could use the port. My security teams would usually fly into Cairo and wait to be brought forward to Suez when their ship arrived in the canal, boarding by a small pilot boat controlled by the Egyptian Navy. In the rising unrest I banned all shore leave therefore my guys would have to sit tight in their Cairo hotel. I needed to keep an eye on the road routes from Cairo to Suez to ensure they were safe. Living in Hugharda proved to be stressful but useful to co-ordinate operations as the chaos unfolded.

I instructed *AL345*, currently in a holding pattern off Oman, to head to Djibouti for further instructions. All my agents in the region regarded it impossible to land the Egyptians without passports. For a nation to refuse the return of its own citizens seemed ludicrous. They were the maritime version of another Tom Hanks film character, Viktor Navorski, instead of being trapped an airport terminal, the Egyptians were confined in a claustrophobic patrol boat with an uncertain future and no Catherine Zeta-Jones for morale, just the ramblings of their eccentric captain and sweaty former bootnecks often clad only in underpants. They were three pieces of jetsam missed only by their families, yet I considered it my duty to get them home. We'd have to smuggle them back in. With the Egyptian military on high alert, it wasn't going to be easy.

I returned to England to devise a plan. I didn't want another vessel detained while Garaad continued his attacks. His recent hijackings of two more vessels added to his tally and the 1027 sailors he currently held hostage. With Garaad running amok, it was even more important that PVI ran efficiently, even if we were about to juggle another politically hot potato.

CHAPTER 23
PVI Headquarters, Tiverton, UK
50'54N 03'21W

I walked into the office. Banks of computer screens hid admin staff typing as if their lives depended on it. Some I hadn't yet met—hallmarks of our increasing administrative burden, others were pleased to see me if only to step away from their screen. Killer remained slumped at his desk. The sleepless nights had taken their toll. His red eyes, heavy within a puffed face, told me he'd ignored the clock. I hugged him. He really needed it, as did I. A small act of brotherly love, a small physical moment just to say, *'You're not alone. I'm with you.'*

In the wilderness of Scottish highlands, surrounded by awe-inspiring mountains stands a monument of three commandos side by side above a plinth that simply reads *United We Conquer*. These small words galvanise commando ethos. In this remote corner, British commandos were born, sculpted from the black peat and granite peaks. Should they survive the rigours of training they would be amongst the first wave to hit the Normandy beaches. This DNA borne of hell is our origins and it runs deep through our veins. No matter how high the mountain, no matter how deep the seabed, we'll always be there for each other.

"Have you heard about Suez?" asked Killer.

"No, tell me." I dreaded the answer.

A large crowd had attacked the police station in Suez looting all the weapons before turning their stolen guns on the police. The military regained control after 24 hours of anarchy but the weapons hadn't been recovered. While I empathised with the public's anger, I couldn't stomach the idea that 200 of my assault rifles secured in the navy armoury could be used against the police in the full glare of the media. Mr Nabil reassured Killer that the military had sent an armoured division to protect the Suez Canal and it would remain open.

I'd left Anna there. Even though I'd advised her to stay in the apartment, I felt immense guilt in not being at her side to protect her. We stood motionless around the office TV watching a nation unravel. Looking less a protest and more a revolution, the unthinkable seemed possible—the fall of a regime that had stood unchallenged for 30 years. Egypt was an unguided missile spiralling out of control. It filled me with a deep sense of foreboding.

We considered all options before drawing up a limited plan regarded the best we could execute under the circumstances. *AL345* was three days from reaching Djibouti; where both S200's were on standby. I sent instructions to Roy to bunker both boats and prepare for sea. I needed *AM230* for my mission to cross deck the Egyptians from *AL345*. *AM230* would then move north up the Red Sea until I concocted another plan possible to implement with havoc running through the country.

"I've booked you into the Globe tonight. I thought you'd want to be off the grid when we meet Karl," Killer said as we broke. After such a stressful time that showed no signs of abating, we both needed time away to keep us sane.

I drove into the wealthy enclave of Topsham, idyllically located on the eastern bank of the River Exe estuary and just three miles from Commando Training Centre on the south Devon coast. Established in Roman times, with a good sheltered harbour for sea trade, in its heyday Topsham rivalled London as a port. Ironically, in the 1600s, Turkish and North African pirates targeted it as a lucrative objective, so much so that Admiral Robert

Blake was sent to drive them out. In 1654 he enjoyed some early success but the pirates continued to harass local shipping. At least now I took the fight to the pirates thousands of miles away from the sleepy shores of England.

I navigated the narrow streets arriving at the Globe Inn, smashing the side of my rather expensive hired Mercedes as I turned into its tiny entrance. I grimaced, just another strange receipt for the accounts department to nag me about producing. It was unlikely I would, my mind more occupied by the frontline than the back office and despite our troubles, the business had increased exponentially—financial difficulties were not one of my worries yet there had been a pernicious sway from admin staff of late. It was something I'd correct when time allowed.

Entering the 12th Century inn, its low ceiling of oak beams embodied everything I loved about England—its great history preserved in the fabulous pubs that abound the island. These weren't only working museums but community hubs as they'd done for centuries. It was also a fitting place to meet my senior captain to discuss a secret plan I had for him in the Red Sea. I'm sure the hidden ghosts of old masters would smile as they listened to our plotting.

Killer joined me at the bar adorned by many brass pumps offering an impressive array of real ales, from 'Pickled Partridge' to 'Black Pearl Oyster Stout'. It would be sociable to try each one in the course of the evening.

Karl Stott soon joined us. He dressed as if he'd just stepped off a boat. His tanned weather beaten face cracked a smile. It'd been a while since we sailed through the Baltic together delivering *AM230* from Stockholm to

London. We retreated to a quiet corner to discuss the Egyptian situation.

Karl spoke first. "So what mission impossible do you have for me this time?" He was rock solid, the epitome of a hardcore mariner and someone I could rely on whatever the sea state or geopolitical situation. I knew he'd say yes before even telling him about the plan, or lack thereof in this case.

I explained the churning of Egyptian politics and that I'd be in country to oversee the operation. He'd move slowly up the Red Sea until I contacted him. He was to leave for Djibouti within 24 hours. With the brief completed we could focus on working our way through the parade of beer pumps before hitting the rum recounting many a sea tale together.

Killer's phone rang so he excused himself. He returned 15 minutes later looking stressed. "That was the CSO from Hapag Lloyd, they've heard a rumour that the Suez Canal is going to close along with the airports."

"How many guys do we have in Egypt?" I asked.

"About 60."

I immediately called a taxi to take me to the airport. I'd book a flight while on the 150-mile journey to Heathrow. I needed to enter Egypt before it shutdown. With a quick farewell and a take away coffee I was back on the move.

Anna rang, her fear rising as the situation deteriorated, the country now in turmoil. I advised her to sit tight, reassuring her that I was on my way.

The flight to Hurghada was virtually empty, it seemed only idiots would fly into a civil war. It was gracious relief as the only flight available was the no frills hell of Easy Jet. I slept most of the way in a real ale stupor, my hop-loaded breath keeping the personality-bypassed cabin crew at a distance. The arrival hall echoed with the sound of nobody, the token customs official stamped my passport without even looking up from his desk. The Russian Embassy had issued advice for all its nationals to leave as the violence played out on the streets leaving the departure hall a stampede of panicked tourists guided by hopeless tour reps failing to keep order. The evacuation was in full swing.

Mustafa faithfully waited. Now released, he avoided further detention. I asked him about the mood in the town.

"Here only some small protests. Everywhere else is crazy, like you." Our eyes met in his rear view mirror, his crow's feet pronounced in a smile.

Killer rang. "Dom, Suez has closed for armed guards. I've scrambled both S200's to support our Red Sea operations."

Killer was a genius. His quick thinking would save the day, as all the other maritime security companies would be screwed with no mechanism to cross deck weapons. He'd carefully set up a series of cross decks between the different ships we protected, exchanging men and equipment via the ships' lifeboats. This would mean no ships heading south would be unprotected in Pirate Alley.

"Good work, brother. Hurghada is safe and the airport is still working. I want all the guys in country to come here. I'll try and deploy them locally by sea."

I needed to get some command and control of the situation before things worsened. Having my men in one safe place gave us options. Hurghada had boats, Cairo didn't. Suez had boats but also a vengeful mob armed with AK47's.

Anna waited at my apartment. We embraced, not wanting to let each other go. She knew I had to work but was just thankful I'd arrived, her colleagues flitting out one by one leaving her ever-more nervous watching events unfold.

Six hours later, I had 60 PVI guys in the Hurghada Hilton Resort. It showed how much of a family we were when each and every man asked about the boys in Eritrea. It was good to be with the guys again even if I was getting it the ear about the office staff in the UK giving them a rough ride. I was surprised to see morale so low. After speaking to a number of Team Leaders something in the company had changed.

I gathered them all for a briefing. "I'm looking at deploying you from here within the next 48 hours. No move for 18 hours, so enjoy a beer tonight on the company. Please stay in the hotel." It was only a revolution, after all.

That night 11 protestors were killed in Suez along with 170 injured. The US Embassy advised all US citizens to leave the country. The protestors in Cairo, Alexandria, Nile Delta and Suez continued to stand their ground and in Sinai, tribes exchanged gun fire with the authorities, yet the Canal remained open—it was imperative East met West.

The following evening I arranged a boat to take two teams out to ships waiting offshore but the boat never showed up. Local vessels were permitted to move during daytime hours only. The military had imposed martial law with a night-time curfew. Anyone on the streets after 8pm would be shot.

Mustafa found a captain willing to take us out for a massively inflated price. I gathered three teams together and escorted Mustafa to the fishing port. As we all boarded the boat ready to meet the three ships, the police showed up and ordered us into the back of their vehicles.

It would not be a wise move to resist under the circumstances, besides I hid over $20,000 in my jeans that, in theory, could make all this go away. I sighed audibly when we drove into the familiar compound of the SSI.

"Right lads, this is the local secret police headquarters. Stay switched on and don't say a fucking word, revert any questions to me," I warned.

I exited the vehicle with Mustafa. This would be a great risk for him so it was best for him to play the dumb driver who didn't know anything and stay in the vehicle, but he insisted staying with me. We'd created a strong bond since setting up *Sea Scorpion*. He was fiercely loyal, a commitment that could have him tortured and killed by SSI. I couldn't forget such bravery.

The protestors in other cities had ransacked many SSI buildings forcing many officers to leave their posts and seek refuge underground. Their reign of terror now crumbling like the regime for whom they did their bidding. It was their turn to feel fear. Those that stayed were either the most stupid, conceited or more worryingly, sadistic.

I was led into the house of pain. The finery of the opulent oak panelled office seemed to be closed on this visit. I entered a bare concrete room, the flaking paint the most interesting part of the décor. Behind a scarred veneered desk were two officers, one seated the other standing; both needed a wash. The armed escort left the room. There was something I'd witnessed many times lingering in the air—fear. These guys were more scared than me, they knew their empire was about to crumble and here was a citadel to the furore outside.

As I stood alone, for one fleeting moment I toyed with the idea of taking them down, crushing the standing man's head against the back wall and choking out the seated one before he'd had the chance to stand. These thoughts were glitches in my human software, ones that I struggled to supress. The idea of killing these cowards was immensely appealing. Their misguided sense of power when torturing people unable to fight back gave them sickening delusions of being tough guys. They thought we were alone; however, they could not see my blood thirty evil twin with murder on his mind, his aggression always worse after a night on the rum. I towered above them and stared at the seated officer.

He blinked and broke the silence. "Mr Dom isn't it? You met with our commanding officer a few months back," he stated in perfect English.

"Yes, we met regarding my filming with National Geographic Channel," I replied, my red mist thankfully lifted.

I continued to explain that my day job was providing security to ships but Suez had been closed due to the recent unrest. I furnished them with Mr Nabil's number who would confirm everything that I stated was the truth. They returned 20 minutes later. It was clear that they'd smoked themselves half to death to calm their own fears of what was happening outside the gate. At least we had one thing in common.

"OK, go." It was a simple demand and one I wasn't keen to dwell on.

I returned to the van where my guys were waiting. I said nothing but gave Leon a cheeky wink. We were released but it was obvious we couldn't deploy to the ships. Killer, already ahead of me, was booking flights to redeploy the guys from Hurghada airport before it closed. Mark Wilson, an old cohort from 40 Commando had been extremely helpful in organising everybody while in Egypt. He agreed to stay on and assist with another problem I had to overcome.

Killer somehow managed to get all the guys on flights out of Dodge. Hurghada airport was chaos, everyone realised the situation was degenerating into anarchy and threat to life a distinct reality. I bid a fond farewell to Leon at the security point. If I'd known it would be the last time I'd see him alive I'd have hugged him a little tighter.

My phone rang. Derek in Durban. With disorder in one ear I heard despair in the other.

"Dom, I've been arrested and all your weapons have been impounded. I swear to God I've done nothing wrong, Kerk has betrayed me." He went on to explain that Kerk had made a play for his business using his wife's influence within the Directorate for Priority Crime Investigation, commonly known as the Hawks, that targeted organised crime in South Africa.

I reassured Derek we'd back him up the whole way and cover any legal bills and would never do business with Kerk. With South Africa off line I needed to activate our Madagascar contingency that currently sat as a desktop exercise.

Back at the hotel I briefed Mark on the next operation—smuggling the three Egyptians back into the country. It came with a great deal of risk so offered him a flight if he didn't fancy it.

"I'd only be bored sat at home," he smiled.

Back at the apartment I briefed Anna on the situation. I wasn't used to operating with a loved one in tow. That my murky world was now irrevocably entwined with my personal life filled me with dread. It seemed everything conspired to wreck our relationship.

CHAPTER 24
Hurghada, Egypt
25'57N 34'28E

AM230 was half way up the Red Sea towing the Red RIB due to it being sabotaged while in Djibouti. After severing the HT leads, someone had unscrewed the seacocks causing the boat to fill with water. That 'someone' didn't want the RIB to leave Djibouti and we all surmised it was most probably an Eritrean intelligence agent. Having the RIB gave us more options and would hopefully not compromise *AM230* in returning our three Egyptians to the mainland.

Mark and I rented a car and drove along the coast to find a discreet location to land the Egyptians. It proved harder than anticipated. The Egyptian military had established exceptionally robust coastal defences. Along the pristine tourist beaches stood newly erected sangars and infantry outposts with interlocking arcs to ensure machine gun fire covered the entire coast. As a former anti-tank specialist, Mark happily identified tank battalions, air defence units and infantry companies en route. After 110 miles we finally found a one-mile gap in the defences between machine gun nests and a network of dunes.

We drove off the metal road, the dunes providing excellent cover. We dismounted and scanned for any signs of human habitation, it was thankfully clear. The RIB had berthed in Hurghada marina when refitting *Sea Scorpion* so would be easy to check her back in again, although at a highly inflated price.

We made our plan: *AM230* would stay offshore as her military profile would lead to a defence unit opening fire thinking she was a hostile.

The RIB, with Sharky as coxswain and the three Egyptians, would follow a steady course up the coast. Upon nearing the dune location, Mark and I would signal by torch and the Egyptians would dive over the side and swim ashore. We'd recover them before dropping off each one individually inside Hurghada where they could lie low. The RIB would continue to Hurghada marina where we'd RV with Sharky. *AM230* would then leave the area and head back south.

I rang Karl to brief him on the plan, sending the co-ordinates of the dunes. Mark and I were sure this could work provided we didn't get stopped and searched on the return to Hurghada. Finding three drenched Egyptians in the trunk on an isolated desert road could be hard to explain.

***

I lay on my bed picking through the plan to ensure I hadn't missed anything until satisfied this was the way to go. My eyes closed in relief. In eight hours it would hopefully all be over.

My phone rang. Karl. "Dom, we have a problem. We've been working on the RIB all day but we can't start it. I think this storm has trashed the electrics."

"Fuck," I exclaimed. "OK, stay on course, I'll think of something." I hung up and called Mark.

This was a bitter blow. All vessels entering port under martial law would be subject to boarding and searched by the navy before being cleared to proceed alongside. Attempting to do such a port call would lead to the Egyptian's discovery and result in *AM230's* crew being detained. I cursed Egypt for its draconian rules and prayed for a revolution of common sense. With the country in meltdown and a military on high alert, pulling up in a battleship grey military patrol boat would draw plenty of attention.

We'd need another vessel to cross-deck the Egyptians and any plan would have to be executed at night before *AM230* could make a run for it.

Mark found an agent near the marina who said he could resupply *AM230* so we arranged a meeting. The stairwell to the office was a partially built concrete staircase that would be easier to navigate should I not have consumed a bottle of rum the night before. The office was surprisingly smart, and despite the encompassing turmoil the agent bore a lustrous countenance borne, no doubt, from enjoying ring-fenced wealth. It was evident he was of privileged stock and led an easy life, which in Egypt, is the same thing. His arrogance was pronounced in his insinuation that he thought himself smarter than everyone else in the room, encouraged further by me sounding dumb.

I offered an introductory smile to the captain of the boat who'd undertake the resupply. Together they oozed greed and were both out to fleece me. I was going to let them. We agreed on $20,000. The trip would take around 40 minutes. *Stupid Westerners*. They left wearing big smiles. So did we.

Mark and I returned to the hotel to finalise the plan before briefing Karl and his crew. I plotted the location, noting a good spot between the islands of Giftun el Saghir and Abu Rimathi offered shelter for the cross deck and hopefully cover from naval radar. The guys needed any edge in the circumstances.

"I don't like this one bit, mate," said Mark.

"Neither do I Brother, but this is the only option left."

Mark headed over to the agent's office with the primary role of ensuring the captain did as agreed and actually sailed out to meet *AM230*. He'd also be my eyes and ears in the agent's office when we cross decked the three Egyptians into the resupply boat—a detail I'd kindly missed when arranging the deal.

With a degree of reticence I roped Anna into the operation, tasking her to sit on our apartment's balcony and look for any coastguard boats leaving port. I'd be at a vantage point overlooking the harbour to act as early warning for *AM230* if the Navy base scrambled any vessels. We'd all be in breach of the curfew.

I took the back streets to the Sheraton Road tourist district. It was eerily quiet, without a soul to cast a shadow upon the lamp lit sidewalks. Normally it would be seething with stunning Russians alluring in sexy super short miniskirts followed by an entourage of sexually repressed Egyptian males pathetically offering them tat or marriage. I quickly turned into a side street to avoid a BTR60 armoured personnel carrier guarding the HSBC bank ahead. Following the dusty coast road I arrived at the top of the cliffs offering a sweeping vista of the area looking towards the islands where the exchange was about to happen.

"Dom, we're in position. All quiet here," radioed Karl.

"Roger. All quiet here also. The resupply boat left the dock 20 minutes ago so should be with you in the next five minutes." I scanned the bay for activity.

I exited the car and fired up a Marlboro to calm my shattered nerves. The RV was too far out for me to observe, but thankfully the only movement in the naval base came from small patrol crafts bobbing on the tide, occasionally banging into the pontoon from poorly tied knots.

My phone rang. Anna. "There's a small boat with a blue light on leaving the coastguard base."

The port was obscured from my position but I saw the blue light atop a small patrol craft travelling at around 15 knots heading south. This didn't bode well. It would not have the range of *AM230;* hopefully Karl could lose it.

I immediately called him. "Do the exchange now and get the fuck out there, you have company. Head for the Saudi coast at full speed."

I jumped into the car and headed for the apartment.

Mark called en route. "The captain's radioed the agent about the three Egyptians. It's all kicking off down here."

"Fuck him off. Get back to the hotel, check out and meet me at the apartment as soon as you can."

I reached the apartment with Anna still observant on the balcony watching things unfold on the water. I grabbed the binoculars noting the coastguard vessel closing in to intercept the exchange. This was going pear shaped by the minute. Time was of the essence. It wouldn't take long before SSI started joining up the dots leading them to yours truly.

Anna gazed at me with sad eyes. "What does this mean?"

I didn't want her knowing the answer. "Just go back to your hotel. Deny you ever knew me, no matter who asks, understand?" I tried to cosset my orders in sympathy but couldn't soften them to a degree where Anna didn't recognise the consequences. SSI would ensure she suffered if they linked her to me.

We fell into each other's arms. Her tears soaked through my shirt and her golden hair shook in my cupped hands. Mustafa arrived and took her bag.

"Mustafa, hide Anna in the car, she can't be seen after dark. Whatever happens do not link her, or yourself for that matter, to here."

Our lingering fingers separated as she exited the door with one last look. I held onto the sound of her echoing steps until they too were gone. My muscles weakened as if curare passed my lips. I slumped down in the hollowness of her leaving. There was never any time. Mark knocked at the open door.

He must have seen loss etched across my face. "You OK, mate?"

"Yeah, I'm fine," I lied as I stood stoutly, my vacant stare offering the truth. "We need to get out of Egypt at first light."

This way of life had cost me everything. A litre of Bacardi Gold stood neglected in the kitchen. It would be a shame to waste it. If SSI came to pick me up it may be the last drink I ever had.

I filled an iced tumbler to give just enough room for a splash of coke and took a gulp. I needed quiet.

My phone rang. Karl. "Dom, bad news." It seemed to be the prefix for every call. "The towline to the RIB has snapped. What do you want me to do?"

"Leave it." A $50,000 RIB was a loss, but freedom was worth much more.

He'd picked up the coastguard interceptor on radar, shadowing their every move from exactly half a mile. Noting her size leaving the port I estimated that she'd have a maximum range of 250 miles, *AM230* could go for 2000 miles, Karl just had to hold her off.

The weather conditions prevented Karl from heading to the Saudi coast, his fastest course set to SSE, the Volvo engines powering her at a comfortable 18 knots. With her in international waters I felt more relaxed. I hoped the coastguard vessel would lose interest and head back when she'd used too much fuel. Hope is often the prelude to disappointment.

***

Karl was on watch with Si securing the deck in preparation for strengthening winds. With a moderate sea on the starboard quarter they ran with the waves. Karl checked the radar—the coastguard vessel lagged further behind.

"It looks like the coastguard vessel has given up. Happy days," Karl announced, before cracking a joke with Sharky to try and lighten the mood.

He quickly checked his position. He was around three days from *DM234* currently in the southern Red Sea. They were about to settle into their watch routine when Si, still on deck, banged on the window pointing out to sea.

To Karl's horror he saw the silhouette of a warship heading towards them at full speed. "Fucking hell, have you seen this thing?"

Sharky stared through the binoculars intensely at the warship heading straight towards them. "It's a Tiger Class."

"Can we outrun her?" Karl asked optimistically.

"Not a chance. Top speed 38 knots, she has a 40mm main gun upfront and a 12.7mm off the stern and if we really piss them off she's equipped with four Exocet missiles," he stated, trying not to laugh. "And yes, I am a ship spotter."

The warship approached from the stern at around 30 knots. Si sat on the deck watching the ship storm alongside. The warship captain meant business, pulling alongside just 10 feet from *AM230*. Ten sailors, pointed their AK47's nervously at Si. In return, he gave them a friendly wave and a smile.

***

I watched Mustafa for 20 minutes talking to the infantry officer who offered nothing but hostile body language and a face burnt with an unerring grimace. I left the air-conditioned capsule to see if I could assist. The heat hit me; my internal Bacardi infused sprinkler system activated in response so by the time I reached the officer I was in the advanced stages of melting. Hurghada's perimeter checkpoint was well protected by an infantry battalion and here, four BTR-60's and a T-62 tank parked on the hill overlooking the main road.

The officer sneered at me until he saw the big wedge of $100 bills tactically placed in my top right-hand pocket.

I took him to one side and pulled out my trusty Royal Navy ID. "I have orders to report to the British Embassy without delay."

He looked at my pocket. I smiled. Corruption was so endemic, even simple truths had been stolen.

We bumped along a desert road that hugged the coastline overlooking the Gulf of Suez, passing through small non-descript villages and mini cities of oil storage tanks. Military check points became more frequent as we neared Suez.

I told Mustafa to turn off Highway 65 at Alin Sokhna and take the smaller desert road to bypass Suez, still locked in virtual anarchy.

Mustafa talked on the phone looking stressed. "That was the agent at the marina. He says the Egyptian resupply boat has been arrested."

"Were our lads on board?"

"He said they dived over the ship and escaped."

"How far out were they?"

"He did not say, but he is very angry with you."

I couldn't give two shits. He was happy enough to take $20,000. My concern was for Sammi, Mohammed and

Chesni. They could well be floating face down and be washed up on a beach somewhere already. With their passports still in Eritrea, this could look really bad once the two governments linked their fantasist ideas together.

Mark and I needed to split up at the airport and escape on the earliest available flight as the agent and boat captain would now be singing like canaries to save their skins.

A wispy pall of acrid smoke hovered like a threadbare blanket between the vivid blue skies above and the murkiness of Cairo below. A mobile wall of military checkpoints manned by surly armed guards and M1 American Abrams tanks protected the city's outskirts. The ancient capital sounded surreally quiet, an altogether pleasant experience not having to spend the usual three hours overheating in congested traffic surrounded by beggars. We made good progress and although I knew Cairo pretty well, the route seemed strange, perhaps due to it being the scene of post apocalyptic serenity. Paranoia and my natural Satnav took over. We were in the middle of a military district. "Where are we going?"

Mustafa didn't reply. My one ally now silent when I needed him the most. We slid around a sharp corner kicking up a dust storm alerting the M1 Abrams tank in the middle of the road. The turret swung around to point at us.

"Fucking stop you stupid twat. What the fuck are you doing?" I shouted.

"Sorry Mr Dom, I am lost."

"Turn the car around." Being lost was far better than being betrayed even if it meant narrowly avoiding vaporisation by a 700mm heat round.

I sat in the departure lounge furtive to meet anyone's glimpse. Mark had managed to get away with no hassles, yet I still harboured nerves that I'd receive the dreaded tap on my shoulder before my plane's wheels left the tarmac. SSI could conjure up a list of criminal acts longer than my arm to go with the three drowned Egyptians still taking up space in my conscience.

On the bus heading to the aircraft my phone rang. Karl. "Dom they're pointing the 12.7mm at us and threatening to open fire if we don't stop. What do you want us to do?"

"They're bluffing. Get the captain to give you the number for his boss I'll call him in two hours when I land in Athens. Stay on course." I hung up. I needed more than 200 Marlboro to clear this up.

***

Red Sea Naval Headquarters, Safaga, Egypt
26'45N 33'57E

Karl and the crew had managed to hold off the Tiger Class vessel for 110 miles, pretty impressive against such overwhelming odds. I'd managed to speak with the Admiral in charge of the Red Sea region after touching down in Athens. I agreed to let his officers from the Tiger class vessel board and search *AM230* to reassure him we were unarmed. *AM230* would be escorted back to his naval base; the crew would not be arrested and instead be checked into a local hotel. He added he'd provision my vessel with fuel and food. I gave him my word that I'd personally come to Safaga to pay for the provisions and any other costs incurred during the Red Sea chase. He sounded a man of honour and despite my reservations of Egyptian morality, my instincts told me he was trustworthy.

The regime crumbled by the day. Defiant protestors grew in number and there seemed to be a wave of optimism across the country that people power would prevail. The return flight to Egypt was packed with the Western media brat packers wanting to be in the middle of this historic moment. *This is Fox News live from Cairo, blah, blah blah'* happy in the moment until the next tragedy where they could again play God with their shiny studio anchors reporting government endorsed 'facts'.

I turned on my phone and listened to my messages. Most were business orientated that could wait, others were about AM230 that couldn't, but none were about the *Sea Scorpion* crew still detained in Eritrea. They were the priority. The last message finally brought a smile. Chesni. All three Egyptian crew had made it back to land. I'd ensure they were cared for.

I showed my papers to the main gate sentry before being accompanied by an armed sailor to the HQ building. Like most military headquarters, the base smelled spotless and devoid of any litter—a heinous crime requiring a harsh punishment from the officer of the day. White painted rocks surrounded grassed areas that would never feel a human foot and large polished brass cannons glittered in the sun.

From Annapolis to Yokosuka, main naval headquarters buildings offer authoritarian décor and here appeared no different—perfect white steps led to impressive double doors guarded by two large anchors. I noted *AM230* tied to the adjacent pristine jetty. Whilst serving I avoided headquarters if I could help it, preferring commando units where time was better spent preparing to take out anyone who displeased Her Majesty rather than polishing and painting to please her; yet understood the stakes so dressed accordingly in my signature beige suit with a pink shirt and matching handkerchief.

I was directed to a side room where I hugged all my guys and reassured all would be well. I was soon led to the largest office in the building to meet my fate with the admiral. I didn't care what happened to me, the release of my men was my only concern. My instincts were correct. The admiral seemed a man of his word and immediately released *AM230*. I disclosed the whole *Sea Scorpion* story including my issues returning our Egyptians from *AM230*. My confession had merit, I banked on this intelligence being passed to Asmara via Egyptian diplomatic channels to back up my statement already sent to the Eritrean government. He accepted my story but would need proof by me providing him with any one of the Egyptians. I feared for their safety should they attend. The Admiral assured they would only be liable for a sizeable fine, which, in reality, amounted to a paltry sum, a sad reflection of an Egyptian worker's net worth.

We shook hands firmly as we concluded the meeting. I truly hoped he would survive regime change. A new Egypt needed men like him.

The following day I brought Chesni back to Navel Headquarters. If things turned sour he was the only one of the three without a wife and children and his motor mouth would be ideal to recount the Romiyah Islet situation. Chesni was immediately hand cuffed and led away by the military police.

"We cannot have Egyptian nationals on Eritrean soil without permission," explained the Admiral apologetically. " He will do six months in prison. He will be OK," he added as if sending Chesni to boarding school.

It was clear the Eritrean and Egyptian security services were communicating. This was a breakthrough. If Chesni had to be the sacrificial lamb to open negotiations with the Eritreans, then so be it. I'd look after him financially; he was young, fit and a character, prison would not be his death knell—something that could not be guaranteed with the *Sea Scorpion* crew.

I'd been consumed with darkness for so long, I hoped this small chink of hope wouldn't blind me, unlike the sun's brilliance as I descended the grand headquarter steps. My phone rang. Killer. My outlet.

"Hey shippers, I was just about to call. All OK?" I said, mustering my most positive tone.

"Dom, there's no easy way to say this. Leon Green is dead."

I searched for clear air trying to compute Killer's blow. Leon was in Djibouti on *AL345* and had suffered a heart attack while in the water trying to retrieve a fender. Noting Lee's distress, Nora had dragged him back on board and despite the best efforts of the crew Leon could not be resuscitated.

Killer jumped on the next flight to Djibouti to get our brother home.

CHAPTER 25
Didim, Turkey
37'22N 27'15E

Droplets of crimson blood exploded on the white porcelain like an excerpt from a psychological horror movie. My razor hadn't been changed for weeks and painfully cut my flesh trying to hack through the rough beard. The mirror haunted me, the only person I could see looked pale, old and tired. The image could never answer the same scary question I'd asked every day for the last four months, *"What if they don't get released?"*

After leaving Egypt Mark had offered me his villa in Turkey to live off the grid for a while. Another country to wake up in, just to confirm that 'home' was just a word. Hiding was all I could do to stay alive. If the Eritrean President really did think I was out to assassinate him he may do a pre-emptive strike—it's what I'd have done. I walked down the marble staircase to the darkened rooms below, curtains drawn in protracted paranoia; the lounge still strewn with maps, charts and empty rum bottles, the scars of late night planning tattooed with madness. My contingency plan seemed more like a Tarantino film script.

I crawled outside, the sun blinding me as I fumbled toward the patio table to the comfort of a cigarette butt molehill. I needed to clean up but my mind darted with distraction. I'd reached out to my intelligence network on the prison network. The more I heard the tighter insanity grabbed. If diplomatic channels didn't work there was only one solution. It was time to meet my Waterloo.

My phone rang. Killer. "Hi Dom, have you seen the papers?"

"No, tell me," I said, firing up my fifth Marlboro in succession.

"One of the guys on the Romiya gig is apparently a minor celebrity and The Sun newspaper has run a story."

The one thing that the Foreign Office had told us, above all, was not to insult the Eritrean Government in the media as it could have grave implications. Killer sent me the link. I read in despair:

TV Gladiator flees despot's hell hole.
One of TV's Gladiator's was among former Commandos who escaped from an African depot's henchman after a gun battle at sea, The Sun can reveal.

The article showed a stock photo of the guy flexing his tattoos in some kind of lycra gimp outfit. Hope was already gossamer thin for the *Sea Scorpion* lads but could be cut all together thanks to an immensely selfish publicity stunt. While he promoted his pecs on screen, our concerns were for the guys whose ordeal could only be made worse. As the head of the company I'd been the spokesperson trying throughout to be sympathetic to the Eritreans, dealing with difficult interviews from probing journalists. I held no malice toward the Eritreans per se, we'd fucked up and I could see their point of view, irrespective of emotive and dangerous journalism. Yet they still prevented consular access, their pride of independence cluttering common sense leaving the lads to suffer further. There was no end in sight.

My phone rang again. Blocked. "There are two prisons you'll need to focus on: Eiraeiro between Massawa and Asmara and a political prison on the island of Dahlak Kebr. I'll send more details shortly." The Israeli voice hung up.

The details came through as I smoked feverously, sucking in as much information as possible. My Israeli contact was a former member of Kidon—a specialist assassin unit within Mossad; his intelligence always registered A1. It had to—we were going to bust the lads out of jail.

Successfully attacking Eiraero prison was going to be an extremely tall order. Denied to even exist by the government, we knew it held high-level political prisoners and journalists. 21 miles from the coast was a lot of ground to cover if the balloon went up, which it would big time—it was heavily guarded by 150 well trained and loyal guards. After checking the schematics generally, it was a no go. The Israeli's assessment was that the more likely location would be the maximum-security facility on Dahlak Kebr Island. Surrounded by sharks, like Alcatraz, it would seem a highly secure location, but I deemed myself an amphibian—I'd have an edge approaching from sea. To add further jeopardy, the Emir of Qatar was building his own private resort on the island. However, from danger comes resource, the construction company would provide ideal cover to infiltrate and gather vital intelligence before we hit the prison. I sat down in the darkened room, poured rum and pored over the charts and satellite imagery.

The prison was well hidden, almost camouflaged from prying eyes in space. The report indicated it held 800 political prisoners, mainly ex-military deported from Libya and Malta. There was likely to be a battalion guarding the installation meaning stealth was key to success. We'd need to conduct a number of reconnaissance missions to the island over the course of two months, inserting teams for a few days at a time to establish troop movements and size of the force including naval activity and establishing fire bases to be used. I'd procure the usual smorgasbord of RGP's, AK47's, PK Light machine Guns, Dragunov sniper rifles and enough grenades to eradicate a small country via another French intelligence contact based in Yemen. Personnel wasn't an issue, I'd already sourced some of the meanest gunslingers on the planet, war-hungry South Africans with the appetite to commit any atrocity should the money be right. I'd normally stay away from cold-hearted mercenaries, but I was in no normal situation. A traditional dhow would be utilised as a floating base using local skiffs fitted with more powerful engines to infiltrate teams back and forth from the island so not to draw too much attention. We'd jam the island's communications, completely cutting it off from the mainland 30 miles away.

The attack would be brutal, every paid killer knowing his individual and team objective, death would be inevitable for some. Upon releasing the four prisoners we'd extract under heavy fire from our outlying fire bases. Providing the jammers worked it was unlikely air force jets would be scrambled from Asmara to respond. We'd run for Eilat in Israel where my new identity had been promised. The released prisoners would be handed over to the UK embassy in Tel Aviv. The operation would cost around $3.5 million, a sum I didn't have but could raise now a Greek ship owner courted me to sell my company shares. There was no way I could compromise PVI with my actions, I had to do this alone, the company would survive without me; the lads may not.

My morality seethed as I finished the final page of planning. I personally commanded over 1000 former Royal Marines within the biggest private navy since the East India Company, and had been named one of the most influential figures in world shipping having created a business hailed as the fastest growing company in Europe, setting the benchmark in maritime security; but here I was in a darkened room amongst the detritus of binge drinking and imaginary savagery planning to invade a sovereign country using the attack methods of my enemies. The ghost of Major 'Mad' Mike Hoare danced upon my shoulder. Maybe Sir Peter was right. I'd become a mercenary, a pirate. I emptied the last remaining bottle of rum. I'd reached rock bottom.

***

MV *PACIFIC OPAL*
16'42N 59'45E

Nige watched two skiffs running parallel with the ship. They were too far away to confirm weapons but intuitive hairs told him everything. In Nigeria he'd developed the same feeling prior to 400 militants lighting up the oil platform in a kaleidoscope of broken glass and molten metal as bullets strafed the rig.

"Nige, the skiffs are changing course," said Arron from the bridge wing.

The first skiff looked pristine and equipped with newer, more powerful engines—the pirates were reinvesting wisely. The team fanned out taking up firing positions as the first skiff opened fire, the rounds whizzing overhead. Arron responded with two shots from his sniper rifle. The water erupted five feet in front of the skiff causing the helmsman to swerve and stop. The second skiff appeared less obliging, firing wildly as it approached the ship despite the team firing a volley of shots. The helmsman stood his course undeterred. Nige pondered he may have to use deadly force on this guy if he kept coming. If they boarded or even got close he'd shoot them but in the water he'd give them every chance to stop their course of action. It was not our job to kill pirates it was to protect the crew and the ship. Nige brought up his SIG 542 assault rifle equipped with an Advanced Combat Optical Gunsight and lined up his final warning shot. He slowed his breathing bringing the skiff into line before gently squeezing off the action. He watched the round hit the front of the skiff splintering fibreglass. The skiff stopped dead in the water before changing course to join the first skiff. Nige smiled to himself. Job done. He kept his team on high alert.

Nige joined the captain on the bridge busy speaking to UKMTO on the ship's phone. "They want to speak to you." The captain handed Nige the handset.

"This is UKMTO. Are you sure these were pirates?"

Nige's eyes rolled. "Yes 100% confirmed. Two armed skiff opened fire and were repelled." Nige added they'd also taken video and photographic evidence of the attack and noted the skiffs had returned to a mother ship two miles away from the attack location. UKMTO stated that a Finnish warship was on the way and for Nige to assist when the ship reached the area.

The Finnish warship intercepted the dhow and skiffs and by using our photographic evidence they were able to confirm this particular pirate group had attacked other ships. I issued a statement that we'd support legal action with international agencies to bring the men to justice. After my dark planning it felt good for a moment to be on the right side of justice. Part of Nige's sitrep was of major concern. The Finnish had recovered children from the pirate skiffs.

I paused trying to process the information. In an attempt to breach ships' defences, some pirate groups were using children to gain access through small access points. I was horrified that Garaad had stooped so low to exploit children for his filthy trade. For Nige, a father of four, it was particularly poignant. He'd not seen them in the boats so thankfully had held back on the use of lethal force. It wouldn't be long before these kids were being used as human shields.

The two boys, aged seven and eleven, waited on the Finnish warship with an uncertain future, *personae non gratae* who no one wanted. The complexity of the international laws governing piracy was about to fail again, in this case not just against armed criminals but in not saving two vulnerable children.

Pacific Opal flew under the flag of Singapore whose courts advocated the death penalty for piracy. The arresting warship was under European jurisdiction therefore wouldn't handover the pirates to face the noose as it contravened the European convention. The pirates and children were released and sent back to Somalia to re-arm. The fate of the children was unknown.

European navies were trying to fight medieval style criminals with 21st century morality, this lack of resolve further emboldened the pirates but our approach was to answer in the only language they understood—violence. No matter the ever-decreasing opposition to armed guards, we were winning the war. We stopped over 50 hijacks and were not alone. In the two years since my rag tag Brothers entered the region on *DM234*, the whole industry mushroomed from eight companies providing security for ships to 233 arming over 900 ships each month. The pirates were feeling the pinch, Garaad and his men were getting more desperate and, like a wounded animal, more dangerous committing more determined attacks by the day. Killer sent me updates by the day:

"MV *Alina* attacked by three skiffs thwarted by PVI team."

"Nine skiffs attacked MV *Stella Kosan*. Craig Nelson's team had to throw down a heavy rate of fire to hold them off."

"Attackers refused to comply with Nic the Greek's US team's warning shots. Eight pirates killed."

It was getting intense on the high seas. It felt like the final show down.

***

Heathrow Airport, UK
51'28N 00'29W

The lads had been holed up in Eritrea for 172 days. I waited nervously at the gate scanning for any paparazzi photographers. I'd only just landed after receiving the welcome phone call from Sandra Tyler-Hywood in Asmara. Through the British government she'd negotiated the release of the four prisoners thanks to the Qatari's throwing support behind her quest. The Emir had sent his Royal private jet to Asmara to pick up my men. He may not have been so keen if he knew I'd planned to attack the island near his private resort. After her herculean effort over the previous six months to get access to the guys, the Eritrean Minister of Foreign Affairs' final snub to Sandra was only to inform her of their release once the jet was airborne. The Qatar ambassador brokered a deal so that the Eritreans would not lose face—I was charged with terrorism and espionage. Fair enough.

Reconnected families, long distance reunions and the tearful beam of rekindled love mean airport arrivals halls are the perfect display case for humanity. I felt no different to the crowd of friendly faces waiting to take a loved one home. Butterflies flittered in my stomach as I watched red-eyed travellers passing through the arrivals gate eyes scanning for a recognisable smile. The Qatar Air

313

flight had been on the ground for 40 minutes. I wondered what state the guys would be in after six months detention fingered as assassins. A huge wave of guilt descended over me. At these times the loneliness of command is unbearable but accountability comes with the job and if the families wanted someone to blame I stood front and centre to accept responsibility. They'd suffered terribly. All our support could never replace a son, father or husband.

Luggage tags indicated that the Qatar flight passengers were starting to filter through. My nerves rose as each traveller activated the sliding doors. I stared in horror as Adrian Troy staggered through supported by Chris Collinson. He appeared gaunt and sallow and seemed as if death was only a coughing fit away. He looked a broken man.

I thought I might have to catch him as he closed in. I then smelled his breath. He was in fact totally and utterly drunk.

He gazed up and smiled with a glint in his tired red eyes, "Alright Dom." It was the first time we'd met.

I hugged them as if they were my children. Big Al looked at me with sadness. "Sorry Dom, we let you down."

"It was my call and mine alone. Welcome home." Tears stung my eyes.

They'd all done a remarkable job to keep it together in the most difficult circumstances, I was immensely proud of them. Our business often gets dirty and they and their families had paid the price.

I led them into a private room at a nearby hotel to reunite them with their families. I then moved discreetly to one side—we all needed some time to ourselves so sought refuge in a quiet bar. The bar tender poured a large rum and coke while I sat processing what had just happened. I downed the drink in two gulps almost disbelieving their ordeal was finally over, it had happened so quickly. I motioned to the bar tender for a larger measure.

Barry had organised a small press conference. I knew most of the journalists after having to fend off months of difficult questions. I humbly apologised to the Eritrean government for the misunderstanding I'd caused. It was a strange affair where, in the main, I was ignored, Barry positioning himself centre stage taking credit for the release. His ego had grown in my absence creating a dynamic change I felt had been engineered.

After the press conference, Killer rang. "I need to talk to you in private." His tone was reminiscent of the bar in Djibouti.

"Book me into the Globe, I'm on the way."

I drove down the M4 reflecting on the last 24 hours. For the first time in six months I felt a future, I could start again.

I arrived at the Globe without damaging the Mercedes. We exchanged our customary hug at the bar before retreating to the corner where we'd met with Karl three months earlier to discuss the Egyptian recovery operation. Killer explained he'd been sidelined, Barry preferring to use the many new corporate employees engendered to a developing culture where office staff paid higher regard to administration than the welfare of the guys fighting pirates. I pondered back to the press conference.

"I think this Colonel Cully may be a saboteur," he continued.

"With his background it wouldn't surprise me."

I'd met Cully only once, Barry was star stuck, hanging on his every word. I, on the other hand, immediately lodged him in the category of quisling. I'd warned Barry about recruiting him as he'd previously approached Phil Shaw with an offer to audit us—an oft used excuse for outsiders to collate a company's workings with a view to setting up as a competitor, yet here he was parking on my driveway leaking oil everywhere. His contemptuous tone amplified his jealousy of my success, and as a former Special Forces officer he clearly felt he should be in my position and not the other way around. This didn't bode well. In my absence, Cully's and Barry's egos and arrogance strengthened, spreading their influence throughout the office staff with negative effects on the frontline. With ammunition requests mounting and pirates becoming ever more dangerous, office politics was the last thing I needed to focus on.

The following day I visited PVI HQ to watch and observe what was happening. I felt a stranger in my own company—a Steve Jobs in a 1980's Apple. We'd built an empire through sweaty polo shirts and operational graft, now everyone seemed to be a director with a PA obscenely gorging at my table. Barry was a corporate suit, not a leader and used the weakest trick in the book of playing people against each other in a point-scoring circus of self-justification. His meddling had managed to turn an efficient and committed operationally sound model into a toxic environment of inane job titles, endless administrative bullshit and pointless meetings. My heart sank. I hated micro managing; however, due to *Sea Scorpion* and Eritrea I'd left Barry unchecked for too long. People had jobs and were paid well to do them, loyalty I shouldn't need to pay for. If we were to defeat Garaad and his men PVI HQ was no longer the place to direct operations. I needed a plan. I headed to Cornwall to spend the weekend with Killer to work out a new strategy before someone was killed.

I navigated the narrow winding roads synonymous with the old county famous for smugglers and pirates—an apt place for Killer to reside. In the days before life became complicated I often travelled to Cornwall to surf the Atlantic swells. That simple memory conjured a subconscious smile as I tried to avoid tractors along the high-banked lanes adorned with confident throstles—the bird of my childhood. I entered the medieval village of Pentewan where Killer had recently bought an old fisherman's cottage offering commanding views over the harbour, his faithful VW camper 'Clockwork Orange' a beacon for his property. I sucked in the sea air and for a moment felt at peace.

Killer greeted me. "Afternoon shipmate, I'll get the kettle on."

He too had managed to find some space in his life rather than sleeping on the office floor. I felt pleased for him. We'd done well to keep our sanity sharing this relentless journey. He was a remarkable planner and in a crisis was the best in the business, managing to keep every ship protected during the Egyptian revolution and the Eritrean crisis, I didn't know how he did it. Barry trying to move him out of operations showed he knew nothing beyond the stationery store. I cast these negative thoughts from my mind, there were more important things at hand—how to contain Garaad and his men.

We needed to set up a tactical headquarters in the field but the question was where? Killer jokingly suggested Egypt, I immediately dismissed it but felt a pang of sadness for Anna's love I'd lost.

Sri Lanka had become our busiest hub and after considering all other options it would be as good as place as any to set up. I rang Anil in Colombo and tasked him to find a villa. We'd move out in two weeks.

CHAPTER 26
East of Dar es Salaam
06'30S 44'01E

Captain Sergei Ordinartsev stood proudly on the bridge of his Udaloy Class anti-submarine destroyer. They'd spent the summer months escorting ships through the IRTC working with the European and American navies, the captain now glad to be rid of them so he could refocus on spending the autumn destroying pirates. His crew were bored and keen to get some action. In contrast to the weak West, the Russian Navy executed captured pirates with impunity. The rarity of pirate attacks on Russian ships was not lost on those in the know.

The Udaloy Class bristled with weaponry—two 100mm main guns, port and starboard mounted 30mm Gatling guns capable of firing 10,000 rounds per minute, plus ship-to-ship and anti-air missiles. With an anti-submarine arsenal including depth charges and torpedoes, she was a formidable beast. Captain Ordinartsev was old school, joining the Soviet Navy as a cadet and once a committed member of the communist party. The politics in Russia may have changed but this old sea dog loved the homeland. If any pirates attacked ships of Mother Russia they would die.

"Russian bulk carrier under attack 10 miles south of our position," the radio operator reported.

"Action stations," the old Soviet bellowed.

The navigation officer plotted a course as the captain ordered the engineering officer to give him maximum speed. The four mighty gas turbine engines thrust the destroyer forward cutting through the aquamarine water like a switchblade as it accelerated to 38 knots. They were too late. The Russian bulk carrier had evaded the attackers.

The radar operator reported a dhow, possibly a mother ship, in the area. The captain quickly turned course to intercept the vessel. Coming alongside, the Russian sailors lined the deck pointing their AK47's at the twenty Somali's cowering on the bow.

The captain tutted at the pathetic wretches below, then addressed them casually through a load hailer. "Hey Somalis, we warned you not to attack Russian ships but you did not listen. I am a fair man, you have five minutes before we start firing," he said with a glaze of satisfaction.

The gunnery officer approached. "Sir, may we fire off all the old ammunition for the Gatling gun, the two forward turrets and small arms."

"Permission granted. Engage the target at 500 metres. After pussy footing around with the Americans the men could use a little sport." The steward extended the captain's smile with steaming black *kophe*.

***

Scarface peered through his binoculars. Once he realised their attack on the Russian tanker had failed he instructed the helmsman to return to the mother ship, now within visual distance with a warship nearby. His jaw dropped as the splashes of gunfire hit the water before the sonic gunfire hit his ears. The splashes crept up on the mother ship until Scarface saw the horror of her fracturing and smoking as she was cut to pieces. His friends jumped overboard to escape the storm of bullets only to be turned into pink mist forever lost on the sea breeze by the Gatling gun as they floundered in the water.

He sat motionless with his six crewmen as they watched the Russian warship disappear over the horizon, remnants of its wake rocking their small skiff as if offering them a gentle goodbye. The relief of not being turned into blancmange from a wall of 30mm hell was short lived as they stared at the meagre supplies lying in the bottom of the water-soaked skiff. Even just using one Yamaha 60HP engine, six gallons of petrol could cover only 18 miles. The Somali coast was 55 miles away. They held half a gallon of water, a small bag of khat and a tiny pile of dried fish. Exposed to the elements and the unrelenting sun they'd suffer a prolonged death in four days.

Scarface pulled down the peak of his Sacramento Kings baseball cap to shade his eyes. He filled his mouth with khat. "We hijack a ship or we die."

***

The Russian bulk carrier attack was never reported, nor the Russian warship's response. Jason Day and the crew of the Liberian flagged container ship *Emirates Zambezi* were nearby en route to conduct their port call at Dar es Salaam. His recent promotion to TL would be a baptism of fire as the ship had never sailed through pirate-infested waters. There'd been a considerable amount of work to get the ship hardened and crew drilled into emergency procedures. Thankfully, the PVI team was highly experienced with a combined military service time of 61 years. None were spring chickens and they jokingly called themselves 'Team Saga' after the travel company specialising in holidays for the over 50's.

They were 12 hours from port. The voyage south had been quiet but attacks had happened around them. Jason advised the captain on the best course to avoid reported pirate activity. He felt calm on the bridge wings as daylight dwindled, and confident he'd delivered exemplary service to the new client.

Gary joined him, gently laying two peli weapon cases on the floor. "I'm just going to give these weapons a once over before we reach port."

There was a morbid therapy in the slow and careful cleaning of every nook and cranny of intricate components of death. Fresh oil was applied evenly, not too heavy not too light, to protect against corrosive sea air. On completion, the working parts were drawn back then released, the spring loaded steel rammed forward with a satisfying clunk as the working parts hit the breech.

It was a dark, moonless night by the time Jason finished his watch. Morton relieved him but to allow his eyes to adjust to the dark, Jason waited 20 minutes before heading down to his cabin. He opened his door and was immediately stunned by a huge flash momentarily blinding him. His throat rasped as the cabin filled with smoke. He stumbled, totally disorientated and slumped to his knees.

His radio exploded with Morton's rapid call. "Contact! Security team on the bridge now."

Jason collided into Gary as they both headed to the bridge where the captain was bent over the chart table in shock.

"Call UKMTO now," Jason shouted, shaking the captain from his trance.

"We've been RPG'd," Morton reported.

"Where are they?" Gary shouted.

"We've a boat on starboard inbound, not sure where, my night vision's gone," Morton replied.

Gary stared through the night sight into darkness. "Just one boat?"

"Dunno, the radar's offline and we've lost half the power on the bridge."

Darkness cloaked the attackers, but the familiar outboard engine noise told Gary that they were extremely close. As he crawled parallel to the lifeboat one deck below the noise of the outboard engine sounded loudest. He leaned over to see a silhouette firing a magazine of green tracer rounds. Gary fell back against the bulkhead and watched the deadly fireflies light up the night. Morton avoided another magazine of tracer by crouching behind the sand bags placed behind the bridge wing bulkhead for such eventualities.

The pirates were about to put the ladders on the ship to board. Gary had to react quickly while under heavy fire. The last time he'd encountered incoming green tracer was as a teenager on the final assault of Mount Harriet in the Falklands War. He was young no more, but bravery isn't bound by age.

He spoke into the radio, "Jason, on three, light up the skiff. Morton, let's give it to them."

On three, Jason hit the skiff with eye piercing light. Gary and Morton followed with a volley into the skiff. Screams told them they were hitting targets that fell when hit. Two pirates continued to spray automatic fire of green tracer bullets that ricocheted from the bridge wings and the superstructure.

The gunfire stopped, it didn't matter whether it was a magazine change or a stoppage it was now their turn. Gary and Morton knelt up into their firing positions and focussed on the exposed skiff lit up like a Christmas tree in open sea. 7.62mm rounds spat into the skiff from Gary's SLR, Morton mirroring the heavy fire with his own. Pirates fell where they stood, Gary swooping on the last pirate about to raise his AK. The pirate fell, his Sacramento Kings baseball cap falling into the sea as his head smashed against the skiff.

The skiff's motors stopped, the humming of the ship's engine a lullaby casting off the skiff as it drifted into the darkness. It was over. The sulphuric smell of cordite lingered in the gun smoke and empty shells littered the deck.

Gary smiled at Morton. "Not bad for old men."

"Speak for yourself," Morton smiled. "I think I need a new hip."

***

Tactical HQ, Galle, Sri Lanka
06'02N 80'13E

Although the south western monsoon season was due to stop in September, it had continued for another four weeks, and the rain drumming on my window seemed therapeutic as I sat at my desk poring over the intelligence reports, transferring co-ordinates of attacks or suspicious sightings of pirate craft to my master chart. The time I'd spent on the Omani dhow with the fisherman and his son was invaluable and by fusing this knowledge of a dhow's wind and tide voyage with my skill as a sailor and navigator I'd been successfully tracking five long range pirate groups across the Indian Ocean. Seen by ship owners as a toothless tiger, the international anti-piracy force had finally made a concerted effort to hit the pirates, not only to discourage attacks, but also to regain credibility. The newly created Maritime Police Force in Puntland arrested 250 pirates but would only bring them to justice should the international community pay for it—corrupt Somali officials could now suck from the breast of two mothers. They'd skimmed piracy income and now the anti-piracy bandwagon was another good source of income.

On the high seas international navies had arrested 70 pirates and the Indian Navy had captured 120 pirates now rotting in Mumbai's Arthur Road jail. In a secret operation, the Royal Marines sabotaged the beaches of Puntland. From a warship four miles out, they observed the pirates loading their boats for the following day's

323

piracy before going into town for their last night of vice and debauchery—a warped tradition for mariners either side of the sword. The Royal Marines then covertly inserted onto the empty beach where in a hit and run operation of 15 minutes, they destroyed all thirty skiffs and vessel fuel.

"Chris Rowland is here to see you," said Killer through the doorway.

It was good to see Chris again. I was his first TL on *Cosmic Jewel*. It seemed a lifetime ago. He'd just been attacked on the tanker *North Sea* en route to Galle so I was keen to get as much intelligence from him for my morning briefing. He personally had used 60 rounds to repel one attacking skiff. This tallied with reports I'd heard from other teams leaders—pirates were not backing down. In this case, the skiff approached with the sun directly behind them in an attempt to blind snipers. They fired around 200 rounds at the vessel before finally aborting the attack. Pirate intelligence suggested that security companies only carried 20 rounds of ammunition—they were trying to out-gun security teams.

Companies had formed in the mushrooming maritime security business, many naively unaware of initial costs, administrative hurdles and operational requirements of a business they saw as a cash cow. As a result they were totally unprepared, deploying unskilled and low paid operators into a high threat environment with dangerously low ammunition states. Should pirates out gun them and board, these security guys, many from low economic countries, would be immediately executed, yet companies were still prepared to put profits before the safety of their men. I baulked at the thought of PVI becoming the same.

I'd set up reporting procedures for my teams at sea to gather intelligence and appointed Roman to act as my intelligence officer back in the UK. Dave Seaton was promoted as my training officer to maintain the high standards and inform them of new industry regulations of which we were at the forefront of promoting. Tim Welford, with whom I'd rowed across the Pacific, was now in charge of patrol boats—the operational side of the business was now how I'd envisaged it when freezing my gonads off looking over the scrap of S200 on Hogmarso Island. We couldn't let our guard down at such a crucial time in the fight against Garaad.

Tactical headquarters was getting results, the guys were getting optimal support and I held the UK office staff accountable, putting the priority back to where it belonged—our frontline men. I sensed this rattled the cages of empire builders who dithered in the detachment of boardroom procrastination. I cared little, our men's lives were on the line and we had innocent sailors to protect.

My phone rang. Nic the Greek. "Hey mate, we've had a ship attacked in the Gulf of Oman."

It was my worst fear. We had the Indian Ocean locked down apart from one area in the Gulf of Oman, north of Muscat due to the UAE not allowing armed guards to land on their territory. Garaad was no mug, he'd figured out our weakness. This was the first major attack in the area for a while but I could guarantee it wouldn't be the last. As we could only disembark in Muscat, the tankers that transited through the narrow Straits of Hormuz into the Persian Gulf were not protected for 200 miles. I needed a plan to shut down the threat.

Killer and I headed to the Lucky Tuna bar on the iconic bikini clad backdrop of Unawatuna beach to discuss the development over rum to help the grey cells along. I rang Sanjeev, our agent in Fujairah, to ask about the possibility of landing guards there as he was close to the Sheik of the Emirate.

His response was unusual. "Hey Mr Dom, I was going to call you. Do you know a Bruno from Djibouti?"

Bruno, seeing an opportunity, had arrived off Fujairah in a charter vessel full of weapons causing major concern to the port authority. Bruno's presence highlighted how amateurish some of the other companies were. Sanjeev was keen for me to meet the Sheik in person to discuss the situation. I agreed immediately on the proviso he didn't tell anyone in the industry I was in country, and as the biggest player I was keen to broker a better deal than everyone else. If we could launch a S200 and provide logistical support from Fujairah we would have a solution and reinforce our position as industry leader.

***

Fujairah, UAE
25'07N 56'21E

The drive from the ever-expanding Dubai airport to Fujairah was featureless and slightly depressing, pink sands have a unique romance when not the conduit to plastic cities of consumerism.

The meeting with the Sheik would be conducted at one of his palaces, so imperative I asserted my strength as the market leader. While waiting for his highness, Bruno pulled up in a rented Range Rover Sport, his silver tongue an accompaniment to his sharply tailored Parisian suit. He confidently walked towards the palace.

I hid from view as he walked in. "Morning Bruno, you're rather a long way from home?"

"Oh, hi Dom," he blushed through his French accent. "How are you? I heard about Eritrea. I can get you anything you want if you're having trouble."

I smiled and declined his offer. *Same old Bruno.*

The meeting was far easier than envisaged, the Sheik was impressed by the impact PVI had made on securing the region and could see the merit in what we were trying to achieve. With permission to operate out of Fujairah, I hotfooted it back to Sri Lanka. Time was of the essence. I rang Tim en route to the airport and told him to ready the S200 to move from Djibouti to Fujairah. I'd give him more details when back at HQ.

Killer picked me up from Colombo airport. His red face, a caricature of angst against Galle's humidity, could not hide a troubled mind.

"Barry's instructed Tim not to move the S200."

I was flabbergasted; it made no sense. I immediately rang Barry. "What the fuck are you playing at?"

"Don't be like that, Dom, it's all OK; we just to have follow procedure and present it to the board for approval."

"Procedures and presentations? Are you on fucking drugs? How many times have we discussed this Barry, you do admin I do guns and kung fu. Stick to shit you know. By the time you limp dicks have finished having meetings, pedicures and ego stroking, the pirates will have hijacked a ship. Move the S200 now." I hung up. I slumped into the car seat and shook my head in disbelief.

"Barry and Cully are as thick as thieves." Killer mirrored my deflation.

"They're sabotaging the company, but for what gain?" I struggled to understand. "Are they that clueless?"

Maybe Killer was right. Cully could be working to bring down the company as the inside man for the opposition aided by Barry's lack of knowledge and personal ambition.

CHAPTER 27
East of Oman
20'58N 59'54E

Garaad strained his itching eyes through the binoculars. He needed khat. Two skiffs closed in on the southbound tanker, his pulse raced as the first skiff opened fire. The skiffs closed in, the bowman raising his ladder in anticipation of boarding the fully laden tanker sitting low in the water. A figure appeared on the bridge wings and the recoil of a rifle preceded the shots that rang out. Another figure followed, then another then another, four rifles all firing death upon the skiff, now retreating.

The captain rushed towards Garaad. "Have they boarded it?"

"No. More armed guards," Garaad scowled. This was their third failed attack since the new year, each one stopped by onboard security teams.

Big Mouth had warned him to come back with a ship or not come back at all. The criminal syndicates were starting to withdraw pirate funding due to the lack of return. Previous financial reports saw them enjoy big profits, turning as little as fifty thousand dollars into a million within six months. The Yakuza were putting serious pressure on the pirate corporation to deliver. Garaad also had the complication of losing contact with four of his pirates dhows in the last month. They were either lost or had been taken out by Russians. He wished he still had *Asian Glory* rather than the squalid dhow he now found himself roaming the ocean on. He may be number one on the ocean but was finding the land-based profiteers more interested in financial returns than the efficiency of piracy.

After a further five days drifting north they'd not seen a single ship as they paralleled the Empty Quarter of the Omani Coastline.

The dhow captain approached Garaad as he sat by the wheel. "We don't have enough fuel to return home if we go any further north."

"When I hijack a ship you'll have plenty."

"What if we don't?"

Garaad thrust his AK47's barrel into the captain's chest causing him to fall heavily on the deck. He then stuffed the barrel in his mouth cracking two teeth. "You know how many ships I've hijacked? Stop asking stupid questions."

The weary crew had been at sea for over three months shuffling around the deck like sea zombies. Having hijacked no ships they were moved around on various dhows as unwanted hand-me-downs. Filthy and gaunt, they survived on khat, dried fish and the hope of seeing Somalia. As light repeatedly transited through darkness, they slept out of sheer boredom and despair, drifting north at 1.3 knots under the punishing sun.

Garaad despaired at the catatonic stares devoid of will. He needed to hijack a ship fast before they all died. He'd lead the next night attack using only the fittest on board. He wouldn't have to wait long—the dhow was approaching the cape at Ras al Hadd and beyond, the busy shipping lanes of the Gulf of Oman.

"Ship ahead." The captain's call pierced the night air.

Garaad leapt up and observed the tanker heading north around three miles behind. He hastily boarded a skiff and started the twin 60HP engines picking five armed men to quickly join him. Needing to get on the tanker's course he sped full throttle towards the target before putting the engine into neutral to allow the tanker to pass before making his approach. He judged the ship's course perfectly before stopping. The sea tapped musically on the skiff hull, it was peaceful as he sat and watched the moon illuminate gun metal, the sea's calmness reflecting the stars upon which many people wished upon, but it was pointless, how could a star protect them from him? They watched the dark hull of the ship pass 100 metres away. They held their breath fearing even a cough would be carried upon the light wind and over the hum of the tanker's engines.

The moonbeams lit up the tanker's name—*African Sanderling*. The name rekindled sweet memories—she'd been hijacked previously with a nice $2million ransom paid. This may mean they'd learned their lesson and established more robust countermeasures. They needed surprise.

They gained on the tanker with ease in the tranquil sea. Garaad scanned the bridge wings as they closed in he saw a figure moving before it disappeared.

"Hold fire until I say," he whispered before instructing the ladder man to position himself. The ladder man readied to board as they drew up the hull just 10 metres away from the tanker. Garaad spotted another figure on the bridge wings, this one armed. He fired a burst of AK47 machine fire sparking up the bridge wings as the guard took cover. "Get on board," Garaad shouted to his ladder man before spraying an indiscriminate volley into the bridge.

The weak ladder man stumbled in the skiff, Garaad lunged to help him, dropping his AK47 as the tanker security team opened fire from the superstructure. Water around the skiff erupted as the onslaught of rounds rained down. The helmsman convulsed as two bullets hit him in the chest, cartwheeling him into the sea, propelling the skiff out of control sending the ladder man into the depths. Bullets smashed through the skiff as the tanker left the scene.

"We're sinking," shrieked a panicked voice from the bottom of the skiff.

Ripped clothing was stuffed into the holes to prevent swift leakage, salvaging the engines and fuel was paramount to give them a chance of limping back to the mother ship before it sank below the waves.

Garaad would have to move even further north.

***

Tactical HQ, Galle, Sri Lanka
06'02N 80'13E

The attack on the *African Sanderling* confirmed my projection of a northbound pirate group clearly heading to the Gulf of Oman. Looking at my master chart, after plotting the position of another company that had also been attacked in the same area, it confirmed that another pirate group also headed north. This would have grave implications for shipping in the Gulf of Oman.

"Surely they can see now the threat is real and we should move the S200 to cover the area," said Killer stating the obvious.

"The problem is it'll be too late unless they leave today and have good weather en route," I replied.

The stress of being so exposed was telling. We had a large number of guys in country and so I took the opportunity to conduct a briefing. Everyone raised the same question—what were the plans to secure the Gulf of Oman? All of us on the frontline recognised this as the priority.

I told them I was onto it. The problem was the suits back in the UK weren't. I rang Barry to tell him we needed to ready the S200s.

"I'll report it to the board when I return from vacation in two weeks."

I slammed down the phone. I rang Tim in Djibouti to ready them anyway.

"I can't Dom, Andy has prevented me from buying fuel and provisions until Barry authorises it on his return."

There was no board decision to be made. In trying to unseat me, Barry and Cully had ignored the implications of their actions. Cully arranged a conference call with all the company directors and managers in a corporate ambush to prevent the S200 move. Barry was too much of a snide to do it himself. It was a heated call with Cully challenging my intelligence. It was an amateur move. I promised that on conclusion of the meeting I'd furnish them with the daily intelligence outlining the danger we faced.

I could feel my anger rising, Cully was ruining the company that I'd given my life and soul trying to create. I collated the intelligence report and gave it a once over before attaching it to the email.

Immediate threat assessment

PVI teams have been attacked three times in the past ten days—a useful indicator to confirm all incidents as genuine. Pirates continue to operate off the Omani coast due to the lack of resources available to the Omani Coastguard. The general behaviour of pirates in the area bounded by 15-17 N 55-58E is to hold and attack vessels entering or leaving the IRTC, they can stay in the area for two weeks or so depending on coalition activity.

The trend of vessels sighted north of 17N is to continue north towards the Gulf of Oman where busy shipping lanes can be encountered. The vessel attacked at 16'58N 062'48E could be a north mover with another vessel attacked at 14'18N 062'48E confirmed by PVI team. This is likely to be the same pirate team.

I believe this pirate group has moved north and is responsible for the attack on African Sanderling at 21'37N 059'59E. We have a gap of 9 days, which is conducive to a dhow drifting north on a rhumb line roughly of due north with the prevailing winds to save fuel.

Their average speed will have been around 1.3 knots, which fits the assessment on their current track they are likely to be in the area of 23'50N 060'00E. This could be shortened due to changing wind conditions off Sur. We have another pirate group also on course to the Gulf entering from the east.

We are likely to see an attack in the Gulf of Oman in the next 48-96 hours.

After sending the email I collected my board and took to the surf. I needed to clear my head of malevolence. I sat out back, rising up on the Indian Ocean swell trying to make sense of what had happened. The suits didn't understand the ocean nor how high the stakes. We'd built our reputation on guaranteeing ships under our protection wouldn't be boarded, if one of our clients was hijacked PVI would fold. It was that simple. More importantly, sailors would endure hell as a hostage. I thought back to all the challenges we'd overcome, the great bravery of my men and the opportunities PVI had given them. We'd always snatched victory for the jaws of defeat time after time. It was an incredible journey with some of the greatest people I'd ever known—a true brotherhood to protect mariners. I caught the last wave of the day slipping down the face to a drop knee turn at the base and rode the tide into shore. The wave gave me a rare moment of peace and a brief snapshot of who I used to be when life was simple. I thought about Lee. Life was short. I needed to live again.

***

I sat on the sand watching the solace of the sea being touched by the orange glow of the April sun. Peace, as always was fleeting. My phone rang. Killer. "There's been two hijacks north of Muscat."

"Any of ours?"

"I don't know," he replied.

I could tell he was stressed. I immediately headed back to HQ.

Killer sat outside gagging. "Have we failed the lads?"

I put my hand on his shoulder. "I'll put the kettle on."

The first scant details of the hijacks came from Paul Storey in Muscat. It was an agonising wait monitoring news feeds, praying none involved our ships. I received an email from Roman confirming the hijack of Chinese ship *Xianghuamen*. All our ships were accounted for. Our relief was palpable. We were lucky but pirates would still be out there hunting vessels. I started plotting the attack positions to warn our ships in transit. I received compliments on how insightful I'd been to predict the hijacks and how wrong Cully was. Their sycophancy angered me even more. For them it was all about scoring points in the boardroom not about reality, not one had the balls to speak up when we'd had the conference call. For every caller I told them there was no reason to congratulate me, we'd collectively contributed to increasing our vulnerability.

I'd been through all levels of emotion on the run up to the Gulf of Oman debacle. There was some irony that after spending my waking days focused on stopping ships being seized by pirates that my own business had been hijacked, not by khat-chewing thugs, but by slippery suits sharing the same motivation of power and greed.

Barry and Cully's manipulative words had swung the fickle shareholders, locking me out. Despite having the loyalty of the men on the front line, cutthroat business was taking over and unbeknown to them their livelihood hung in the balance that day.

I needed to ponder my own future. The hapless pair had virtually taken over the company through demonstrating they were a liability, this in itself showed me I was outnumbered, my position as President becoming a title of servitude. With their unstable hands on the wheel the ship could founder or worse. I'd handed over all my assets to Angela in the divorce and had little to show for my time on planet earth, I couldn't risk ruin again.

My phone rang. Roman. "Have you heard the news?" he said excitedly. "It was Garaad who hijacked the *Xianghuamen*, the Iranians have captured him."

Garaad had pulled another masterstroke knowing I couldn't protect ships north of Muscat, but in his planning he'd underestimated the elite Iranian Revolutionary Guard. When surrounded, he turned to default mode by threatening to kill the crew if the warship came any closer. The Iranian's don't entertain that sort of nonsense so deployed their commandos to storm the ship, releasing the hostages in the process. Garaad and his cowardly thugs surrendered.

I sat down trying to process the information. My nemesis had finally been apprehended. The fact it was the Iranians who'd caught him gave some satisfaction that he'd do hard prison time. He'd have the rest of his life to reflect on the misery he'd caused so many sailors.

As my Moriarty, Garaad had become an important part of my life and a figure I was driven to defeat. As such, the news was tinged with poignancy. I wondered if he'd be replaced by a pirate corporate wanker equivalent or was this the end of his operation? He'd been the benchmark for modern day piracy and while there were other pirate groups, all admired him. Things would never be the same again. We'd both been pushed over the Reichenbach Falls.

The suits may have hijacked my ship but I'd call the ransom. I thought of Loyaan the pirate negotiator. I didn't require an airdrop to be flown by Fang but I'd need it quick before the suits made a mess of things.

Killer joined me in the office. I pulled out a bottle of my favourite Caol Ila whisky from my desk's bottom draw and poured out two very generous measures. "I have some news; Garaad has been captured."

"That's worth drinking to," said Killer downing the amber fire in one gulp.

I poured him another. "You may want this one as well. I'm leaving PVI."

***

Galle, Sri Lanka
06'02N 80'12E

Nige and Killer entered the briefing room. I meticulously thought through the final stages of planning before we hit the ground for rehearsals. On this gig nothing would be left to chance, timings were key to the success of the operation. Scotty and Ryan were currently delayed flying in from Sudan and Roman was already in country along with Titch getting ready for their phase of the job.

We arrived at the target location—a high-class 5 star hotel. As in Casablanca, skin privilege allowed us to casually walk in unchecked to get a full heads up on the venue. Killer took charge of controlling all exits while Nige and I would work together to back each other up. We ran on limited mobile phone communications, due to the country's network, regularly monitored by the security forces. Back to basics, just how I liked it.

Nige and I chatted through the plan. "Transport?" I quizzed.

"Mustafa will arrive out front in the Jag," Nige replied, sedulous as ever.

"Make sure Mustafa has proper training on the car the last time he drove me we nearly got blown up by a tank."

"Never mind Mustafa, you're on an elephant, have you rode one before?"

"How hard can it be? We've rode camels across deserts."

The following day we assembled as rehearsed. My heart raced. I gave everyone the green light. Killer stood in position while Mustafa drove around in a holding pattern waiting to be called forward. Nige and the rest of the team were all inserted and in position.

A text. Killer. *By the Pool.'* It was safe to enter.

I peeled off into position. I approached the elephant nervously, the Mahout kindly helping me onto her back. Clearly I should have practised, as I nearly fell off as we ascended the hill. I quickly dismounted to join Nige. I couldn't afford this op to fail.

I tensed as butterflies welled. I turned to see the first Kandyan drummers enter the lobby, the noise increasing—a perfect cover for my heart that I swear could be heard jumping from my chest. I then noted the target. My heart missed a beat as I saw her. Anna. She looked beautiful adorned in her spectacular white dress surrounded by a throng of traditional dancers. I could

337

hardly believe how life had changed as she walked towards me to embark on a new life together.

The soothing call of the waves woke us both on our first morning as man and wife. The wind gently billowed the window lace to reveal a perfect blue sky that smiled radiantly upon us.

"I have a surprise for you," I said over our breakfast on the beach.

She studied me suspiciously for obvious reasons—our journey had been far from conventional. We took a car and drove up the coast before stopping at a large gate— the welcoming guardian of a lavish villa. Rose petals lay on the driveway as the mighty Indian Ocean became the beautiful backdrop to the house we now approached. I opened the massive double doors and picked up Anna to carry her across the threshold.

"What is this place?" she asked.

"Home."

I picked up a bottle of Bollinger from the fridge and headed to the water's edge. This ocean had stole into my soul through the most troubled of journeys. I'd been ranked number 30 in the Lloyds List of world's most influential figures in international shipping. Garaad had been ranked number four. He was welcome to it; it wasn't much use to him in a squalid Iranian jail cell.

I put my arm around Anna. "Not a bad place to raise a family," I said before kissing her.

No one dare hijack this ship.

Printed in Great Britain
by Amazon